Windows 10 Development Recipes

A Problem-Solution Approach in HTML and JavaScript

Senthil Kumar

Lohith Goudagere Nagaraj

Pathik Rawal

Pryank Rohilla

Apress®

Windows 10 Development Recipes: A Problem-Solution Approach in HTML and JavaScript

ISBN-13 (pbk): 978-1-4842-0720-8

ISBN-13 (electronic): 978-1-4842-0719-2

Trademarked names, logos, and images may appear in this book. Rather than use a trademark symbol with every occurrence of a trademarked name, logo, or image we use the names, logos, and images only in an editorial fashion and to the benefit of the trademark owner, with no intention of infringement of the trademark.

The use in this publication of trade names, trademarks, service marks, and similar terms, even if they are not identified as such, is not to be taken as an expression of opinion as to whether or not they are subject to proprietary rights.

While the advice and information in this book are believed to be true and accurate at the date of publication, neither the authors nor the editors nor the publisher can accept any legal responsibility for any errors or omissions that may be made. The publisher makes no warranty, express or implied, with respect to the material contained herein.

Managing Director: Welmoed Spahr
Lead Editor: Gwenan Spearing
Technical Reviewer: Fabio Claudio Ferracchiati
Editorial Board: Steve Anglin, Pramila Balen, Louise Corrigan, Jim DeWolf, Jonathan Gennick,
    Robert Hutchinson, Celestin Suresh John, Michelle Lowman, James Markham, Susan McDermott,
    Matthew Moodie, Jeffrey Pepper, Douglas Pundick, Ben Renow-Clarke, Gwenan Spearing
Coordinating Editor: Melissa Maldonado
Copy Editor: Kim Burton
Compositor: SPi Global
Indexer: SPi Global
Artist: SPi Global

Distributed to the book trade worldwide by Springer Science+Business Media New York, 233 Spring Street, 6th Floor, New York, NY 10013. Phone 1-800-SPRINGER, fax (201) 348-4505, e-mail orders-ny@springer-sbm.com, or visit www.springer.com. Apress Media, LLC is a California LLC and the sole member (owner) is Springer Science + Business Media Finance Inc (SSBM Finance Inc). SSBM Finance Inc is a Delaware corporation.

For information on translations, please e-mail rights@apress.com, or visit www.apress.com.

Apress and friends of ED books may be purchased in bulk for academic, corporate, or promotional use. eBook versions and licenses are also available for most titles. For more information, reference our Special Bulk Sales–eBook Licensing web page at www.apress.com/bulk-sales.

Any source code or other supplementary material referenced by the author in this text is available to readers at www.apress.com. For detailed information about how to locate your book's source code, go to www.apress.com/source-code/.

I dedicate this book to my late father, Shree. H.B Rawal

—Pathik Rawal

Contents at a Glance

About the Authors...xxiii

About the Technical Reviewer xxv

Acknowledgments xxvii

Introduction xxix

■Chapter 1: Getting Started with Windows 10 Applications 1

■Chapter 2: WinJS Fundamentals 15

■Chapter 3: Basic WinJS Controls 31

■Chapter 4: List Controls, AppBar, and ToolBar 55

■Chapter 5: Data Binding and Navigation... 83

■Chapter 6: Adapting the UI for Different Screens 115

■Chapter 7: Application Lifecycle and Navigation..................................... 127

■Chapter 8: Globalization and Localization 145

■Chapter 9: Data Storage and App Data 159

■Chapter 10: Sharing Data 181

■Chapter 11: Background Tasks... 213

■Chapter 12: Location and Maps in Windows Apps 221

■Chapter 13: Building Apps That Connect to the Cloud............................. 251

■Chapter 14: Tiles and Notifications 275

■Chapter 15: Device Capabilities.. 287

■**Chapter 16: Additional Tools**...**307**

■**Chapter 17: Sideloading and Windows App Certification Kit**..........................**327**

■**Chapter 18: Store and Monetization**...**347**

Index...**365**

Contents

About the Authors...xxiii

About the Technical Reviewer xxv

Acknowledgments xxvii

Introduction xxix

■Chapter 1: Getting Started with Windows 10 Applications 1

1.1 Examining the Universal Windows Platform...1

    Problem 1

    Solution..1

1.2 Development Tools for Universal Windows Platform 3

    Problem 3

    Solution..3

1.3 Creating Universal Windows Platform Application 4

    Problem 4

    Solution..4

    How It Works...5

1.4 Running Universal Windows Platform Apps 7

    Problem 7

    Solution..7

    How It Works...8

■Chapter 2: WinJS Fundamentals 15

2.1 Namespaces in JavaScript 15

Problem 15

Solution 15

How It Works 15

2.2 Add a Namespace to an Existing Namespace 18

Problem 18

Solution 18

How It works 18

2.3 Creating a Class in WinJS 19

Problem 19

Solution 19

How It Works 19

2.4 Deriving a Class in WinJS 22

Problem 22

Solution 22

How It Works 22

2.5 Create Mixins in WinJS 24

Problem 24

Solution 24

How It Works 24

2.6 Encapsulation in WinJS 26

Problem 26

Solution 26

How It Works 26

2.7 Using Promise in WinJS 29

Problem 29

Solution 29

How It Works 29

■Chapter 3: Basic WinJS Controls **31**

3.1 Declaring a WinJS Control on a Page 31

Problem 31

Solution..31

How It Works..31

3.2 Setting Options for WinJS Controls 34

Problem 34

Solution..34

How It Works..34

3.3 Adding WinJS Controls from Your JavaScript Code 35

Problem 35

Solution..35

How It Works..36

3.4 Getting the WinJS Controls from an HTML Document..................................... 38

Problem 38

Solution..38

How It Works..39

3.5 The ToggleSwitch Control 40

Problem 40

Solution..40

How It Works..41

3.6 The DatePicker Control 43

Problem 43

Solution..43

How It Works..43

3.7 The TimePicker Control 46

Problem 46

Solution..46

How It Works..46

3.8 The Tooltip Control **49**

Problem 49

Solution 49

How It Works 49

3.9 Displaying Text **50**

Problem 50

Solution 50

How It Works 51

3.10 Editing Text in an App **52**

Problem 52

Solution 52

How It Works 52

■Chapter 4: List Controls, AppBar, and ToolBar **55**

4.1 Using the Repeater Control **55**

Problem 55

Solution 55

How It Works 55

4.2 Using the FlipView Control **59**

Problem 59

Solution 59

How It Works 59

4.3 Using the ListView Control **62**

Problem 62

Solution 62

How It Works 62

4.4 Filtering Items in the ListView Control **66**

Problem 66

Solution 66

How It Works 66

4.5 Grouping Items in the ListView Control **68**

Problem 68

Solution 68

How It Works 68

4.6 Semantic Zoom in ListView **71**

Problem 71

Solution 71

How It Works 71

4.7 Using the AppBar Control **75**

Problem 75

Solution 75

How It Works 75

4.8 Using the ToolBar Control **79**

Problem 79

Solution 79

How It Works 79

■Chapter 5: Data Binding and Navigation **83**

5.1 Data Bind to Simple Objects **83**

Problem 83

Solution 83

How It Works 83

5.2 Data Bind Style Attributes of DOM Elements **86**

Problem 86

Solution 87

How It Works 87

5.3 Use Templates for Data Binding **89**

Problem 89

Solution 89

How It Works 90

5.4 Data Bind WinJS Controls 93

Problem 93

Solution 93

How It Works 94

5.5 Navigational Structures in UWP Apps 97

Problem 97

Solution 97

5.6 Navigational Elements in UWP Apps 98

Problem 98

Solution 98

5.7 Pivot Navigation in UWP Apps 98

Problem 98

Solution 98

How It Works 98

5.8 SplitView Navigation in UWP Apps 100

Problem 100

Solution 100

How It Works 101

5.9 Hub Navigation in UWP Apps 105

Problem 105

Solution 105

How It Works 106

5.10 Master/Detail Navigation Using ListView in UWP Apps 108

Problem 108

Solution 108

How It Works 109

■Chapter 6: Adapting the UI for Different Screens 115

6.1 Design Breakpoints for Different Screens 116

Problem 116

Solution 116

6.2 Adaptive UI Technique: Reposition 116

Problem 116

Solution 116

How It Works 117

6.3 Adaptive UI Technique: Fluid Layouts 121

Problem 121

Solution 121

How It Works 121

■Chapter 7: Application Lifecycle and Navigation 127

7.1 Application States and Events 127

Problem 127

Solution 127

How It Works 127

7.2 Handling the Unhandled Exception in Your App 131

Problem 131

Solution 131

How It Works 131

7.3 Handling the Termination and Resuming of the App 133

Problem 133

Solution 133

How It Works 133

7.4 Using SessionState to Store the State 135

Problem 135

Solution 135

How It Works 135

7.5 Navigate Between Pages Using Hyperlinks 137

Problem 137

Solution 137

How It Works 138

7.6 Navigate Between Pages Using Single-Page Navigation 138

Problem 138

Solution 138

How It Works 138

Chapter 8: Globalization and Localization 145

8.1 Using Resource Strings 145

Problem 145

Solution 145

How It Works 145

8.2 Formatting Date, Time, Number, and Currency 150

Problem 150

Solution 150

How It Works 150

8.3 Localizing WinJS Controls 154

Problem 154

Solution 154

How It Works 155

Chapter 9: Data Storage and App Data 159

9.1 How to Create and Delete a Local App Data Settings Container 159

Problem 159

Solution 159

How It Works 159

9.2 How to Create and Read Local App Data Settings 163

Problem 163

Solution 163

How It Works 163

9.3 How to Create and Retrieve Local Composite Settings 166

Problem 166

Solution 166

How It Works 166

9.4 How to Create a Roaming App Data Store Container 167

Problem 167

Solution 167

How It Works 167

9.5 How to Create and Read Roaming App Data Settings 169

Problem 169

Solution 169

How It Works 169

9.6 How to Register the Data Change Event 173

Problem 173

Solution 173

How It Works 173

9.7 How to Create, Write, and Read a Local File 175

Problem 175

Solution 175

How It Works 175

■Chapter 10: Sharing Data **181**

Share Contract 181

10.1 Set up an Event Handler for a Share Option for a Source App 182

Problem 182

Solution 182

How It Works 182

10.2 Share Plain Text Data to Other Apps 184

Problem 184

Solution 184

How It Works 184

10.3 Share Web Links to Other Apps 187

Problem 187

Solution 187

How It Works 188

10.4 Share an Image to Other Apps 190

Problem 190

Solution 190

How It Works 190

10.5 Declare App As a Share Target 194

Problem 194

Solution 194

How It Works 195

10.6 Handle Share Activation and Receive Plain Text 198

Problem 198

Solution 198

How It Works 198

10.7 Receive Images Shared by Other Apps 203

Problem 203

Solution 203

How It Works 203

10.8 Share Custom Data Type 207

Problem 207

Solution 207

How It Works 207

■Chapter 11: Background Tasks 213

11.1 System Event Triggers for Background Tasks 213

Problem 213

Solution 213

11.2 Create and Register a Background Task 214

Problem 214

Solution 214

How It Works 214

11.3 Setting Conditions for Running a Background Task 218

Problem 218

Solution... 218

How It Works.. 219

11.4 Monitor Background Task Progress and Completion... 220

Problem 220

Solution... 220

How It Works.. 220

■**Chapter 12: Location and Maps in Windows Apps** **221**

12.1 Get the Current Location 221

Problem 221

Solution... 221

How It Works.. 221

12.2 Respond to Geolocator Location Updates... 226

Problem 226

Solution... 226

How It Works.. 226

12.3 Detect the User's Location with HTML5 231

Problem 231

Solution... 231

How It Works.. 232

12.4 Detect Location Updates with HTML5 235

Problem 235

Solution... 235

How It Works.. 235

12.5 Display Maps in the Built-in Maps App 238

Problem 238

Solution... 238

How It Works.. 238

12.6 Display Directions in the Built-in Maps App 242

Problem 242

Solution... 242

How It Works... 243

12.7 Bing Maps Control in the Windows Store App 245

Problem 245

Solution... 245

How It Works... 246

■Chapter 13: Building Apps That Connect to the Cloud.......................... 251

13.1 Creating a New Mobile Service in Microsoft Azure 251

Problem 251

Solution... 251

How It Works... 251

13.2 Creating a Database Table in Mobile Services 258

Problem 258

Solution... 258

How It Works... 258

13.3 Installing Mobile Services for the WinJS Client Library............................ 260

Problem 260

Solution... 260

How It Works... 260

13.4 Performing the CRUD Operation 262

Problem 262

Solution... 262

How It Works... 262

13.5 Data Retrieval with Paging 267

Problem 267

Solution... 267

How It Works... 267

13.6 Sorting Returned Data from the Mobile Service 269

Problem 269

Solution 269

How It Works 269

13.7 Performing Validation in a Server Script 270

Problem 270

Solution 270

How It Works 271

■Chapter 14: Tiles and Notifications 275

14.1 Create a Default Tile 275

Problem 275

Solution 275

How It Works 275

14.2 Create Adaptive Tiles 276

Problem 277

Solution 277

How It Works 277

14.3 Create a Toast Notification with Visual Content 279

Problem 279

Solution 279

How It Works 280

14.4 Create a Toast Notification with Actions 281

Problem 281

Solution 281

How It Works 281

14.5 Create a Scheduled Tile and Toast Notification 283

Problem 283

Solution 283

How It Works 283

14.6 Create or Update a Badge on a Tile 285

    Problem 285

    Solution... 285

    How It Works.. 285

■ **Chapter 15: Device Capabilities** **287**

15.1 How to Specify Device Capabilities in an App Package Manifest......................... 287

    Problem 287

    Solution... 287

    How It Works.. 287

15.2 How to Specify Device Capabilities for Bluetooth for Windows Apps.................. 289

    Problem 289

    Solution... 289

    How It Works.. 289

15.3 How to Find Devices Available for a UWP App... 290

    Problem 290

    Solution... 290

    How It Works.. 290

15.4 How to Create an Audio Stream and Output Speech Based on Plain Text........... 292

    Problem 292

    Solution... 292

    How It Works.. 293

15.5 How to Specify Recognition Constraints for Speech Recognition 300

    Problem 300

    Solution... 300

    How It Works.. 300

15.6 How to Launch Your App with Cortana Voice Command in Foreground 303

    Problem 303

    Solution... 303

    How It Works.. 304

■Chapter 16: Additional Tools... 307

16.1 JavaScript Console Window 307

Problem 307

Solution... 307

How It Works.. 307

16.2 DOM Explorer 310

Problem 310

Solution... 311

How It Works.. 311

16.3 Diagnostic Tools 314

Problem 314

Solution... 314

How It Works.. 314

16.4 Windows 10 Mobile Emulator: Additional Tools 318

Problem 318

Solution... 318

How It Works.. 318

■Chapter 17: Sideloading and Windows App Certification Kit............................. 327

17.1 Sideload Your App.. 327

Problem 327

Solution... 327

How It Works.. 327

17.2 Install Certificate and Package Separately... 330

Problem 330

Solution... 330

How It Works.. 330

17.3 Validate Your Windows App Using the Windows App Certification Kit 336

Problem 336

Solution... 336

How It Works.. 336

17.4 Validate an App Package on a Remote Windows 10 Device 342

Problem 342

Solution 342

How It Works 342

■Chapter 18: Store and Monetization 347

18.1 Create a Windows App Developer Account 347

Problem 347

Solution 347

18.2 Package a Universal Windows Platform Application for Windows 10 349

Problem 349

Solution 349

How It Works 349

18.3 Submit an App to the Windows Store 358

Problem 358

Solution 359

18.4 Use Windows Ad Mediation in Your UWP Apps 360

Problem 360

Solution 360

18.5 Show Ads in Your Application 362

Problem 362

Solution 362

Index 365

About the Authors

Senthil Kumar leads the Windows app development team at Cleartrip Pvt. Ltd. He previously worked for Trivium eSolutions in Bangalore. His experience spans across various technologies within the Microsoft stack, including Windows Phone, WinForms, ASP.NET, SQL Server, C#, and Entity Framework. He is a Microsoft MVP (Most Valuable Professional) in Windows Platform Development and a Microsoft Certified Technology Specialist (ASP.NET). He is a technical presenter, blogger, mentor, and a Geek. Senthil is actively involved in the local developer communities and is an active member and UG lead for the Bangalore .NET User Group (BDotnet). He is a regular speaker in local user groups and conferences. He has presented in conferences like the Great Indian Developer Summit and Microsoft DevCamps and WebCamps. He blogs at DeveloperPublish.com. You can reach out to Senthil via the Twitter handle @isenthil.

Lohith Goudagere Najaraj is a production engineer by education and a software engineer by profession. He has 15 years of industry experience in Microsoft .NET technology. He specializes in building web applications using .NET as a platform. He is well versed in the WebForms and MVC ways of building a web application. He has been awarded the prestigious Microsoft Most Valuable Professional (MVP) award five years in a row. In his day job, Lohith works as a Technical Evangelist in India. He is a regular speaker in local user groups and conferences. He has presented in uber conferences such as Microsoft TechEd India, the Great Indian Developer Summit, and the Mobile Developer Summit, to name a few. He can also be seen presenting in Microsoft DevCamps across India. He is a lead for the Bangalore Dotnet User Group and helps run the group.

He lives in Bangalore with his lovely wife, Rashmi, and son Adithya. He likes to listen to Bryan Adams, Raghu Dixit, and Sonu Nigam. He also likes to watch the *Ocean's* Trilogy, *Italian Job*, and *National Treasure* all the time.

Pryank Rohilla works as a collaboration solutions architect for a Microsoft Gold partner in London. Pryank has 15 years of software development experience in Microsoft technologies. He is Microsoft certified and has worked as developer, consultant, architect, tech lead, and delivery lead in various engagements. He lives in Reading, UK. His Twitter handle is @Pryankrohilla. In his free time, Pryank enjoy watching sports and spending time with family and friends.

Pathik Rawal is a successful technical architect and working as a Microsoft technology architect. He has 15 years of software development experience and he has worked on many consulting and technical assignments. Pathik is Microsoft Certified and enthusiastic about cloud and mobile platforms. He lives in London. He can be reached on Twitter at @Pathikrawal. Pathik enjoys socializing with friends and family in his free time.

About the Technical Reviewer

Fabio Claudio Ferracchiati is a senior consultant and a senior analyst/developer using Microsoft technologies. He works at BluArancio SpA (`www.bluarancio.com`) as Senior Analyst/Developer and Microsoft Dynamics CRM Specialist. He is a Microsoft Certified Solution Developer for .NET, a Microsoft Certified Application Developer for .NET, a Microsoft Certified Professional, and a prolific author and technical reviewer. Over the past ten years, he's written articles for Italian and international magazines and coauthored more than ten books on a variety of computer topics.

About the Technical Reviewer

Acknowledgments

Writing a book is a challenging task that takes lot of time and effort. This requires tremendous support from family and friends. Thanks to my parents for their endless support. Not to forget few of my mentors—Sree Kumar (VP, Trivum eSolutions), Ananda Kumar (project manager, Trivium eSolutions), Jayaprakash (principal engineering manager, Cleartrip) who have been very much supportive of me in writing this book. I also need to thank my coauthors and friend Lohith GN, and the Apress team.

—Senthil Kumar

To Dad, Mom, my wife, Rashmi, and my son, Adithya.

—Lohith GN

Writing a book was not an easy task for me. It takes a lot of time and lot of support. Thanks to my wife for her endless support. I also need to thank coauthor and friend Pathik Rawal, and the talented team of editors and reviewers at Apress. It would have not been completed without your collaboration.

—Pryank Rohilla

I wish to personally thank the following people for their contributions to my inspiration and knowledge and other help in creating this book.

Pryank Rohilla (coauthor)

Gwenan Spearing (editor)

Melissa Maldonado (coordinating editor)

Douglas Pundick (development editor)

My family (wife, Mittu, and two kids, Aayu and Jigi)

—Pathik Rawal

Introduction

With Window 10, Microsoft has brought in the concept of a "universal" application architecture to Windows, where the apps designed using UWP can run across different Windows-powered devices like PCs, tablets, smartphones, Xbox One, iOT, Surface Hub, and HoloLens.

You could develop Universal Windows Platform (UWP) apps using various technologies, like C# and XAML, web technologies (HTML, CSS, JavaScript, and WinJS), C++, and so forth.

Examples in the book cover the development of a Universal Windows Platform (UWP) app using web development technologies (HTML, JavaScript, and CSS). Once you have knowledge of web development technologies and you have mastered the UWP app development examples in this book, you will have a head start in building some great Windows apps that can run on almost all the devices powered by Windows.

Who This Book Is For

This book is targeted at developers with some basic knowledge in web development technologies like HTML, CSS, and JavaScript and who are interested in developing Windows apps. The step-by-step approach taken in the book will help developers understand the concepts much easier.

What You Will Learn

Chapter 1: Get introduced to the Universal Windows Platform, its features, and how to get started with the development of a UWP app. You'll learn about the development tools required for UWP app development and how to create the app and run it on a Windows machine.

Chapter 2: Learn the fundamentals of the WinJS library. In this chapter, you'll explore how to use namespaces, class, and promise in WinJS.

Chapter 3: In this chapter, you'll explore various controls that are available in the WinJS library for building the Windows apps. You will learn how to add a WinJS control in the HTML page and setting its properties. Additionally, you get to explore some of the commonly used WinJS controls.

Chapter 4: Learn about ListControls like Repeater Control, FlipView, ListView, AppBar, and ToolBar. Explore options on how to filter and group items in the ListView control.

Chapter 5: In this chapter, you'll learn about databinding in WinJS and the navigation structure used in Universal Windows Platform apps.

Chapter 6: Universal Windows Platform runs on various devices with different screen sizes, which provides a challenge for developers and designers to adapt their app to these scenarios. In this chapter, you will learn how to adapt your UI for different screens.

Chapter 7: Learn about application states and lifecycle events. Also learn how to handle the termination and resumption of the app, as well as state management in the app.

Chapter 8: Are you targeting your UWP app for multiple regions and languages? This chapter provides the necessary recipe to add globalization and localization support in your UWP app built using WinJS.

Chapter 9: This chapter provides an overview of the data storage techniques to store app data in a Windows 10 app. You will learn about app settings, how to store and retrieve app settings as app data, and working with app data folders.

Chapter 10: This chapter covers how to share data between Universal Windows Platform apps. Sharing data enables developers to build features that allow users to share information, copy/paste, and drag and drop from one app to another app.

Chapter 11: Learn about the background tasks in UWP. Explore topics like system event triggers, creating and running a background task, and more.

Chapter 12: Do you want to integrate Location APIs in your Windows app? This chapter covers topics such as maps and locations that can be used by developers to integrate in their UWP JavaScript apps.

Chapter 13: In this chapter, you learn about the integration of Microsoft Azure Mobile Services in your Universal Windows Platform app. This includes recipes that explain how to create the mobile services back end in Azure and how you can connect from your app to perform CRUD operations.

Chapter 14: This chapter provides insights about the tiles and notifications features of Windows 10. Here you learn about the creation of default tiles, adaptive tiles, and toast notifications.

Chapter 15: In this chapter, you'll explore the various device capabilities and sensors in your Windows device and how you can use them in your UWP app.

Chapter 16: In this chapter, you'll learn about additional tools, like the JavaScript Console window, DOM Explorer, diagnostic tools, the Windows 10 Mobile emulator, and more. These tools let developers easily debug and test their Windows apps.

Chapter 17: In this chapter, you'll explore sideloading and installing your Windows app on devices. You'll learn about using the Windows App Certification Kit to test your app and generate reports to see if it is ready for the Windows Store.

Chapter 18: Once app development is complete, you need to submit it to the Windows Store so that users can download your app. In this chapter, you'll learn how to create the application package and submit it to the Store. You will also learn how to monetize your Windows app.

Source Code

The source code for this book can be found at www.apress.com/9781484207208. Scroll down and select the Source Code/Downloads tab to view the Download link.

■ ■ ■

CHAPTER 1

Getting Started with Windows 10 Applications

Windows 10 is the new operating system released by Microsoft on July 29, 2015. It has been much awaited since Windows 8.1. For application developers (Store and Phone), Windows 8.1 and Visual Studio 2013 gave a unique programming model called Universal Windows 8 applications. Universal Windows apps were able to target both Windows and Windows Phone from a shared code base. With Windows 10, it goes beyond Windows and Windows Phone and introduces what is known as Universal Windows Platform (UWP) apps. With the new platform, you are guaranteed a consistent core API layer across devices. A single package developed on UWP can be installed on a wide range of devices and device families. The device family includes desktop OS, Mobile OS (phones and tablets), Xbox, and Internet of Things (IoT) devices and headless device families. This means that your apps can run on any variety of devices, including phones, tablets, PCs, Xbox consoles, and more. This chapter introduces Windows 10 Universal Windows Platform application development.

1.1 Examining the Universal Windows Platform

Problem

You have decided to develop a Universal Windows Platform application that targets PCs, phones, tablets, and the Xbox. You want to understand the Universal Windows Platform—device families and universal controls.

Solution

Let's go through some of the highlights of the Universal Windows Platform.

One Windows Platform

Windows 10 brings one Windows platform to the table (see Figure 1-1). In Windows 10, the OS has been refactored and now has a common core across different Windows 10 platforms. This means that you have a common Windows kernel, one file I/O stack, and one app model. Simply put, the Universal Windows Platform is a collection of contacts and versions. With Windows Phone 8.1 and Windows 8.1 applications, you have to target the OS—either Windows or Windows Phone, whereas with Universal Windows Platform apps, you target the devices.

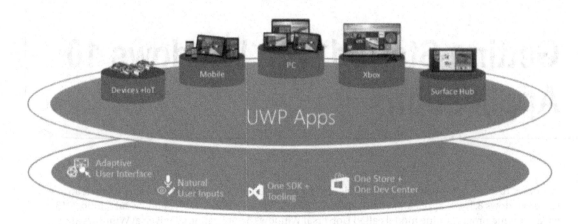

Figure 1-1. Universal Windows Platform apps model

UWP apps can run on a variety of devices that have different form factors and input mechanisms. When you develop UWP apps, you need to make sure that you tailor the experience to each device and take advantage of the respective device's capabilities. There is a common core or kernel on Windows 10. Each device adds its own API to the base layer. So to access the devices' unique APIs, you need to write conditional code to provide device-specific features in your apps.

Device Families

Windows and Windows Phone are the operating systems that developers targeted their Windows 8.1 and Windows Phone 8 applications. But with Windows 10 now available on various devices, UWP apps target a specific device family. A device family identifies APIs, characteristics, and behaviors that are seen across the devices within the family. It also determines the set of devices that the app can be installed on. Figure 1-2 showcases the device family hierarchy.

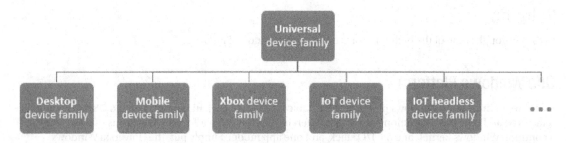

Figure 1-2. Universal device family hierarchy

A set of APIs have a name and a version number. This is the foundation of a device family OS. For example, PCs run the desktop OS and are based on the desktop device family. On the other hand, phones and tablets have a mobile OS that is based on the mobile device family. I hope you now have an idea of what exactly a device family is.

Universal Controls

With UWP, apps run on different form factors, screen resolutions, DPIs, and other device characteristics. Apps have to adapt to these different form factors and resolutions. Windows 10 provides new universal controls, layouts, and tooling that will help you adapt your app API according to the device on which it is run. Windows 10 includes new controls, such as Calendar and Split View. Pivot control, which was specific to Windows Phone apps, is now available for Universal Windows Platform apps.

Common Input Handling

With UWP apps, the universal controls now support various inputs, such as the mouse, keyboard, touch, pens, and controllers (e.g., the Xbox controller). The platform provides some core APIs that can be used in your apps to handle various inputs. The following are some of the input APIs that can be used.

- *CoreInput*: Allows you to consume raw input.

- *PointerInput*: Unifies raw touch, the mouse, and the pen into a single consistent interface.

- *PointerDevice*: A device API that allows you to query device capabilities to understand the available input types.

1.2 Development Tools for Universal Windows Platform

Problem

You want to start developing Universal Windows Platform apps. You want to know which tools you should use for development.

Solution

You need to have the Windows 10 operating system and Visual Studio 2015 Community Edition installed on your development machine.

To install Windows 10, visit Microsoft at http://windows.microsoft.com/en-us/windows/buy. If you are already on any Windows OS, you are able to upgrade your OS to Windows 10 for free.

To install the Visual Studio 2015 (VS 2015) Community Edition, you can visit the Microsoft site at https://www.visualstudio.com/en-us/downloads/visual-studio-2015-downloads-vs. When installing VS 2015, you need to make sure that the Universal Windows app development tools are selected (see Figure 1-3). This is in the optional features list.

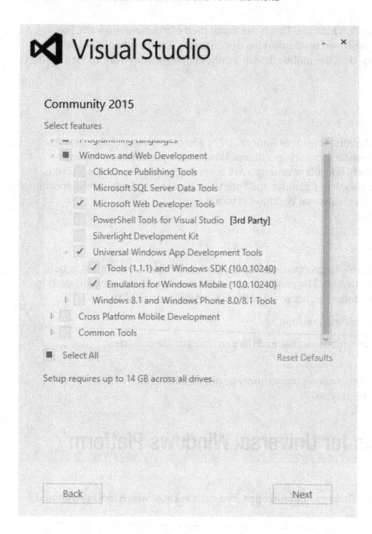

Figure 1-3. *Visual Studio 2015 Community Edition installation*

1.3 Creating Universal Windows Platform Application

Problem

You want to create a simple Universal Windows Platform application.

Solution

Visual Studio 2015 comes with a preinstalled Universal Windows Platform application project template. You will use this template to create your first application.

How It Works

Let's see how to create a new Universal Windows Platform app using Visual Studio 2015.

1. Open Visual Studio 2015 Community edition. Select **File ➤ New Project**. In the New Project dialog window, select **Templates ➤ JavaScript ➤ Windows ➤ Universal** from the Installed Templates section. **Select Blank App (Universal Windows)** from the available project templates (see Figure 1-4). Provide a name and location for the app and click **OK**.

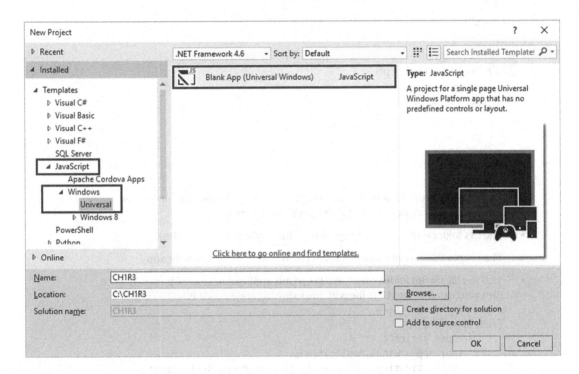

Figure 1-4. *New project template*

2. Visual Studio will prepare the project. Figure 1-5 shows what the new solution looks like.

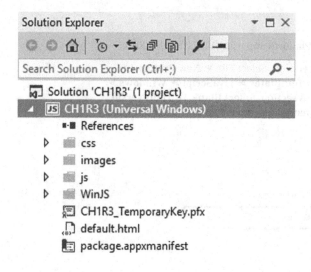

Figure 1-5. *Solution Explorer*

As part of the project template, you get css, images, js, and WinJS folders. You also have a pre-created default.html page to get started.

- The css folder is the place to keep your custom stylesheets (.css files).

- The images folder contains any images you would like to use in your app.

- js is the JavaScript folder where you keep your application-related js files. You see the pre-created default.js file with the following code inside it.

```
(function () {
        "use strict";
        var app = WinJS.Application;
        var activation = Windows.ApplicationModel.Activation;
        app.onactivated = function (args) {
                if (args.detail.kind === activation.ActivationKind.launch) {
                    if (args.detail.previousExecutionState !==
                activation.ApplicationExecutionState.terminated) {
                            //App Initilization code
                    } else {
                            //Restore app sessions state
                    }
                    args.setPromise(WinJS.UI.processAll());
                }
        };
        app.oncheckpoint = function (args) {
            //save any app state here
        };
        app.start();
})();
```

3. The code creates a `WinJS.Application` object instance and starts the application.

4. Open **default.html** by double-clicking the file in Solution Explorer. Here is the default code you see in the file:

```
<!DOCTYPE html>
<html>
<head>
    <meta charset="utf-8" />
    <title>Ch1R3</title>
    <link href="WinJS/css/ui-dark.css" rel="stylesheet" />
    <script src="WinJS/js/basejs"></script>
    <link href="/css/default.css" rel="stylesheet" />
    <script src="/js/default.js"></script>
</head>
<body class="win-type-body">
    <p>Content goes here</p>
</body>
</html>
```

5. It's pretty much empty with just one line of text that reads, "Content goes here." Replace this text with "Hello World!" This will be our Hello World application with UWP ☺.

6. Press **Ctrl+Shift+B** on your keyboard or select **Build ➤ Build solution**. Visual Studio builds the project.

1.4 Running Universal Windows Platform Apps

Problem

You have created a new UWP app and you would like to run the app to see it in action. You want to know how to do this.

Solution

Visual Studio 2015 comes with a lot of options to run your UWP app:

- Run Application on Windows Phone 10 Emulators
- Run Application on Windows 10 Simulator
- Run Application on Local Machine
- Run Application on Device

How It Works

When you install Visual Studio 2015, it also installs Windows Phone 10 emulators and the Windows 10 simulator. These emulators and simulators mimic different devices and screen sizes in Windows Phone and Windows. Visual Studio 2015 allows you to select one of these options to deploy your app. You can also deploy the app on your machine right from Visual Studio and run the app as a local app. Let's look at all of these options, one at a time.

Run Application on Windows Phone 10 Emulator

In Visual Studio, select one of the Windows 10 emulators available from the target combo box. Figure 1-6 shows the list of available emulators.

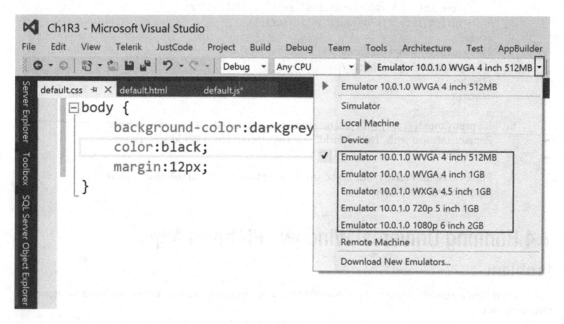

Figure 1-6. *Windows Phone 10 emulators target*

Press **F5** to run the app on the selected Windows Phone 10 emulator. Figure 1-7 shows a screenshot on a 4-inch Windows Phone 10.

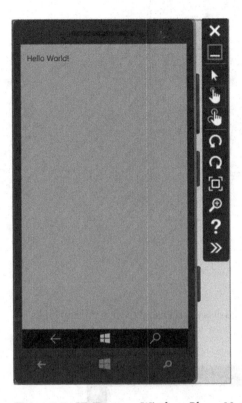

Figure 1-7. *UWP app on Windows Phone 10 emulator*

Run Application on Windows 10 Simulator

In Visual Studio, select **Simulator** from the target combo box. This option allows you to deploy your app to a Windows 10 simulator (see Figure 1-8).

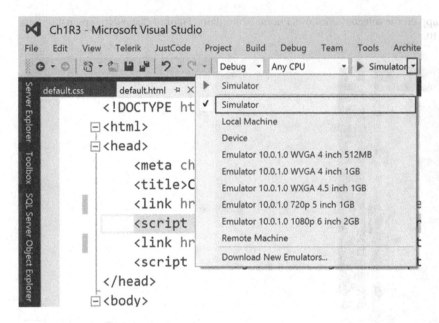

Figure 1-8. *Windows 10 simulator target*

Press **F5** to run the app on the Windows 10 simulator. Figure 1-9 is a screenshot of what the app looks like on a simulator.

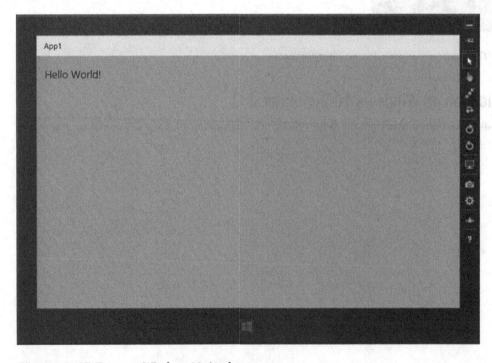

Figure 1-9. *UWP app on Windows 10 simulator*

Run Application on Local Machine

Typically, Windows 10 apps need to be downloaded from Windows Store and then installed on your machine. But this workflow is applicable only for end users, not developers. During app development, a developer can directly deploy and run their app on their development machine.

Before running your app on your local machine, you need to enable what is known as Developer Mode on your machine.

On your machine, go to **Settings ➤ Update & security ➤ For developers**, as shown in Figure 1-10.

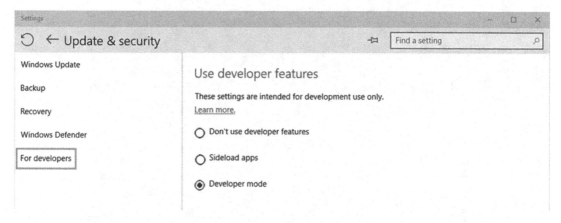

Figure 1-10. *Developer features settings*

7.   Select the **Developer mode** radio button.

8.   In Visual Studio, select **Local Machine** from the target combo box, as shown in Figure 1-11.

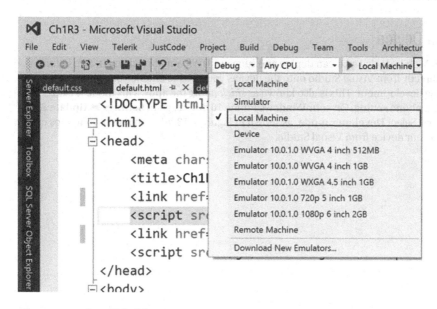

Figure 1-11. *Local Machine target*

9. Press **F5** to run the app on your development machine. Figure 1-12 is a screenshot of the app running on a local machine.

Figure 1-12. UWP app on local machine

Run Application on Device

If you have a Windows 10 Mobile device, you can deploy and run your UWP app directly on it. But, before you can deploy the app directly from Visual Studio onto the device, you need to enable your phone to allow apps to be installed during development. This is also known as *sideloading* the apps. This mode is called as Developer Mode and it is a phone setting. On your Windows Phone 10 device, go to **Settings ► Update & security ► For developers**. Select **Developer mode**, as shown in Figure 1-13. After this step, your apps can be deployed directly onto your device from Visual Studio.

Figure 1-13. *Developer Mode setting on Windows Phone device*

In Visual Studio, select **Device** as your target, as shown in Figure 1-14.

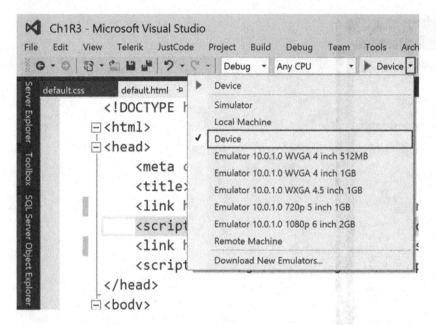

Figure 1-14. *Device target*

Next, press **F5** to run the app on your device. The output should be similar to what you have seen in the emulator.

CHAPTER 2

■ ■ ■

WinJS Fundamentals

When building an app using a library for the platform, it is important to understand the features that the library provides. In this chapter, you'll look at various features that WinJS provides for building Windows Runtime apps using JavaScript, HTML, and CSS. These features include namespaces, modules, promises, and query selectors. These are features used in almost all the applications that you build using WinJS. By taking advantage of the features like namespaces and modules, you can make your app easier to maintain, instead of adding everything under the global namespace.

2.1 Namespaces in JavaScript

Problem

You need to group common functionalities and prevent naming collisions in your JavaScript code when developing using the WinJS library.

Solution

Namespaces allow developers to better group or organize common functionalities. The other programming languages—C#, VB.NET, Java, and so forth—provide this feature. Plenty of JavaScript frameworks do not support namespaces, but WinJS provides a feature in which developers can utilize the namespaces in their projects. Namespaces can come in handy, especially when your app utilizes multiple libraries written by various developers.

Developers can use the `WinJS.Namespace.define` method to declare a namespace.

How It Works

The WinJS library lets developers declare namespaces by using the `WinJS.Namespace.define` method. The `WinJS.Namespace.define` method takes two parameters.

- `Name`: This is the first parameter and represents the name of the new namespace.

- `Members`: This is the second parameter and it is completely optional. This parameter represents the list of objects that need to be added to the namespace being defined.

The following are the steps to create a new namespace in a Windows Store universal app using WinJS.

1. Launch Visual Studio 2015 and select **File ➤ New Project**. In the **New Project** dialog, select **JavaScript ➤ Windows ➤ Universal** from the Installed Templates sidebar. Select **Blank App** (Universal Windows) from the template and name the project **ch2.1WinJSFundamentals**. Click the **OK** button. This created the necessary files within the Visual Studio solution.

2. Add a new JavaScript file in the ch2.1WinJSFundamentals project by right-clicking the project's **js** folder and selecting the **Add ➤ New Item** option. Select the JavaScript file from the **Add New Item** dialog and name the file **WinJSFundamentals.js**. Add the following code to the file.

```
// Define the Namespace Developerpublish
WinJS.Namespace.define("DeveloperPublish");
// Utilities created in the DeveloperPublish Namespace
DeveloperPublish.Utilities = {
    DisplayMessage: function () {
        return "Message from DeveloperPublish Namespace";
    }
};
// Define the Namespace Apress and create the Utilities under it.
WinJS.Namespace.define("Apress",
    {
        Utilities: {
            DisplayMessage: function () {
                return "Message from Apress Namespace";
            }
        }
    });
console.log(DeveloperPublish.Utilities.DisplayMessage());
console.log(Apress.Utilities.DisplayMessage());
```

In the preceding code snippet, the DeveloperPublish namespace demonstrates the usage of the WinJS.Namespace.define method with a single parameter. The objects are added to the namespaces, with the namespace followed by a period and the name of the object.

The Apress namespace is created with the two parameters. The first parameter is the name of the namespace, Apress; whereas the second parameter is the object that is part of the Apress namespace.

1. Open the default.html page and add the reference to the WinJSFundamentals.js file by using the following code snippet:

```
<script src="js/WinJSFundamentals.js"></script>
```

2. Run the Windows app. You will notice that the string that is returned from DisplayMessage of the Utilities class is displayed in the console window, as shown in Figure 2-1.

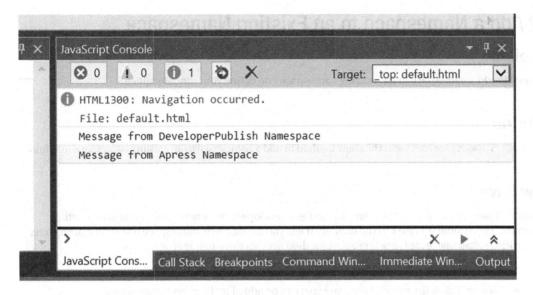

Figure 2-1. Display the string in the Visual Studio 2015 console window

WinJS.Namespace is the default namespace that provides functionalities like

- The promise object
- Functions to define namespaces, log, and xhr.

The following are objects and functions that are part of WinJS.Namespace.

- promise: This object provides the mechanism to implement asynchronous programming in your JavaScript code.

- validation: This property can be set to display the results of the validation.

- define: This function defines a new namespace with the specified name.

- defineWithParent: This function defines a namespace with a specified name under a specified parent namespace.

- log: This function writes the output to the JavaScript console window in Visual Studio 2015.

- xhr: This function wraps the calls made to the XMLHttpRequest in a promise.

Note that you should not refer to a namespace before it is defined. When you try to access the namespace before it is defined, you receive a "Namespace is undefined" error.

The Namespace feature is included in the WinJS library to better handle problems related to the scope. The source code for the Namespaces implementation in WinJS is found in the base.js file, which is under the WinJS/js folder of your project.

2.2 Add a Namespace to an Existing Namespace

Problem

You need to add a namespace to the existing namespace and define your functionalities.

Solution

Use the `WinJS.Namespace.defineWithParent` method to add a namespace to an existing namespace in WinJS.

How It works

The `WinJS.Namespace.defineWithParent` method lets developers add a new namespace to an existing namespace. This is similar to the `define` method; it lets you create a new namespace under an existing one.

The `WinJS.Namespace.defineWithParent` method accepts three parameters:

- *Parent namespace*: The first parameter is the name of the parent namespace.

- *Name*: This is the name of the namespace to be added to the parent namespace.

- *Members*: The list of objects to be added to the new namespace. This is an optional parameter.

Let's use the recipe created in Recipe 2.1. Open the `WinJSFundamentals.js` file in the project and replace it with the following code snippet.

```
WinJS.Namespace.define("Apress");
WinJS.Namespace.defineWithParent(Apress, "Books" ,
    {
        Utilities :
            {
                DisplayMessage: function () {
                    return "Message from Apress.Books Namespace";
                }
            }
    }

);
console.log(Apress.Books.Utilities.DisplayMessage());
```

Run the Windows Store project and you should see the string "Message from Apress.Books Namespace" displayed in the Visual Studio JavaScript console window, as shown in Figure 2-2.

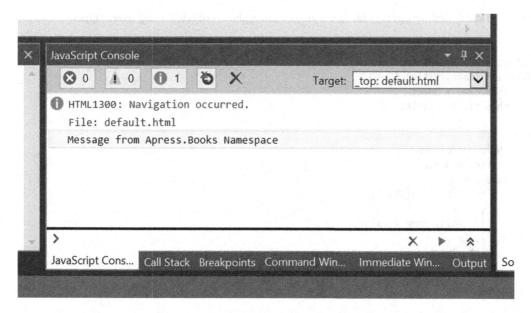

Figure 2-2. Display the string in the JavaScript console window in Visual Studio 2015

Note that the namespaces should only contain classes, functions, constants, and other namespaces.

2.3 Creating a Class in WinJS

Problem

You need to create a class in the JavaScript code within your Windows Runtime apps.

Solution

Use the WinJS.Class.define method to create a class in WinJS.

How It Works

C# and VB.NET are object-oriented languages. They have good implementation and support for the object-oriented concepts within the language; one such feature is the creation of the class. JavaScript, on the other hand, does not have the built-in support for the creation of the class. Everything in JavaScript is treated as an object.

WinJS lets developers create classes and utilize them within their applications.
You can use the WinJS.Class.define method to create a new class in WinJS.
The WinJS.Class.define method takes three parameters.

- *Constructor*: The first parameter lets developers initialize a new object.

- *Instance members*: The second parameter is the collection of instance members, which includes properties and methods.

- *Static members*: The third parameter includes static properties and static methods.

Open the WinJSFundamentals.js file in the project and replace it with following code snippet.

```
// Create a class called Author
var Author = WinJS.Class.define(
    function (name, title) {
        this.name = name;
        this.title = title;
    },
    {
        _Name: undefined,
        _title: undefined,
        name : {
            set :function(value)
            {
                this._Name = value;
            },
            get :function()
            {
                return this._Name;
            }
        },
        title : {
            set :function(value)
            {
                this._title = value;
            },
            get :function()
            {
                return this._title;
            }
        }
    });

// instantiate the author class by invoking the constructor with 2 parameters
var author1 = new Author("Senthil", "WinJS recipes");
// display the name and the title  in the console window.
console.log(author1.name);
console.log(author1.title);
```

In the preceding code snippet, the Author class is created using the WinJS.Class.define method. The first parameter to this method is the constructor, which takes two parameters and initializes the name and title.

The Author class has two properties.

- The title with its backing field _title
- The name with its backing field _name

Both of these properties contain a getter method and a setter method. Look at the following property, for example.

```
title : {
        set :function(value)
        {
            this._title = value;
        },
        get :function()
        {
            return this._title;
        }
    }
```

The `title` property has a `set` method, which lets developers set a value to the property. Similarly, you can retrieve the value of `_title` using the `title` property with the get method. From a developer's perspective, the call to the `<PropertyName>` object is good enough to get or set the value.

Run the Windows project. You should see the name and the title that are used when instantiating the object, as shown in Figure 2-3.

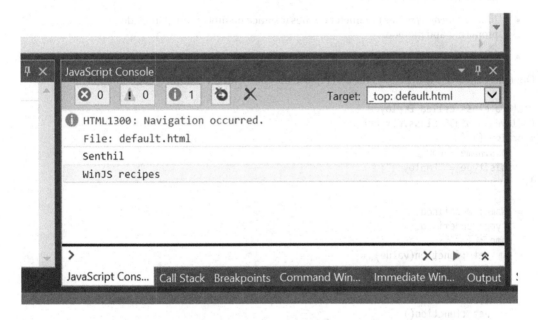

Figure 2-3. Displaying the name and title in the JavaScript console window in Visual Studio 2015

The WinJS.Class Namespace provides the following helper functions for defining Classes.

- `define`: This function defines a class using the specified constructor and instance members.

- `derive`: This function creates a subclass for the specified class by using the prototype inheritance.

- `mix`: This function defines a class using the specified constructor and combines the set of instance members specified by all the mixin objects.

2.4 Deriving a Class in WinJS

Problem

You need to apply the inheritance concept in your WinJS application.

Solution

Use the `WinJS.Class.derive` method to derive one class from another in WinJS.

How It Works

The WinJS library provides the `WinJS.Class.derive` method that lets developers apply inheritance to derive one class from another. The `WinJS.Class.derive` method takes the following parameters.

- *Base class*: The class that the current class needs to inherit from.
- *Constructor*: This parameter refers to the `constructor` function that can be used to initialize the class members.
- *Instance members*: This parameter defines instance members, which includes properties and methods.
- *Static members*: This parameter defines static properties and static methods.

Open the `WinJSFundamentals.js` file and replace the code with the following code snippet.

```
// Create a class called Employee
var Employee = WinJS.Class.define(
    function () {
        this.name = name;
        this.type = "Employee";
    },
    {
        _Name: undefined,
        _type: undefined,
        name : {
            set :function(value)
            {
                this._Name = value;
            },
            get :function()
            {
                return this._Name;
            }
        },
        type: {
            set :function(value)
            {
                this._type = value;
            },
```

```
        get :function()
        {
            return this._type;
        }
    }
});

var ContractEmployee = WinJS.Class.derive(Employee,
    function (name) {
        this.name = name;
        this.type = "Contract Employee";
    });
var ContractEmployee1 = new ContractEmployee("Senthil");
// display the name and the title  in the console window.
console.log(ContractEmployee1.name);
console.log(ContractEmployee1.type);
```

This code snippet creates a class called Employee. Later, another class called ContractEmployee is created; it derives from the Employee class. A contract employee instance is created and the name and the type of employment is displayed in the console window.

Run the Windows Store project from Visual Studio. This displays the name and the type in the JavaScript console window, as shown in Figure 2-4.

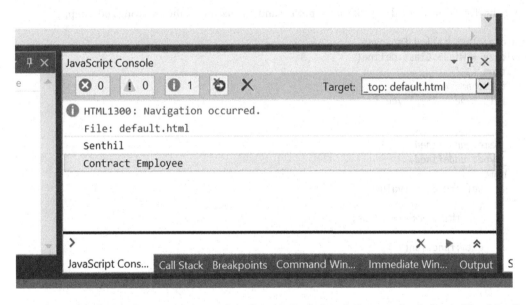

Figure 2-4. Displaying the name and type of employment in the JavaScript console window in Visual Studio 2015

The WinJS.Class.derive function behaves like the WinJS.Class.define function, except that it uses the prototype of the base class using the Object.create function to construct the derived class. The Object.create method derives one type from another by prototyping the parent object; it also adds the properties that are part of the child object.

2.5 Create Mixins in WinJS

Problem

You need to combine methods and properties from multiple JavaScript objects without using the WinJS. Class.derive method.

Solution

Use the WinJS.Class.mix method to combine methods and properties from multiple JavaScript objects in WinJS.

How It Works

The WinJS.Class.derive method uses the prototype inheritance, which has its own advantages and disadvantages. It requires additional time to process and has a performance impact. This can be overcome by using WinJS.Class.mix method.

The WinJS.Class.mix method takes two parameters.

- *Constructor*: The first parameter, which is used to initialize the class members.

- *Mixin*: The second parameter is the array that takes the mixin methods

Open the WinJSFundamentals.js file in the project and replace it with the following code snippet.

```
// Create a class called Employee
var Employee = WinJS.Class.define(
    function () {
        this.name = name;
        this.type = "Employee";
    },
    {
        _Name: undefined,
        _type: undefined,
        name : {
            set :function(value)
            {
                this._Name = value;
            },
            get :function()
            {
                return this._Name;
            }
        },
        type: {
            set :function(value)
            {
                this._type = value;
            },
```

```
        get :function()
        {
            return this._type;
        }
    }
});

var ContractEmployee = WinJS.Class.mix(
    function (name) {
        this.name = name;
        this.type = "Contract Employee";
    },Employee);


var ContractEmployee1 = new ContractEmployee("Senthil");
// display the name and the title  in the console window.
console.log(ContractEmployee1.name);
console.log(ContractEmployee1.type);
```

In this code sample, an `Employee` class is created and later another class called, `ContractEmployee`, is created; it inherits from the `Employee` class. Note that you have used the `mix` method instead of the derive method.

Well, the code might look similar to the one that was used with `derive` method, but the mixin adds more features. One such feature is the support of multiple inheritances. Since the second parameter in the `mixin` method is an array of mixins, you could have the `ContractEmployee` class implement the features from multiple classes.

When you execute this program, you see the name and the type of the employee, as shown in Figure 2-5.

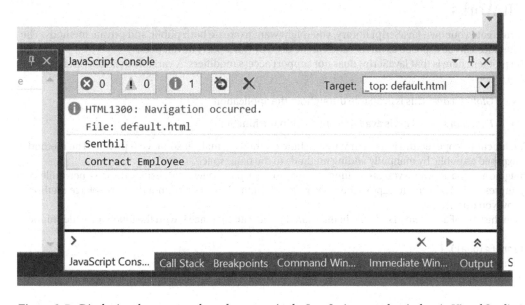

Figure 2-5. Displaying the name and employee type in the JavaScript console window in Visual Studio 2015

Mixins can be used to add functionality to your types. Mixins generally contain implemented functions that can be added to many types in WinJS.

In WinJS, you can manage events as well as bind using one of the following mixins.

- `WinJS.Utilities.eventMixin`: This mixin can be used to add the event management functionality to any type that you define. It includes functions like `WinJS.Utilities.eventMixin.addEventListener`, `WinJS.Utilities.eventMixin.removeEventListener`, and `WinJS.Utilities.eventMixin.dispatchEvent` to raise and handle custom events that you define.

- `WinJS.Binding.dynamicObservableMixin`: This function is used to add binding management functionality, in which developers can bind a user-defined object to a control that is capable of notifying listeners when the value of a property changes.

2.6 Encapsulation in WinJS

Problem

You want to build a library and you want to expose only a few methods from it to outside access. You need to support encapsulation in the WinJS application.

Solution

Use the capabilities of the functions and the namespaces to achieve this. The variable can have global scope or function scope. This feature can be used to bring in the encapsulation functionality in JavaScript.

How It Works

When you create your own JavaScript library, you might want to create both public and private methods. The public methods can be exposed as an API and can be used by third-party developers.

The problem here is that JavaScript does not support access modifiers. A variable in JavaScript has the following scope.

- *Global scope*: This is available throughout the application.

- *Function scope*: This is available only within the function.

The function scope feature is used in WinJS to hide methods to make it somewhat private. The methods can be exposed as public by manually adding methods to the namespace.

Imagine a scenario where you are writing a library to track page views and display the cost-per-million (CPM) impressions. You want to expose the `GetPageViews` method to users but not the `GetCPMRate` method. Here's how you do it...

Open the `WinJSFundamentals.js` file in the shared project and replace it with the following code snippet.

```
(function (global) {
    // public method
    function GetPageViews()
    {
        return 1000;
    }
    //private method.
```

```
    function GetCPMRate()
    {
        return 1;
    }
    WinJS.Namespace.define("DeveloperPublish",
    {
        GetPageViews: GetPageViews
    });
})(this);
```

```
console.log(DeveloperPublish.GetPageViews());
```

The self-executing anonymous function has two methods: GetPageViews and GetCPMRate. The DeveloperPublish namespace is used to expose or export the GetPageViews function and give it public access. GetCPMRate, on the other hand, is a private method. You can call the GetCPMRate method within the global scope method, but not using the DeveloperPublish namespace. For example, the following code snippet demonstrates a scenario where the GetPageViews and GetTotalRate functions are exposed using the DeveloperPublish namespace; the GetCPMRate is only used within the GetTotalRate.

```
(function (global) {
    // public method
    function GetPageViews() {
        return 1000;
    }
    //private method.
    function GetCPMRate() {
        return 2;
    }
    function GetTotalRate() {
        return GetPageViews() * GetCPMRate();
    }
    WinJS.Namespace.define("DeveloperPublish",
    {
        GetPageViews: GetPageViews,
        GetTotalRate: GetTotalRate
    });

})(this);
```

```
console.log(DeveloperPublish.GetPageViews());
console.log(DeveloperPublish.GetTotalRate());
```

Run the Windows project. In Figure 2-6, you see the GetPageViews method displaying 1000 in the Visual Studio JavaScript console window.

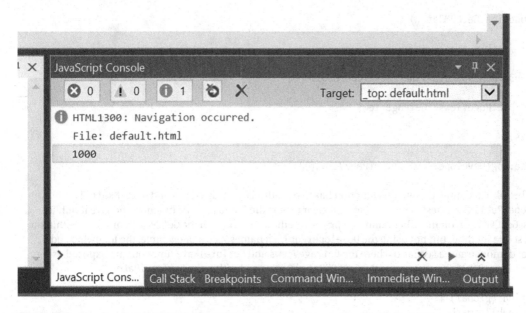

Figure 2-6. *Display the string in the JavaScript console window in Visual Studio 2015*

When you try to access the GetCPMRate method outside of the self-executing anonymous function, you get the following error (also see Figure 2-7).

```
0x800a1391: JavaScript runtime error: 'GetCPMRate' is undefined.
```

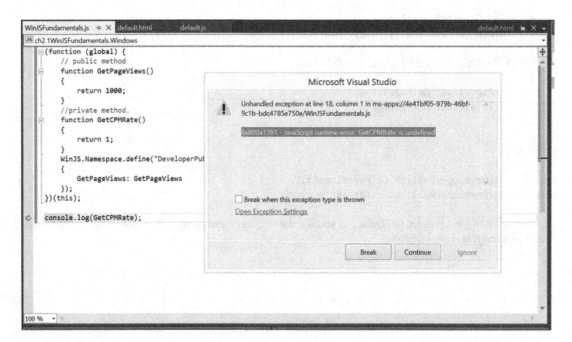

Figure 2-7. *Error when trying to access private methods*

This is a useful feature, especially when you are building a library and you want to restrict access to certain methods in WinJS.

2.7 Using Promise in WinJS

Problem

You need to execute the code asynchronously so that the UI is more responsive.

Solution

You can use the asynchronous programming in your Universal Windows apps so that the processing of certain methods can be done asynchronously. This way, your app's UI thread is free and responsive to user input.

How It Works

Asynchronous APIs in WinJS and Universal Windows apps are represented as promises. One of the common implementations of promise in WinJS is the xhr function, which wraps the XMLHttpRequest in a promise. When you provide a URL and the response type, the xhr function returns the promise, which is fulfilled by returning the data, or it returns an error if it fails.

In this recipe, you are building an app that simply takes the URL as input and tries to connect to it. The result is a success or failure based on the connection.

In Visual Studio 2015, launch the existing Universal Windows app that was built in the previous recipe. Open the default.html page and add the following div elements under the body section. This accepts the URL in the inputurl text box and the status is displayed in the output div tag.

```
<div>
    <input id="inputurl"/>
</div>
<div id="output">
</div>
```

You need to add the change event handler to the input element, which should be triggered when the user enters the text and hits the Enter key. You can add this within the WinJS.Utilities.ready function in the app.onactivated event handler in the default.js file, as shown next.

```
WinJS.Utilities.ready(function () {
                var input = document.getElementById("inputurl");
                input.addEventListener("change", changeEvent);
            }, false);
```

The next step is to add the changeEvent function, which needs to call the xhr function by passing the URL entered by the user; this updates the result accordingly. The return type of the xhr function is promise, which lets developers use the then function of the promise to update the UI asynchronously.

The then function takes up to three parameters, which includes

- The completed function that is executed if the promise was fulfilled without errors

- The error function to handle errors

- The progress function to display the progress of the promise

Let's add the changeEvent, as shown next, to the default.js file after the app.onactivated event.

```
function changeEvent(e) {
    var resultDiv = document.getElementById("output");
    WinJS.xhr({ url: e.target.value }).then(function completed(result) {
        if (result.status === 200) {
            resultDiv.style.backgroundColor = "Green";
            resultDiv.innerText = "Success";
        }
    },
        function error(e) {
            resultDiv.style.backgroundColor = "red";
            resultDiv.innerText = e.statusText;
        });
}
```

This code includes the completed and error functions for the promise. It displays the text *Success* or *Error* based on the result and changes the color of the output div element.

Build and run the app on a local machine, enter the URL, and hit the Enter key. If the URL is valid, the output div tag turns green and displays the Success message. If there is an error, the error message is displayed with a red background, as shown in Figure 2-8.

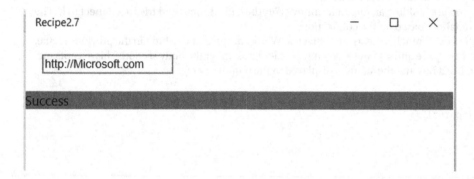

Figure 2-8. *Using the xhr function to demonstrate the promise*

You can stop the asynchronous operation that is currently in execution by using the cancel method of the promise object.

```
xhrPromise.cancel();
```

Note that you can also chain promise operations by invoking the then on the promise that is returned by the previous then function.

CHAPTER 3

■ ■ ■

Basic WinJS Controls

This chapter provides an overview of the controls that are available in the WinJS library, which can be used by developers to quickly build their Windows apps. It explores how to add WinJS controls to a page, as well basic WinJS controls like the ToggleSwitch, Rating, DatePicker, TimePicker, tooltip, text controls, and more.

There are advanced controls in WinJS that can be used to list records, display menus, or add toolbars in an app. (Chapter 4 covers advanced controls like ListView, Toolbar, and AppBar.)

3.1 Declaring a WinJS Control on a Page

Problem

You need to add or declare a WinJS control on a page of your Windows app.

Solution

Use the `data-win-control` attribute within the `div` tag to add the WinJS control on a page.

How It Works

1. Create a new project using the Windows Universal (Blank App) template in Microsoft Visual Studio 2015. This creates a universal app that can be run on Windows tablets and Windows Mobile powered by Windows 10.

2. Open the `default.html` page from the project in Visual Studio Solution Explorer.

3. Declare a WinJS control on a page by using the `data-win-control` attribute. For example, to declare the Rating Control on a page, add the following `div` tag.

```
<div id="rating" data-win-control="WinJS.UI.Rating"></div>
```

In this code snippet, the `div` tag acts like a placeholder for the WinJS control. The `data-win-control` attribute is used to indicate the WinJS control that will be rendered.

The HTML page will look like the following.

```
<!DOCTYPE html>
<html>
<head>
    <meta charset="utf-8" />
    <title>Recipe3.1</title>

    <!-- WinJS references -->
    <link href="WinJS/css/ui-light.css" rel="stylesheet" />
    <script src="WinJS/js/base.js"></script>
    <script src="WinJS/js/ui.js"></script>

    <!-- Recipe3.1 references -->
    <link href="/css/default.css" rel="stylesheet" />
    <script src="/js/default.js"></script>
</head>
<body class="win-type-body">
    <div id="rating" data-win-control="WinJS.UI.Rating"></div>
</body>
</html>
```

The main requirement for using the WinJS controls on the page is to include the JavaScript and the CSS files. You should add the following references in the head section of your HTML page.

```
<link href="WinJS/css/ui-light.css" rel="stylesheet" />
<script src="WinJS/js/base.js"></script>
<script src="WinJS/js/ui.js"></script>
```

The WinJS library provides two CSS (Cascading Style Sheets) files: ui-dark.css and ui-light.css. You can switch between the light theme and the dark theme for all of your controls by changing to ui-light.css and ui-dark.css, respectively.

The base.js and ui.js files are JavaScript files that need to be referenced in the HTML page to use the WinJS controls. The JavaScript source codes for the WinJS controls are defined in one of these JavaScript files.

The WinJS control (in this example, it's the Rating control) does not get rendered until the WinJS.UI.processAll method is called. This method is defined in the default.js file found under the js folder of the project. The main functionality of the WinJS.UI.processAll method is to parse the HTML page, identify the attributes with the data-win-control, and generate the control accordingly.

Hence, it is necessary to include the reference to the default.js file on the page.

Now, let's build the universal app and run it on Windows 10 and the Windows Mobile emulator.

Figure 3-1 demonstrates the appearance of the Rating control on a Windows tablet. Figure 3-2 demonstrates the appearance of the Rating control on Windows Mobile.

Figure 3-1. *Rating control on Windows 10*

Figure 3-2. *Rating control on Windows Mobile emulator*

3.2 Setting Options for WinJS Controls

Problem

You want to set additional options or properties for the WinJS controls on your HTML page.

Solution

Use the `data-win-options` attribute to set additional options or properties for the control.

How It Works

Most WinJS controls support the options attribute to be set. For example, when using the Rating control on the page, you might want to limit the maximum rating that the user can provide.

You can specify this with the `data-win-options` attribute. For example, the following HTML code demonstrates how you can set the Rating control's maximum ratings to 4.

```
<div id="rating" data-win-control="WinJS.UI.Rating"
    data-win-options="{maxRating:4}">
</div>
```

`data-win-options` takes the JavaScript options; it is passed with the property names and its value is surrounded by curly braces.

Here, the `maxRating` is a property. Multiple properties, along with their values, can be passed as well. For example, if you need to set the `enableClear` property along with the `MaxRating`, you would set it with the `data-win-options` attribute, as follows.

```
<div id="rating" data-win-control="WinJS.UI.Rating"
        data-win-options="{maxRating:4,enableClear:false}">
    </div>
```

Figure 3-3 demonstrates the screen and its display on the Window Mobile emulator.

Figure 3-3. *Rating control with maximum rating of 4*

If the enableClear property is set to true, then the user can slide to the left of the control to clear the rating value.

3.3 Adding WinJS Controls from Your JavaScript Code

Problem

You need to add a WinJS control from the JavaScript code instead of adding it in the HTML page.

Solution

You can create a control imperatively; that is, completely use JavaScript to identify the div element and dynamically generate the control and add it to the page.

How It Works

1. Create a new project using the Windows Universal (Blank App) template in the Visual Studio 2015 Community. This creates a Windows universal app that can be run on Windows tablets or on Windows Mobile running in Windows 10.

2. Open the project's `default.html` page from the project in Visual Studio Solution Explorer.

3. Add a `div` tag in the body section of the page where you want the control to be rendered.

   ```
   <div id="rating" >
       </div>
   ```

4. Right-click the `js` folder within the project in the Solution Explorer. Select Add ➤ New JavaScript File and provide a name for the file. In this example, let's name the file **controldemo.js**. This adds the `controldemo.js` file under the `js` folder of the project.

5. Add the following code to the `controldemo.js` file. This creates a new rating control and adds it to the rating `div` tag.

   ```
   (function () {
       "use strict";
       function AddControl()
       {
           var ratingDiv = document.getElementById("rating");
           var ratingCtrl = new WinJS.UI.Rating(ratingDiv);
       }
       document.addEventListener("DOMContentLoaded", AddControl);
   })();
   ```

The preceding code creates a new instance of the `WinJS.UI.Rating` JavaScript class. It is created by passing the rating `div` element to the constructor of the Rating class.

6. Now you need to add a reference to the `controldemo.js` file in the HTML page. Open the `default.html` file and add the following code snippet to the head section of the page.

```
<script src="/js/controldemo.js"></script>
```

The `default.html` page will contain the code, as shown here.

```
<!DOCTYPE html>
<html>
<head>
    <meta charset="utf-8" />
    <title>Recipe3.3</title>

    <!-- WinJS references -->
    <link href="WinJS/css/ui-light.css" rel="stylesheet" />
    <script src="WinJS/js/base.js"></script>
    <script src="WinJS/js/ui.js"></script>
```

```
    <!-- Recipe3.3 references -->
    <link href="/css/default.css" rel="stylesheet" />
    <script src="/js/default.js"></script>
    <script src="/js/controldemo.js"></script>
</head>
<body class="win-type-body">
    <div id="rating">
    </div>

</body>
</html>
```

Let's run the application on the Windows Mobile emulator. Figure 3-4 illustrates the output page on Windows Mobile.

Figure 3-4. *Rating control added from the JavaScript code*

The options or properties for the controls can also be set imperatively from the JavaScript code. The following shows how you can create an instance of the Rating control and set the `maximumRating` property from the JavaScript code.

```
(function () {
    "use strict";
    function AddControl()
    {
        var ratingDiv = document.getElementById("rating");
        var ratingCtrl = new WinJS.UI.Rating(ratingDiv);
        ratingCtrl.maxRating = 4;
    }
    document.addEventListener("DOMContentLoaded", AddControl);
})();
```

This code snippet shows how to set the maxRating property without setting it in the constructor. Alternatively, you can also set it by passing it to the second parameter, surrounded by curly braces.

Figure 3-5 demonstrates IntelliSense support in Visual Studio when setting Rating control properties.

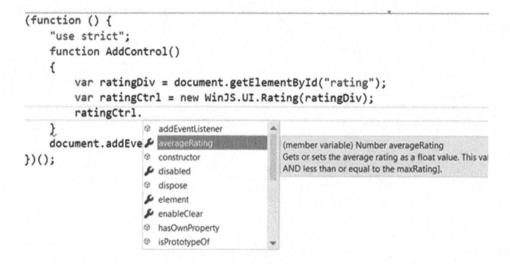

Figure 3-5. *IntelliSense support in Visual Studio 2015*

Intellisense is a great feature in Microsoft Visual Studio that improves developer productivity and provides automatic suggestions to developers based on what the user is typing in the IDE.

3.4 Getting the WinJS Controls from an HTML Document

Problem

You want to get the control from an HTML page and set properties using JavaScript code.

Solution

Use the winControl property to get the control from the page's DOM element.

How It Works

1. Create a new project using the Windows Universal (Blank App) template in Visual Studio 2015 Community. This creates a Windows universal app that can be run on Windows tablets and Windows Mobile running Windows 10.

2. Open the `default.html` page from the project in Visual Studio Solution Explorer.

3. Add the Rating control to the body section of the page.

    ```
    <div id="rating" data-win-control="WinJS.UI.Rating" >
        </div>
    ```

4. Right-click on the `js` folder within the project in the Solution Explorer. Select Add ➤ New JavaScript File and provide a name for the file. In this example, let's name the file **controldemo.js**. This adds the `controldemo.js` file under the `js` folder of the project.

5. Add the following code to the `controldemo.js` file.

    ```
    (function () {
        "use strict";
        function GetControl() {
            WinJS.UI.processAll().done(function () {
                var ratingControl = document.getElementById("rating").winControl;
                ratingControl.userRating = 2;
            });
        }

        document.addEventListener("DOMContentLoaded", GetControl);

    })();
    ```

6. When you invoke the `document.getElementById` method, you get the DOM element. You need to use the `winControl` property to get the associated control.

7. This needs to be surrounded by the `WinJS.UI.processAll` method, which returns the promise. The reason for surrounding your logic with the `processAll` method is that you have to wait until all the controls are created and parsed in the document before trying to retrieve it.

8. Once the Rating control is retrieved, you can start setting the values to the properties of the Rating control instance. In this example, you are setting the user rating to 2.

9. Finally, you need to add the reference of the `controldemo.js` file in the `default.html` page. Open the `default.html` page from Visual Studio Solution Explorer and add the following code to the head tag.

    ```
    <script src="/js/controldemo.js"></script>
    ```

When you run the application on the Windows Mobile emulator, you should see the screen shown in Figure 3-6.

Figure 3-6. *Windows Mobile emulator displaying the Rating control with value 2*

3.5 The ToggleSwitch Control

Problem

You need to provide an option for the user to perform a binary operation on the screen. For example, you need to provide the user with an option to turn a service on or off.

Solution

Use the ToggleSwitch control in WinJS. It is similar to the standard check box control, but has better touch support. You can simply swipe a finger across the ToggleSwitch control to check or uncheck the option. You can declare the ToggleSwitch control on the page using the WinJS.UI.ToggleSwitch value to the data-win-control attribute of the div element.

How It Works

The following shows how you declare the ToggleSwitch control on a page.

```
<div id="locationServices" data-win-control="WinJS.UI.ToggleSwitch"
        data-win-options="{
        title :'Location Services',
        labelOff: 'Disabled',
        labelOn:'Enabled',
        checked: true
        }">
</div>
```

When executed on a Windows tablet or a Windows Mobile emulator, the preceding code snippet will look like what's shown in Figure 3-7.

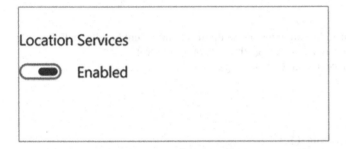

Figure 3-7. *ToggleSwitch on the Windows Mobile and Windows emulator*

The data-win-options attribute is used to set the additional attributes to the ToggleSwitch control. In the preceding example, properties like title, labelOff, labelOn, and Checked are set using this attribute.

The title sets the title content for the ToggleSwitch. The labelOff and labelOn properties identify the text that needs to be displayed next to the ToggleSwitch based on the checked (On) and unchecked (Off) state of the control.

The current state (checked or unchecked) of the ToggleSwitch can be found using the control's checked property.

Let's add a new JavaScript file to the project's js folder and name it **controldemo.js**. Open the default. html page and add the ToggleSwitch control as well as an empty div tag to display a message on a change of the toggle switch state.

The default.html looks like the following.

```
<!DOCTYPE html>
<html>
<head>
    <meta charset="utf-8" />
    <title>Recipe3.5</title>

    <!-- WinJS references -->
    <link href="WinJS/css/ui-light.css" rel="stylesheet" />
    <script src="WinJS/js/base.js"></script>
    <script src="WinJS/js/ui.js"></script>
```

```
    <!-- Recipe3.5 references -->
    <link href="/css/default.css" rel="stylesheet" />
    <script src="/js/default.js"></script>
    <script src="/js/controldemo.js"></script>
</head>
<body class="win-type-body">
    <div id="locationServices" data-win-control="WinJS.UI.ToggleSwitch"
        data-win-options="{
        title :'Location Services',
        labelOff: 'Disabled',
        labelOn:'Enabled',
        checked: true
        }">
    </div>
    <div id="info"></div>
</body>
</html>
```

To identify the state from the JavaScript code, you need to wire up the change event handler of the ToggleSwitch control. This event is triggered when you change the state of the control.

Open the controldemo.js file and replace it with the following code.

```
(function () {
    "use strict";
    function GetControl() {
        WinJS.UI.processAll().done(function () {
            var toggleButton = document.getElementById("locationServices").winControl;
            var InfoElement = document.getElementById("info");
            toggleButton.addEventListener('change', function (args) {
                if (toggleButton.checked) {
                    InfoElement.innerHTML = "Location Services enabled";
                }
                else {
                    InfoElement.innerHTML = "Location Services disabled";
                }
            })
        });
    }

    document.addEventListener("DOMContentLoaded", GetControl);

})();
```

When you run the application on the Windows 10 emulator and the Windows Mobile emulator, you will see the screen as shown in the Figure 3-8.

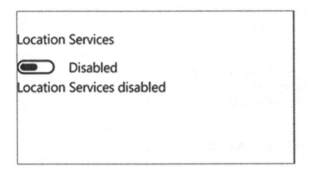

Figure 3-8. *ToggleSwitch with the change event.*

When you toggle the control, the appropriate message is displayed in the Info div element.

3.6 The DatePicker Control

Problem

You want to allow the user to select a date from the application page.

Solution

Use the WinJS DatePicker control that allows the user to pick a date. This control displays three lists: one each for the month, day, and year.

How It Works

You can declare the DatePicker control on the page, like this.

```
<div id="Birthday" data-win-control="WinJS.UI.DatePicker" >
</div>
```

In this recipe, let's try to add the DatePicker control on the page and bind the event in the JavaScript code to display the selected date in a div element.

1.   Create a new project using the Windows Universal App template in Visual Studio 2015.

2.   Open the default.html page and replace it with the following.

```
<!DOCTYPE html>
<html>
<head>
    <meta charset="utf-8" />
    <title>Recipe3.6</title>

    <!-- WinJS references -->
    <link href="WinJS/css/ui-light.css" rel="stylesheet" />
```

```
        <script src="WinJS/js/base.js"></script>
        <script src="WinJS/js/ui.js"></script>

        <!-- Recipe3.6 references -->
        <link href="/css/default.css" rel="stylesheet" />
        <script src="/js/default.js"></script>
        <script src="/js/controldemo.js"></script>
    </head>
    <body class="win-type-body">
        <div id="Birthday" data-win-control="WinJS.UI.DatePicker">
        </div>
        <div id="info"></div>
    </body>
    </html>
```

The default.html page contains the DatePicker control as well as the div tag with the name information to display the selected date. The controldemo.js file is referenced, which you create next.

3. Add a new JavaScript file to the project's js folder from Visual Studio Solution Explorer and name it **controldemo.js**. Add the following JavaScript code to the controldemo.js file.

```
    (function () {
        "use strict";
        function GetControl() {
            WinJS.UI.processAll().done(function () {
                var datepick = document.getElementById("Birthday").winControl;
                var InfoEelement = document.getElementById("info");
                datepick.addEventListener('change', function (args) {
                    InfoEelement.innerHTML = "The selected date is " +
                        datepick.current.toDateString();

                })
            });
        }
        document.addEventListener("DOMContentLoaded", GetControl);

    })();
```

The DatePicker raises the change event as soon as you change the date, or month, or year. You can get the current selected date by handling this event.

The winControl property of the document.getElementById is used to get the DatePicker from the HTML page in the JavaScript code. The addEventListener method is invoked from the DatePicker control to subscribe to the change event.

The selected date is retrieved using the current property of the DatePicker.

Running the application on Windows Mobile or Windows 10 displays the DatePicker and shows the selected date, as demonstrated in Figure 3-9.

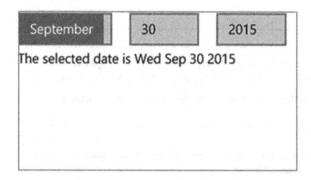

Figure 3-9. DatePicker control demo

You can control the appearance of the year, month, and date fields of the DatePicker control by assigning the format strings.

For example, the DatePicker can be formatted to display the abbreviated month and year, and the date, with a two-digit format, as shown here.

```
<div id="Birthday" data-win-control="WinJS.UI.DatePicker"
    data-win-options="{
    monthPattern : '{month.abbreviated}',
    datePattern: '{day.integer(2)}',
    yearPattern: '{year.abbreviated}'
    }">
</div>
```

The format is set using the `monthPattern`, `datePattern`, and `yearPattern` properties.

The `monthPattern` property defines the display pattern for the month. You can set the month pattern property with one of the values shown in Table 3-1.

Table 3-1. Month Pattern for the date picker

Pattern	Description
month.full	This displays the full name of the month.
month.abbreviated(n)	You can use the month.abbreviated with or without parameters. The parameter specifies the number of letters for the month.
month.solo.full	This represents the month that is suitable for the stand-alone display. And, month.solo.abbreviated can be used with or without parameters.
month.integer(n)	The month.integer is used to specify the number of integers displayed in the month field.

The `datePattern` property is used to get or set the display pattern for the date in the DatePicker control. You can set the `datePattern` with one of the values shown in Table 3-2.

Table 3-2. *Date Pattern for the date picker*

Pattern	Description
day.integer(n)	You can use the day.integer with or without parameters. The parameter specifies the leading zeroes to be included; for example, 02 is displayed if the value is day.integer (2).
dayofweek. abbreviated	This property displays the day of the week. The parameter specifies the number of letters to be displayed.

The yearPattern property gets or sets the display pattern for the year. The default year pattern is year. full. You can modify this to either of the values shown in Table 3-3.

Table 3-3. *Year pattern for the date picker*

Pattern	Description
year.full	Displays the full year in digits
year.abbreviated(n)	Displays the year with the specified set of digits.

3.7 The TimePicker Control

Problem

You want to allow the user to select a time from the application page.

Solution

Use the WinJS TimePicker control that allows the user to pick a time. This control displays three lists: one each for hour, minute, and period (AM/PM).

How It Works

You can declare the DatePicker control on the page, like this.

```
<div id="timeSelector" data-win-control="WinJS.UI.TimePicker" >
</div>
```

In this recipe, let's try to add the TimePicker control on the page and bind the event in the JavaScript code to display the selected time in a div element.

1. Create a new project using the Windows Universal App template in Visual Studio 2015.

2. Open the default.html page and replace it with the following.

```
<!DOCTYPE html>
<html>
<head>
    <meta charset="utf-8" />
    <title>BasicControls</title>
```

```html
<!-- WinJS references -->
<link href="WinJS/css/ui-light.css" rel="stylesheet" />
<script src="WinJS/js/base.js"></script>
<script src="WinJS/js/ui.js"></script>

<!-- Recipe3.7 references -->
<link href="/css/default.css" rel="stylesheet" />
<script src="/js/default.js"></script>
<script src="/js/controldemo.js"></script>
</head>
<body class="win-type-body">
    <div id="timeSelector" data-win-control="WinJS.UI.TimePicker">
    </div>
    <div id="info"></div>

</body>
</html>
```

The default.html page contains the TimePicker control as well as the div tag with the name information to display the selected time. The controldemo.js file is referenced, which you will create in the next step.

3. Add a new JavaScript file to the project's js folder from the Visual Studio Solution Explorer and name it **controldemo.js**. Replace the file with the following JavaScript code.

```javascript
(function () {
    "use strict";
    function GetControl() {
        WinJS.UI.processAll().done(function () {
            var datepick = document.getElementById("timeSelector").winControl;
            var InfoEelement = document.getElementById("info");
            datepick.addEventListener('change', function (args) {
                InfoEelement.innerHTML = "The selected time is " +
                    datepick.current.toTimeString();

            })
        });
    }
    document.addEventListener("DOMContentLoaded", GetControl);

})();
```

The TimePicker raises the change event as soon as you change the hour, or minute, or period. You can get the current selected time by handling this event.

The winControl property of the document.getElementById is used to get the TimePicker from the HTML page in the JavaScript code. The addEventListener method is invoked from the TimePicker control to subscribe to the change event.

The selected time is retrieved using the current property of the TimePicker control.

Running the application on Windows Mobile or Windows 10 displays the TimePicker and shows the selected time, as demonstrated in Figure 3-10.

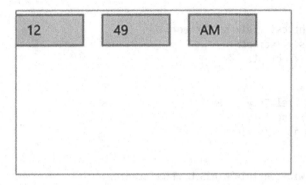

Figure 3-10. *TimePicker control demo*

You can set the TimePicker to support a 24-hour clock format by setting the clock property using the data-win-options attribute, as shown here.

```
<div id="timeSelector" data-win-control="WinJS.UI.TimePicker"
        data-win-options="{
        clock : '24HourClock',
        minuteIncrement : 15
        }">
</div>
```

The increment values of the minute list can be controlled with the minuteIncrement property, as shown next.

When you run the page on Windows 10 or Windows Mobile 10, you see the screen shown in Figure 3-11.

Figure 3-11. *TimePicker with the 24-hour clock format and timeInterval adjustment*

You can control the appearance of the hour, minute, and period fields of the TimePicker control by assigning the format strings.

The format is set using the hourPattern, minutePattern, and periodPattern properties.

The hourPattern property gets to set the display pattern for the hour. The default value of the hourPattern property is hour.integer(2) and you can modify the hourPattern property by changing the values of the parameters. The minutePattern property gets or sets the display pattern for the minute. The default value of this property is minute.integer (2) and you can modify this pattern by changing the number of integers in the parameter. The `periodPattern` property gets or sets the display pattern for the period; the default value of this property is period.abbreviated (2). You can modify the pattern for this property by changing the values of the parameters.

Table 3-4. *Pattern for hours, minutes and period in timepicker*

Pattern	Description
hour.integer(n)	This displays the specified number of digits for hours.
{minute.integer(n)}	This displays the specified number of digits for minutes.
{period.abbreviated(n)}	Display pattern for the period based on the value passed as parameter.

3.8 The Tooltip Control

Problem

You need to display a tooltip when the user hovers over any element on the page.

Solution

Use the WinJS Tooltip control to display the tooltip over the HTML element on the page. When you hover over an element, the tooltip appears for a specified number of seconds. The tooltip should disappear when the user moves the cursor away from the element.

How It Works

You add the Tooltip control for a button like this:

```
<button id="btnSave"
        data-win-control="WinJS.UI.Tooltip"
        data-win-options="{
        innerHTML: 'Saves the <b>Employee</b> record'}">
    Save
</button>
```

The innerHTML property is set via the `data-win-options` attribute, which sets the text for the tooltip control. This text can contain HTML tags too.

Figure 3-12 demonstrates the way that the tooltip is displayed on Windows Mobile 10 and Windows 10 tablets.

Figure 3-12. *Tooltip displayed within the app*

You can customize the styling of the tooltip control by modifying the `win-tooltip` CSS class. Open the `default.css` file from the CSS folder and add the following code to the end of the file.

```
.win-tooltip
{
    background-color: bisque;
    border-radius:30px;
    border-color:red;
}
```

Figure 3-13 demonstrates the appearance of the tooltip control after defining the style mentioned earlier.

Figure 3-13. *Tooltip with styling*

Note that when using the div element as container for the tooltip, you need to set its display property to inline block because the div element has a display setting of block by default.

3.9 Displaying Text

Problem

You need to display text or labels on the page of your Windows app.

Solution

Use traditional HTML elements or tags to display the text on the page of your Windows app. These include divs, labels, paragraphs, headings, and so forth.

How It Works

The HTML elements—like the label, div, paragraph, heading, and so forth—are some of the common controls used for displaying read-only text on Windows universal apps using JavaScript.

You can define a simple label control and set its text, as shown here.

```
<label>Welcome to the Windows 10 App Development World</label>
<div>by Microsoft MVPs</div>
```

The styling can be applied to the display text using one of two approaches: inline or CSS.

The following is a code snippet demonstrating the usage of the inline style attribute to format the text.

```
<div style="font-family:Verdana">Welcome to the Windows 10 App Development World</div>

<p style="margin:0px; color:blue; font-family:Arial; font-size:18px">Welcome to the Windows 10 App Development World</p>
```

Figure 3-14 illustrates the output of the preceding code using the inline style attributes.

Figure 3-14. *Styling the read-only text*

The CSS allows the developers to define a style—once and in a single place—and later reuse it for multiple controls.

3.10 Editing Text in an App

Problem

You need to allow the user to enter text on the page of your Windows app.

Solution

Use HTML elements to allow the user to enter text on the page. This includes text boxes, text areas, password input boxes, rich text boxes, and so forth.

How It Works

Windows universal apps using JavaScript has four different types of text entry elements.

- *Text box*: This control lets the user enter or edit plain text in single line.

- *Text area*: This control has multiline support and lets the user enter or edit plain text.

- *Password input box*: This control lets the user enter a password.

- *Rich text box*: This control lets the user edit text that requires formatting.

Here's the HTML for a simple text box, text area, and password input box.

```
<div><textarea id="textarea1" rows="2"></textarea></div>
<div><input type="text" /></div>
<div><input id="password" type="password" placeholder="Enter password" /></div>
```

Figure 3-15 illustrates how the controls are displayed on the Windows Mobile 10 emulator.

Figure 3-15. *Editable controls*

You can get the content of the control from the JavaScript code, as shown in Recipe 3-4, once the user performs some action such as a button click.

CHAPTER 4

List Controls, AppBar, and ToolBar

This chapter focuses on the controls that are related to the collection of data, including Repeater, FlipView, and ListView. The chapter also covers recipes on menu-related controls, such as AppBar, ToolBar, Flyouts, ContextMenu, and MenuFlyouts.

4.1 Using the Repeater Control

Problem

You need to display a collection of data on the user interface (UI) using the WinJS Repeater control.

Solution

The Repeater control is one of the controls available in the WinJS library to display a collection data on the UI. You can add the Repeater control by setting the `data-win-control` attribute to the WinJS.UI.Repeater value of the container, and later bind the properties to the controls in the UI by using the `data-win-bind` attribute.

How It Works

To demonstrate the use of the Repeater control, let's build a Universal Windows app that displays an HTML table of the employees list, as shown in Figure 4-1.

Recipe4.1   —   □   ×

Recipe 4.1

Employee ID	Employee Name	Employee Designation
1	Senthil Kumar	Mobile Developer
2	Lohith GN	Web Developer
3	Vidyasagar	Game Developer

Figure 4-1. *HTML table with a Repeater control*

Launch Visual Studio 2015 and create a new Windows Universal project using the JavaScript template. Open the default.html page and replace it with the following code snippet.

```
<!DOCTYPE html>
<html>
<head>
    <meta charset="utf-8" />
    <title>Recipe4.1</title>

    <!-- WinJS references -->
    <link href="WinJS/css/ui-light.css" rel="stylesheet" />
    <script src="WinJS/js/base.js"></script>
    <script src="WinJS/js/ui.js"></script>

    <link href="/css/default.css" rel="stylesheet" />
    <script src="/js/default.js"></script>
    <script src="/js/data.js"></script>

</head>
<body style="margin:20px">
    <h1>Recipe 4.1</h1>
    <table>
        <thead>
            <tr>
                <th> Employee ID</th>
                <th> Employee Name</th>
                <th> Employee Designation</th>
            </tr>
        </thead>
        <tbody id="repeaterData" data-win-control="WinJS.UI.Repeater">
            <tr>
                <td data-win-bind="textContent:id"></td>
                <td data-win-bind="textContent:name"></td>
                <td data-win-bind="textContent:designation"></td>
            </tr>
        </tbody>
    </table>
</body>

</html>
```

In the preceding code snippet, the Repeater control is added to the body section; whereas the inner content of the Repeater control is used as the template. Each row from the repeater data is displayed in the body section of the HTML table.

The preceding HTML page has a reference to a data.js page. Let's add this file to the project. Add a new JavaScript file to the project's js folder and name it **data.js**. The following code snippet contains the JavaScript code for setting the data source of the Repeater control.

```
(function () {
    "use strict";
    function Initialize() {
        WinJS.UI.processAll().done(function () {
```

```
            var repeaterControl1 = document.getElementById('repeaterData').winControl;
            var Employees = new WinJS.Binding.List([
                { id: 1, name: "Senthil Kumar", designation: "Mobile Developer" },
                { id: 2, name: "Lohith GN", designation: "Web Developer" },
                { id: 3, name: "Vidyasagar", designation: "Game Developer" }
            ]);
            repeaterControl1.data = Employees;
        })
    }
    document.addEventListener("DOMContentLoaded", Initialize);
})();
```

WinJS.Binding.List is used to bind the Repeater control. In the preceding code snippet, the Repeater control is bound to the employees list, which represents a collection of employee data. The employee object contains the following properties: id, name, and designation. The data is bound using the data property of the Repeater control.

Run the application on a Windows Mobile emulator. You should see the screen shown in Figure 4-2.

Recipe 4.1

Employee ID	Employee Name	Employee Designation
1	Senthil Kumar	Mobile Developer
2	Lohith GN	Web Developer
3	Vidyasagar	Game Developer

Figure 4-2. Repeater control in Windows Mobile 10

If you want the items in the Repeater control to be invokable or selectable, one of the choices is to use ItemContainer control within the Repeater control template.

The following sample demonstrates the usage of the ItemContainer inside the Repeater control, which is bound to the list of employees.

```
<div id="repeaterData" data-win-control="WinJS.UI.Repeater">
        <div data-win-control="WinJS.UI.ItemContainer" data-win-bind="dataset.name:name">
            <div data-win-bind="textContent:name"></div>
        </div>
</div>
```

The ItemContainer has a property called the `data-win-bind="dataset.name: name"` attribute, which associates the name of the each item in the employee list with the ItemContainer.

The Repeater control is bound to the list of employees in the JavaScript file, as shown next.

```
(function () {
    "use strict";
    function Initialize() {
        WinJS.UI.processAll().done(function () {
            var repeaterControl1 = document.getElementById('repeaterData').winControl;
            var Employees = new WinJS.Binding.List([
                { id: 1, name: "Senthil Kumar", designation: "Mobile Developer" },
                { id: 2, name: "Lohith GN", designation: "Web Developer" },
                { id: 3, name: "Vidyasagar", designation: "Game Developer" }
            ]);
            repeaterControl1.data = Employees;
            repeaterControl1.addEventListener("invoked",function(e)
            {
                var name = e.target.dataset.name;
                var message = new Windows.UI.Popups.MessageDialog(name);
                message.showAsync();
            })
        })
    }
    document.addEventListener("DOMContentLoaded", Initialize);
})();
```

When you run the application in Windows, you see the three items being rendered. If you click an item, a message box is displayed with the name of the item, as shown in Figure 4-3.

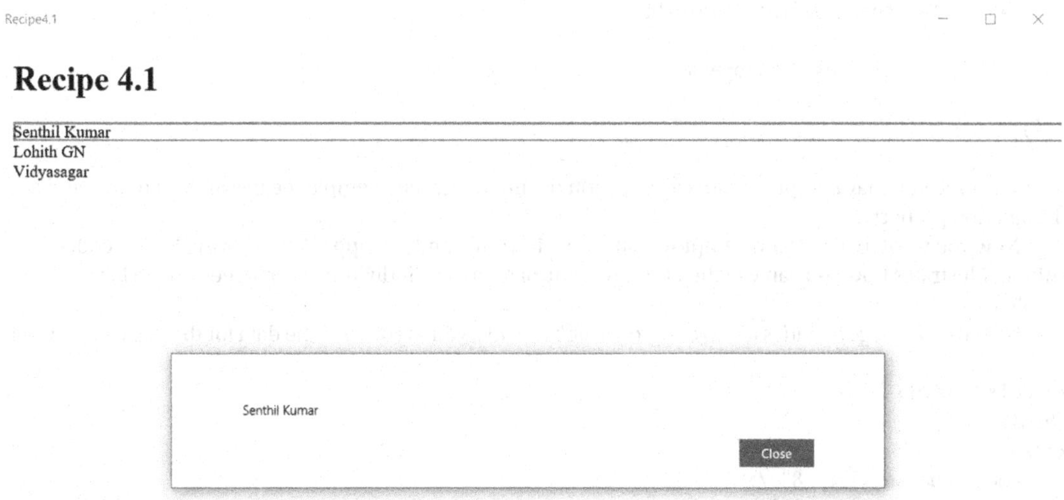

Recipe4.1   — □ ×

Recipe 4.1

Senthil Kumar
Lohith GN
Vidyasagar

Senthil Kumar

Close

Figure 4-3. *Item in the Repeater control that is invokable*

4.2 Using the FlipView Control

Problem

You need to display only a single item from a collection.

Solution

Use the FlipView control in WinJS, which displays only a single item from the collection at a time. A use case of the FlipView control is a photo gallery app, where a user can select an image and then swipe through the list of images.

Although only one item is displayed at a time, the FlipView control displays arrows, which lets you to move to the next or the previous item in the data source.

You can add the ListView control to the page by setting the `data-win-control` attribute of the `div` element with the WinJS.UI.ListView value.

How It Works

Let's create a new Windows Universal project in Visual Studio 2015. Name the new JavaScript file **data.js** under the js folder. This JavaScript file will contain data that can be listed in the ListView. Add the following code snippet to the `data.js` file.

```
(function () {
    "use strict";
    var Employees = new WinJS.Binding.List([
        { id: 1, name: "Senthil Kumar", designation: "Mobile Developer" },
        { id: 2, name: "Lohith GN", designation: "Web Developer" },
        { id: 3, name: "Vidyasagar", designation: "Game Developer" }
        ]);
```

59

```
    WinJS.Namespace.define("recipeData",
        {
            Employees :Employees
        });
})();
```

The preceding JavaScript contains a collection of employees; each employee has an id, a name, and a designation property.

Now you want to display one employee at a time in your Windows app. The following HTML code snippet illustrates how you can use the FlipView control to display individual employees from a list of employees.

Note that the page includes a reference to the data.js file, which contains the data for the FlipView control.

```
<!DOCTYPE html>
<html>
<head>
    <meta charset="utf-8" />
    <title>Recipe4.2</title>

    <!-- WinJS references -->
    <link href="WinJS/css/ui-light.css" rel="stylesheet" />
    <script src="WinJS/js/base.js"></script>
    <script src="WinJS/js/ui.js"></script>

    <!-- Recipe4.2 references -->
    <link href="/css/default.css" rel="stylesheet" />
    <script src="/js/default.js"></script>
    <script src="/js/data.js"></script>
</head>
<body class="win-type-body" style="margin:20px">
    <h1>Recipe 4.2</h1>
    <div id="template" data-win-control="WinJS.Binding.Template">
        <div>
            <h4 data-win-bind="innerText: name"></h4>
            <h6 data-win-bind="innerText: designation"></h6>
        </div>
    </div>
    <div id="flipView1"
        data-win-control="WinJS.UI.FlipView"
        data-win-options="{itemTemplate: select('#template') ,
        itemDataSource : recipeData.Employees.dataSource}">
    </div>

</body>
</html>
```

When you run the app on Windows, you should see the page shown in Figure 4-4.

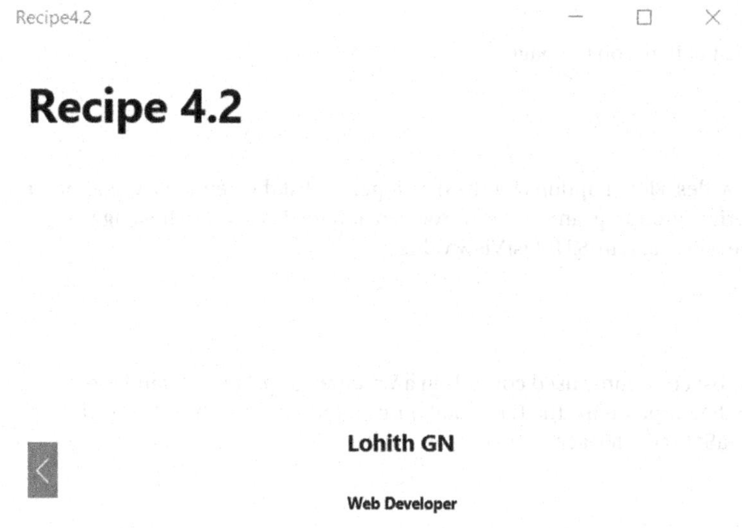

Recipe4.2   —   □   ✕

Recipe 4.2

Lohith GN

Web Developer

Figure 4-4. *FlipView in the WinJS app*

The FlipView is declared with the following HTML tag.

```
<div id="flipView1"
        data-win-control="WinJS.UI.FlipView"
        data-win-options="{itemTemplate: select('#template') ,
        itemDataSource : recipeData.Employees.dataSource}">
</div>
```

The FlipView is bound to the employees list using the `itemDataSource` property. In the preceding code snippet, the FlipView is bound to the employees list, which is of type WinJS.Binding.List.

Note that the FlipView displays data from the data source that implements the IListDataSource interface. An example of this includes the WinJS.Binding.List and WinJS.UI.StorageDataSource.

Additionally, the FlipView's `itemTemplate` property is set to the TemplateControl with the id `template`. This contains the template that is used to format the employee details displayed in the ListView. In this example, the template is configured to display the name and designation.

4.3 Using the ListView Control

Problem

You need to display an interactive list of items on the page.

Solution

Use the ListView control, which provides a lot of options for the developers to list the items, as well as other options, like selection, sorting, filtering, grouping, and so forth. You can add the ListView to the page by setting the data-win-bind attribute with the WinJS.UI.ListView value.

How It Works

The ListView control is one of the most commonly used controls in a Windows app. You can bind the ListView control to the data source that implements the IListDataSource interface. Currently, WinJS has two objects that implement the IListDataSource interface.

- WinJS.Binding.List

- WinJS.UI.StorageDataSource

In this recipe, we will focus on using WinJS.Binding.List data source.

Let's look at how to use the ListView control with WinJS.Binding.List data source.

Create a new Windows Universal app in Visual Studio 2015 and open the default.html page. Replace it with the following code.

```
<!DOCTYPE html>
<html>
<head>
    <meta charset="utf-8" />
    <title>Recipe4.3</title>

    <!-- WinJS references -->
    <link href="WinJS/css/ui-light.css" rel="stylesheet" />
    <script src="WinJS/js/base.js"></script>
    <script src="WinJS/js/ui.js"></script>

    <!-- Recipe4.3 references -->
    <link href="/css/default.css" rel="stylesheet" />
    <script src="/js/default.js"></script>
    <script src="/js/data.js"></script>
</head>
<body class="win-type-body">
    <h1>Recipe 4.3</h1>
    <div id="template" data-win-control="WinJS.Binding.Template">
        <div>
            <h4 data-win-bind="innerText: name"></h4>
            <h6 data-win-bind="innerText: designation"></h6>
        </div>
    </div>
```

```
<div id="listView1"
    data-win-control="WinJS.UI.ListView"
    data-win-options="{itemTemplate: select('#template')}">
</div>

</body>
</html>
```

The following code is used to add the ListView control to the page.

```
<div id="listView1"
    data-win-control="WinJS.UI.ListView"
    data-win-options="{itemTemplate: select('#template')}">
</div>
```

The ListView control shown in the preceding code snippet uses the template to display each employee.

Note that you have referenced the data.js file in the HTML page. This file contains the array of employees. Add a new JavaScript file to the project's js folder and name it **data.js**. Replace the data.js file with the following code.

```
(function () {
    "use strict";
    function Initialize() {
        WinJS.UI.processAll().done(function () {
            var listControl1 = document.getElementById('listView1').winControl;
            var Employees = new WinJS.Binding.List([
                { id: 1, name: "Senthil Kumar", designation: "Mobile Developer" },
                { id: 2, name: "Lohith GN", designation: "Web Developer" },
                { id: 3, name: "Vidyasagar", designation: "Game Developer" },
                { id: 4, name: "Michael", designation: "Architect" }
            ]);
            listControl1.itemDataSource = Employees.dataSource;
            listControl1.addEventListener("iteminvoked", function (e) {
                var index = e.detail.itemIndex;
                e.detail.itemPromise.then(function (item) {
                    var message = new Windows.UI.Popups.MessageDialog(item.data.name);
                    message.showAsync();
                })
            })
        })
    }
    document.addEventListener("DOMContentLoaded", Initialize);
})();
```

A list is created from the array of employees, which is bound to the ListView control using the itemDataSource property.

When you run the app, you see the employee data shown in list view.

The JavaScript code also includes the code, which handles the invoked event of the ListView, which displays the selected employee from the list.

The ListView control uses the ItemContainer control for each ListView item internally. You can handle the ListView control's item-invoked event to detect when a particular ListView item is clicked.

Figure 4-5 illustrates the screen rendered in Windows with the code snippet in this recipe.

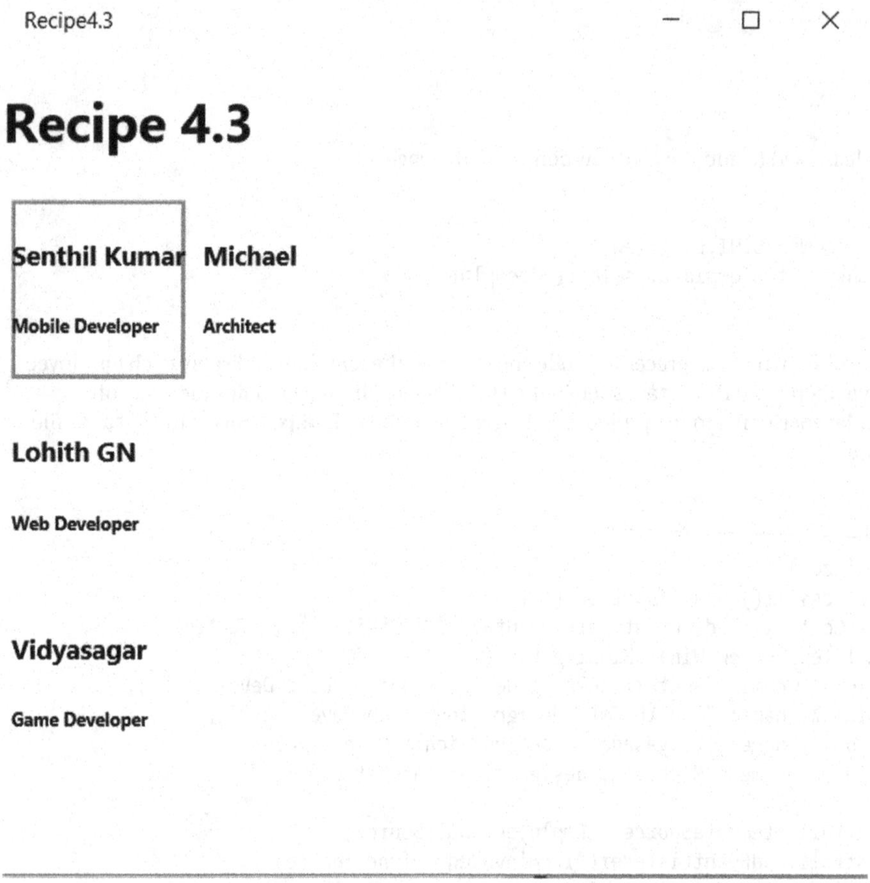

Recipe4.3   —   □   ✕

Recipe 4.3

Senthil Kumar **Michael**

Mobile Developer   **Architect**

Lohith GN

Web Developer

Vidyasagar

Game Developer

Figure 4-5. *ListView control in Windows app with the invoked event handling*

The ListView control supports different layouts, which can determine the overall appearance of the control. These layouts include

- The grid layout

- The list layout

- The cell-spanning layout

The grid layout shows the ListView items in grid format, with rows and columns. The list layout displays the list items in a single list. The cell-spanning layout displays the list items as a grid layout, but supports multiple column cells.

To set the ListView to a grid layout, set the `layout` property to WinJS.UI.GridLayout under the `data-win-options` attribute, as shown next.

```
<div id="listView1"
        data-win-control="WinJS.UI.ListView"
        data-win-options="{itemTemplate: select('#template'),
        layout : {type:WinJS.UI.GridLayout,maximumRowsOrColumns : 1}}">
</div>
```

Figure 4-6 shows the UI that is rendered when using grid layout.

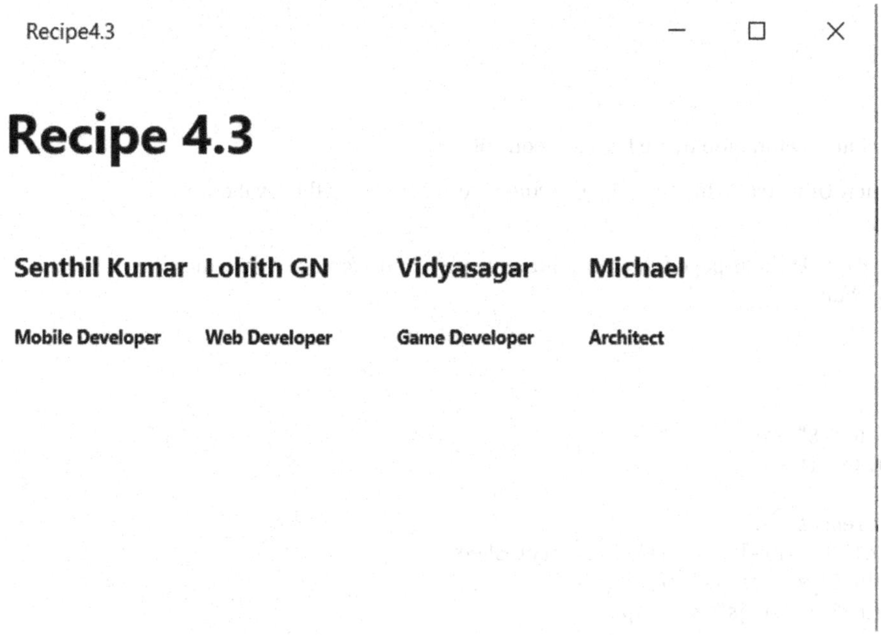

Recipe4.3   —   □   ✕

Recipe 4.3

Senthil Kumar **Lohith GN**   **Vidyasagar**   **Michael**

Mobile Developer   Web Developer   Game Developer   Architect

Figure 4-6. *Grid layout in ListView*

You can also set the layout to the following values:

- WinJS.UI.cellSpanningLayout
- WinJS.UI.ListLayout

4.4 Filtering Items in the ListView Control

Problem

You need to filter the items displayed in a ListView by filtering it from the data source associated with the ListView.

Solution

You can use the WinJS.Binding.List that is set as the data source and then create a new filtered list using the createFiltered method. The createFiltered function creates a filtered projection over the input item from the list.

How It Works

Let's demonstrate the filtering function in the ListView control.

1. Create a new Universal Windows app in Visual Studio 2015 using the JavaScript template.

2. Open the default.html page from the Solution Explorer and replace it with the following code.

```
<!DOCTYPE html>
<html>
<head>
    <meta charset="utf-8" />
    <title>Recipe4.4</title>

    <!-- WinJS references -->
    <link href="WinJS/css/ui-light.css" rel="stylesheet" />
    <script src="WinJS/js/base.js"></script>
    <script src="WinJS/js/ui.js"></script>

    <!-- Recipe4.4 references -->
    <link href="/css/default.css" rel="stylesheet" />
    <script src="/js/default.js"></script>
    <script src="/js/data.js"></script>
</head>
<body class="win-type-body">
    <h1>Recipe4.4</h1>
    <div>
        <input id="txtSearch" />
    </div>
    <div id="template" data-win-control="WinJS.Binding.Template">
        <h3 data-win-bind="innerText:name"></h3>
    </div>
    <div id="lstEmployees" data-win-control="WinJS.UI.ListView"
        data-win-options="{itemTemplate:select('#template')}">
    </div>
</body>
</html>
```

Note the inclusion of the data.js file where the data source is set and the filtering operation is performed. This HTML page contains a simple text box with the id txtSearch and a ListView control. The ListView has a custom template associated, which is used to display the data in a formatted way.

Let's add the JavaScript file to the project's js folder and name it **data.js**. Add the following code to the data.js file.

```javascript
(function () {
    "use strict";
    // List of Employees to be used a datasource.
    var lstEmployees = new WinJS.Binding.List([
        { id: 1, name: "Senthil Kumar" },
        { id: 2, name: "Lohith GN" },
        { id: 3, name: "Senthil Kumar B" },
        { id: 4, name: "Vidyasagar" },
    ]);
    function Initialize() {
        WinJS.UI.processAll().done(function () {
            // Get the Listview from the DOM
            var lstControl = document.getElementById('lstEmployees').winControl;
            // Get the Search Tex from the HTML Page
            var filterText = document.getElementById('txtSearch');
            lstControl.itemDataSource = lstEmployees.dataSource;
            filterText.addEventListener("keyup", function () {
                filterEmployee(lstControl, filterText.value);
            });
        });
    }
    // Function to filter the list
    function filterEmployee(listEmployee,searchtext)
    {
        var filtereddata = lstEmployees.createFiltered(function (item) {
            var result = item.name.toLowerCase().indexOf(searchtext);
            return item.name.toLowerCase().indexOf(searchtext) == 0;
        });
        listEmployee.itemDataSource = filtereddata.dataSource;
    }
    document.addEventListener("DOMContentLoaded", Initialize);
})();
```

This JavaScript code includes a method called filterEmployee, which accepts a ListView control and a search string for filtering. This function filters the ListView and displays the employees, which match the search string.

Here's the function within the createFiltered method to filter the data source in the ListView control.

```javascript
var fileteredData = lstEmployees.createFiltered(function (item) {
    var result = item.name.toLowerCase().indexOf(searchtext);
            return item.name.toLowerCase().indexOf(searchtext) == 0;
 });
```

This function acts like a live filter and returns the item when the item begins with the search text string.

Run the app on Windows. You should see the screen shown in Figure 4-7.

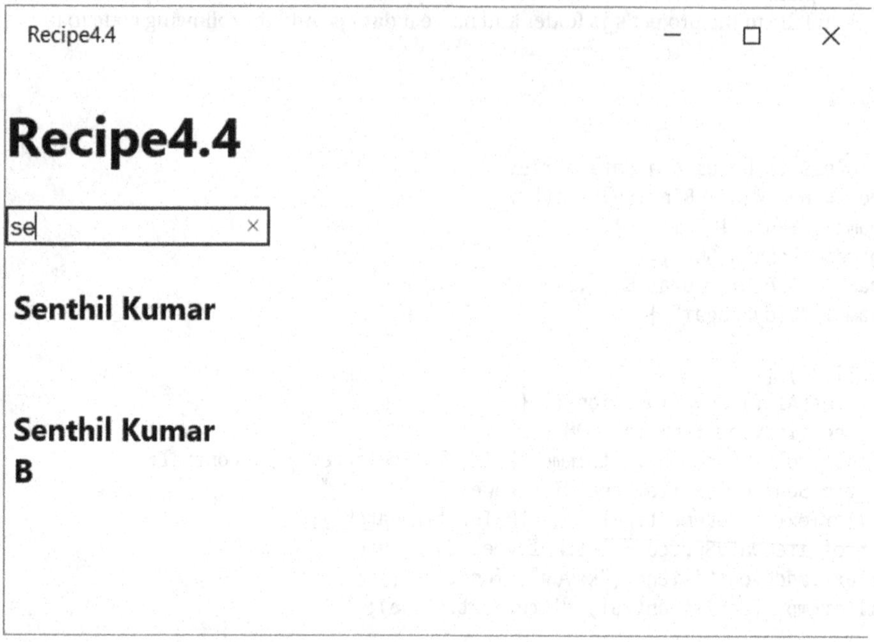

```
Recipe4.4                                    —    □    ✕


Recipe4.4

se                                    ✕


Senthil Kumar


Senthil Kumar
B
```

Figure 4-7. *Filtering the ListView*

When you start entering text in the text box, you see the items filtered and displayed on the screen.

4.5 Grouping Items in the ListView Control

Problem

You need to group the items by category in the ListView instead of as a flat list.

Solution

To group the items in the ListView, you need to use the grouped data source. This can be achieved by using the `WinJS.Binding.List.createGrouped()` function in WinJS.

How It Works

To group the items in the ListView control in WinJS, it is necessary to include two templates: one for the group header and one for the individual item.

Let's create a new Windows Universal project in Visual Studio 2015 and open the default.html page. Replace it with the following code snippet.

```
<!DOCTYPE html>
<html>
<head>
    <meta charset="utf-8" />
    <title>Recipe4.5</title>

    <!-- WinJS references -->
    <link href="WinJS/css/ui-light.css" rel="stylesheet" />
    <script src="WinJS/js/base.js"></script>
    <script src="WinJS/js/ui.js"></script>

    <!-- Recipe4.5 references -->
    <link href="/css/default.css" rel="stylesheet" />
    <script src="/js/default.js"></script>
    <script src="/js/data.js"></script>
</head>
<body class="win-type-body">
    <h1>Recipe 4.5</h1>
    <div id="GroupHeader" data-win-control="WinJS.Binding.Template">
        <h3 data-win-bind="innerText: technology"></h3>
    </div>
    <div id="employee" data-win-control="WinJS.Binding.Template">
        <h4 data-win-bind="innerText:name"></h4>
    </div>
    <div id="lvEmployees" data-win-control="WinJS.UI.ListView"
        data-win-options="{
        itemTemplate: select('#employee'),
        groupHeaderTemplate: select('#GroupHeader')
        }">

    </div>

</body>
</html>
```

This code snippet included a ListView control named as lvEmployees, which has the group header template and the itemTemplate associated with it.

Note the reference to the data.js JavaScript file.

Let's create a new JavaScript file in the Visual Studio 2015 Solution Explorer under the js folder and name it **data.js**. Add the following code snippet to it.

```
(function () {
    "use strict";
    function Initialize() {
        WinJS.UI.processAll().done(function () {
            var listView1 = document.getElementById("lvEmployees").winControl;
```

```
            var employeeList = new WinJS.Binding.List([
                { id: 1, name: "Senthil Kumar", technology: "Mobile" },
                { id: 2, name: "Michael", technology: "Web" },
                { id: 3, name: "Lohith", technology: "Web" },
                { id: 4, name: "Stephen", technology: "Mobile" },
                { id: 5, name: "Vidyasagar", technology: "Game" },
                { id: 6, name: "Joseph", technology: "Mobile" },
            ]);
            var groupedEmployees = employeeList.createGrouped(
                function (item) {
                    return item.technology;
                },
                function (item) {
                    return { technology: item.technology }
                },
                function (group1, group2) {
                    return group1 > group2 ? 1 : -1;
                });
            listView1.groupDataSource = groupedEmployees.groups.dataSource;
            listView1.itemDataSource = groupedEmployees.dataSource;
        });
    }
    document.addEventListener("DOMContentLoaded", Initialize);
})();
```

This JavaScript code creates the item data source, as well as the grouped data source. The list contains employee records, with each item containing the properties id, name, and technology.

The grouped data source is created using WinJS's createGrouped method, which requires three functions to be passed as parameters.

- GroupKey: This function is used to associate each of the items in the list with a group. The preceding example returned the technology property associated with each employee.

- GroupData: This function returns the data item displayed by the group header. In the preceding example, GroupData returns the technology for the group that is displayed in the header.

- GroupSorter: This function handles the order of the group; for example, listing the groups in the header in ascending order.

Note that the grouped data source is live, which can work with a filtered data source as well.

Once the item data source and the grouped data source is prepared, they are set to the ListView's groupDataSource property and itemDataSource property, respectively, as shown next.

```
listView1.groupDataSource = groupedEmployees.groups.dataSource;
listView1.itemDataSource = groupedEmployees.dataSource;
```

When you run the application on Windows, you should see the screen shown in Figure 4-8.

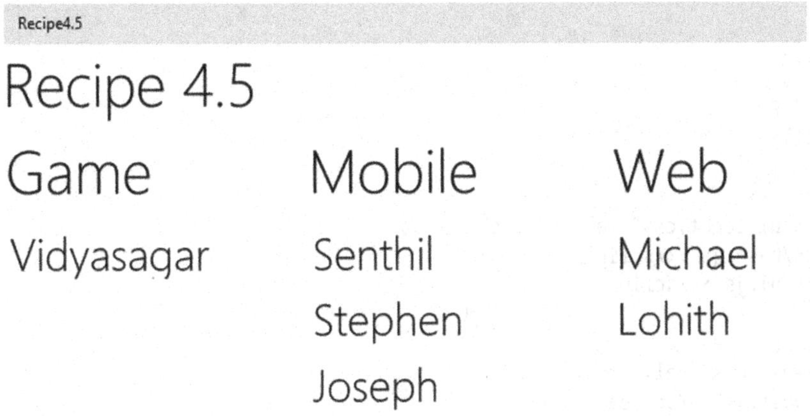

Recipe4.5

Recipe 4.5

Game	Mobile	Web
Vidyasagar	Senthil	Michael
	Stephen	Lohith
	Joseph	

Figure 4-8. ListView with grouped data

Notice that the items are grouped by the technology and displayed on the page.

4.6 Semantic Zoom in ListView

Problem

You want to provide an option for the user to view data at two different zoom levels when working with the ListView.

Solution

You can use the SemanticZoom control in WinJS to bring in the semantic zoom functionality within your app. The SemanticZoom control enables you to provide two different views of the same data when working with the ListView.

You can add the SemanticZoom by setting the `data-win-control` attribute of the div element to the WinJS.UI.SemanticZoom value.

How It Works

Semantic zoom can be implemented using the SemanticZoom control in WinJS. Think of a scenario where you have a list of employees that can be grouped by the technology that they are working with. To allow the user to navigate between the technologies easily, you can use the semantic zoom, in which you see the employees grouped into categories by default, and when you zoom out, you see only the list of technologies.

Create a new Universal Windows app in Visual Studio 2015 and open the default.html page. Replace the existing code with what's provided next.

```
<!DOCTYPE html>
<html>
<head>
    <meta charset="utf-8" />
    <title>Recipe4.6</title>

    <!-- WinJS references -->
    <link href="WinJS/css/ui-light.css" rel="stylesheet" />
    <script src="WinJS/js/base.js"></script>
    <script src="WinJS/js/ui.js"></script>

    <!-- Recipe4.6 references -->
    <link href="/css/default.css" rel="stylesheet" />
    <script src="/js/default.js"></script>
    <script src="/js/data.js"></script>
</head>
<body class="win-type-body">
    <h1>Recipe 4.6</h1>
    <!-- Zoom In-->
    <div id="GroupHeader" data-win-control="WinJS.Binding.Template">
        <h1 data-win-bind="innerText: technology"></h1>
    </div>
    <div id="EmployeeTemplate" data-win-control="WinJS.Binding.Template">
        <h2 data-win-bind="innerText:name"></h2>
    </div>
    <!-- Zoom out-->
    <div id="TechnologyTemplate" data-win-control="WinJS.Binding.Template">
        <h6 data-win-bind="innerText: technology"></h6>
    </div>
    <div id="szEmployee" data-win-control="WinJS.UI.SemanticZoom">
        <!-- Zoom In-->
        <div id="lvEmployees" data-win-control="WinJS.UI.ListView"
            data-win-options="{
         itemTemplate: select('#EmployeeTemplate'),
         groupHeaderTemplate: select('#GroupHeader')
         }">

        </div>
        <!-- Zoom Out-->
        <div id="lvTechnologies" data-win-control="WinJS.UI.ListView"
            data-win-options="{
        itemTemplate: select('#TechnologyTemplate')
        }">
        </div>
    </div>

</body>
</html>
```

The preceding page contains a SemanticZoom control that has two ListView controls. The following is code in which the SemanticZoom control and the ListView are used.

```
<div id="szEmployee" data-win-control="WinJS.UI.SemanticZoom">
      <!-- Zoom In-->
      <div id="lvEmployees" data-win-control="WinJS.UI.ListView"
           data-win-options="{
        itemTemplate: select('#EmployeeTemplate'),
        groupHeaderTemplate: select('#GroupHeader')
        }">

      </div>
      <!-- Zoom Out-->
      <div id="lvTechnologies" data-win-control="WinJS.UI.ListView"
           data-win-options="{
        itemTemplate: select('#TechnologyTemplate')
        }">
      </div>
</div>
```

The SemanticZoom control includes two ListView controls with varied zoom levels. When the user tries to zoom in or zoom out, the ListView controls are switched accordingly.

Let's add a new JavaScript file to the project under the js folder and name it **data.js**. This file contains the item source and grouped data source for the ListView. Add the following code to the data.js file.

```
(function () {
    "use strict";
    function Initialize() {
        WinJS.UI.processAll().done(function () {
            var listView1 = document.getElementById("lvEmployees").winControl;
            var listView2 = document.getElementById("lvTechnologies").winControl;
            var employeeList = new WinJS.Binding.List([
                { id: 1, name: "Senthil Kumar", technology: "Mobile" },
                { id: 2, name: "Michael", technology: "Web" },
                { id: 3, name: "Lohith", technology: "Web" },
                { id: 4, name: "Stephen", technology: "Mobile" },
                { id: 5, name: "Vidyasagar", technology: "Game" },
                { id: 6, name: "Joseph", technology: "Mobile" },
            ]);
            // Grouped Datasource
            var groupedEmployees = employeeList.createGrouped(
                function (item) {
                    return item.technology;
                },
                function (item) {
                    return { technology: item.technology }
                },
                function (group1, group2) {
                    return group1 > group2 ? 1 : -1;
                });
```

```
            listView1.groupDataSource = groupedEmployees.groups.dataSource;
            listView1.itemDataSource = groupedEmployees.dataSource;
            listView2.itemDataSource = groupedEmployees.groups.dataSource;
        });
    }
    document.addEventListener("DOMContentLoaded", Initialize);
})();
```

When you run the application, you should see the screen shown in Figure 4-9.

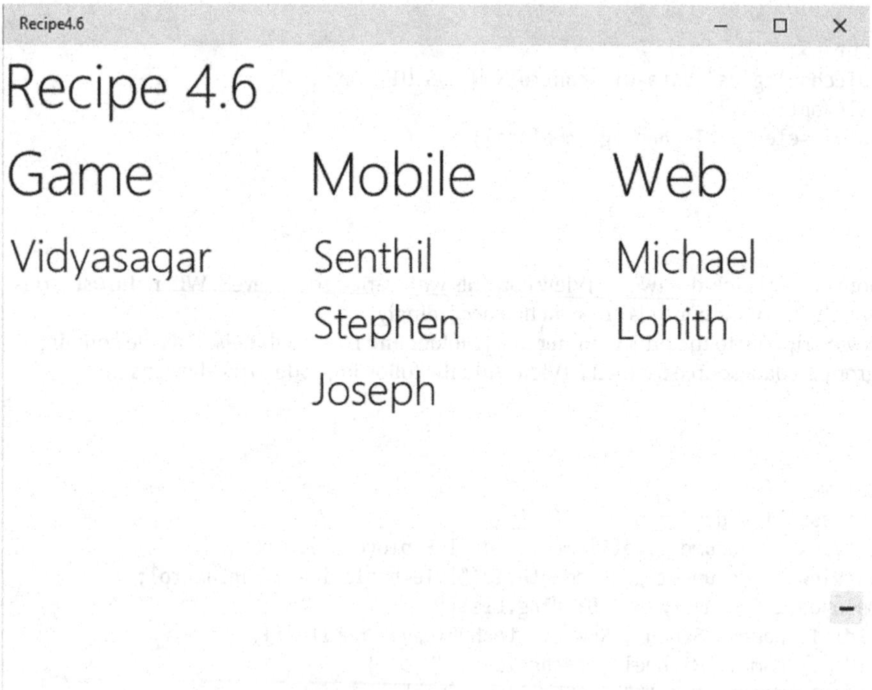

Figure 4-9. SemanticZoom in the default view

Click the – button that is displayed in the top-right corner of the screen, or zoom out using the stretch gesture.

The alternative view is displayed in Figure 4-10.

Recipe4.6   —   □   ✕

Recipe 4.6

Game

Mobil

Web

Figure 4-10. *Alternate ListView shown using SemanticZoom*

4.7 Using the AppBar Control

Problem

You need to provide quick access to the common tasks that are relevant to the current page or the current selection.

Solution

You can provide quick access to the common tasks that are relevant to the current page or the current selection by adding an app bar to your page. You can add the AppBar control to the page by setting the data-win-control="WinJS.UI.AppBar" attribute for the div element.

How It Works

The app bar is a row that contains icon buttons and an ellipsis at the bottom of the app screen. When the user taps on the ellipsis, it displays the labeled icon buttons and menu items that are available.

The following is the syntax to add the AppBar control to the HTML page.

```
<div data-win-control="WinJS.UI.AppBar"></div>
```

The AppBar control can be added using JavaScript code as well as using the following syntax.

```
var object = new WinJS.UI.AppBar(element, options);
```

AppBarCommand is added within the AppBar. This is simply the command or the buttons displayed within the AppBar.

```
<button data-win-control="WinJS.UI.AppBarCommand"></button>
```

You can specify if the AppBarCommand should be displayed as a menu by setting the section property to secondary for the data-win-options attribute of the control.

Let's create an app that demonstrates the functionality of the AppBar, which includes the following functionalities.

- AppBarCommands (buttons) to demonstrate the Add and Remove options.

- AppBarCommands (menu items) to demonstrate the menu items displayed when the user taps on the ellipsis.

When the user taps on a button or a menu item, the corresponding events are handled and an appropriate message is displayed.

Create a new Universal Windows project in Visual Studio 2015 and open the default.html page. Replace its content with the following code.

```html
<!DOCTYPE html>
<html>
<head>
    <meta charset="utf-8" />
    <title>Recipe4.7</title>

    <!-- WinJS references -->
    <link href="WinJS/css/ui-light.css" rel="stylesheet" />
    <script src="WinJS/js/base.js"></script>
    <script src="WinJS/js/ui.js"></script>

    <!-- Recipe4.7 references -->
    <link href="/css/default.css" rel="stylesheet" />
    <script src="/js/default.js"></script>
    <script src="/js/appbarevents.js"></script>
</head>
<body class="win-type-body">
    <div id="appBar" data-win-control="WinJS.UI.AppBar">
        <button data-win-control="WinJS.UI.AppBarCommand"
                data-win-options="{id:'cmdAdd', label:'Add', icon:'add', section:'primary',
                tooltip:'Add'}"></button>
        <button data-win-control="WinJS.UI.AppBarCommand"
                data-win-options="{id:'cmdRemove', label:'Remove', icon:'remove',
                section:'primary', tooltip:'Remove'}"></button>

        <button data-win-control="WinJS.UI.AppBarCommand"
                data-win-options="{id:'cmdCamera', label:'Click Photo', icon:'camera',
                section:'secondary', tooltip:'click'}"></button>
    </div>
    <div id="Message"></div>

</body>
</html>
```

The HTML markup adds the two AppBarCommands (Add, Remove) in the primary section and one AppBarCommand (Camera) in the secondary menu. The data-win-options attribute provides additional options for the controls. Some of these properties include the following:

- Id: This uniquely identifies the AppBarCommand.

- label: The content displayed in the AppBarCommand.

- icon: The built-in icons for the AppBarCommand.

- section: The section within the AppBar where the command should be displayed. This value can be primary or secondary.

- tooltip: The text to be displayed when you mouse-over the command button.

Note that the page contains the reference to the appbarevents.js JavaScript file. This contains the logic to handle the events on the AppBarCommands. Let's create a new JavaScript file in the project under the js folder and name it as **appbarevents.js**. Add the following code to it.

```
(function () {
    "use strict";

    WinJS.UI.Pages.define("default.html", {
        ready: function (element, options) {
            element.querySelector("#cmdAdd").addEventListener("click", AddMethod, false);
            element.querySelector("#cmdRemove").addEventListener("click", RemoveMethod, false);
            element.querySelector("#cmdCamera").addEventListener("click", CameraMethod, false);
        }
    });

    // Command button functions
    function AddMethod() {

        var message = new Windows.UI.Popups.MessageDialog("Add Button Pressed");
        message.showAsync();
    }

    function RemoveMethod() {
        var message = new Windows.UI.Popups.MessageDialog("Remove button pressed");
        message.showAsync();
    }

    function CameraMethod() {
        var message = new Windows.UI.Popups.MessageDialog("Camera button pressed");
        message.showAsync();
    }
})();
```

The preceding JavaScript code handles the click event of the AppBarCommand buttons. On click of the button, it displays a message.

Run the app on Windows. You should see the screen shown in Figure 4-11.

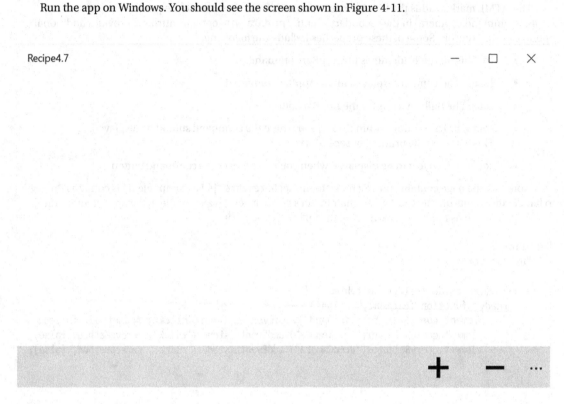

Figure 4-11. *Windows app with the AppBar*

Click the ellipsis button in the app bar, which displays the secondary section, as shown in Figure 4-12.

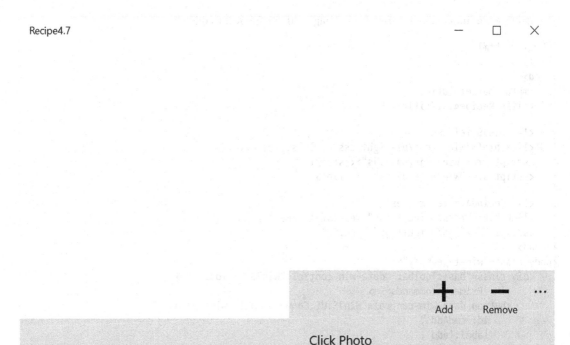

Figure 4-12. *Windows app with the AppBar and secondary section*

When you click the menu button, it displays an appropriate message.

4.8 Using the ToolBar Control

Problem

You need to display a set of commands that can appear in any location; for example, flyouts or an app bar at the top of the screen.

Solution

You can use the ToolBar control to display as many commands as possible in the action area. This control is not constrained to a single location within the app. It can be found in the splitView, Flyouts, and so forth.

How It Works

Create a new Universal Windows app in Visual Studio 2015 using the JavaScript template. Open the default.html page.

Replace the content of the default.html page with the following code.

```
<!DOCTYPE html>
<html>
<head>
    <meta charset="utf-8" />
    <title>Recipe4.8</title>

    <!-- WinJS references -->
    <link href="WinJS/css/ui-light.css" rel="stylesheet" />
    <script src="WinJS/js/base.js"></script>
    <script src="WinJS/js/ui.js"></script>

    <!-- Recipe4.8 references -->
    <link href="/css/default.css" rel="stylesheet" />
    <script src="/js/default.js"></script>
</head>
<body class="win-type-body">
    <div class="basicToolbar" data-win-control="WinJS.UI.ToolBar">
        <!-- Primary commands -->
        <button data-win-control="WinJS.UI.Command" data-win-options="{
            id:'cmdAdd',
            label:'add',
            section:'primary',
            type:'button',
            icon: 'add',
            onclick: recipes.clickcommand}"></button>
        <button data-win-control="WinJS.UI.Command" data-win-options="{
            id:'cmdEdit',
            label:'Edit',
            section:'primary',
            type:'button',
            icon: 'edit',
            onclick: recipes.clickcommand}"></button>
        <button data-win-control="WinJS.UI.Command" data-win-options="{
            id:'cmdDelete',
            label:'delete',
            section:'primary',
            type:'button',
            icon: 'delete',
            onclick: recipes.clickcommand}"></button>

        <!-- Secondary command -->
        <button data-win-control="WinJS.UI.Command" data-win-options="{
            id:'cmdShare',
            label:'share',
            section:'secondary',
            type:'button',
            onclick: recipes.clickcommand}"></button>
    </div>

</body>
</html>
```

The preceding code snippet adds three buttons in the primary command and one button (Share) in the secondary command. The secondary command is hidden by default and is displayed when you tap the ellipsis button.

The ToolBar control is added by setting the `data-win-control` attribute of the div element to the WinJS.UI.ToolBar value.

You can add the buttons inside the toolbar by setting the `data-win-control` attribute to the WinJS.UI.Command value. The `data-win-options` attribute is used to set the command properties. The following are some of the properties set for the command.

- `id`: Defines the identifier for the command.

- `label`: Defines the text to be displayed for the command.

- `section`: Defines the area in the toolbar where the command should appear. This can take a primary or secondary value.

- `type`: The value is set to "button" to display a button control.

- `onClick`: An event that fires and calls the corresponding JavaScript method.

- `icon`: Displays a built-in icon for the command.

Note that we have set the `OnClick` event for the command. Let's add the event for it.

Open the `default.js` file found under the `js` folder of the project. Add the following code before the `args.setPromise` method.

```
WinJS.Namespace.define("recipes", {
                    clickcommand: WinJS.UI.eventHandler(function (ev) {
                        var command = ev.currentTarget;
                        if (command.winControl) {
                            var message = Windows.UI.Popups.MessageDialog(command.
                            winControl.label);
                    message.showAsync();
                        }
                    })
                });
```

The preceding code snippet defines the namespace called `recipe` and adds an event handler with the name `clickcommand`. This displays a MessageDialog when the event is invoked.

Now, let's run the app on Windows. You should see the screen shown in Figure 4-13.

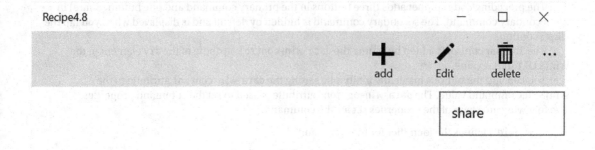

Figure 4-13. Toolbar in Windows app

When you click the command button, you see a message dialog describing the button that was clicked.

CHAPTER 5

■ ■ ■

Data Binding and Navigation

Typically, when you look at any application, it is composed of a user interface (UI) and an underlying business logic. Data binding is a process in which you connect the application UI and the business logic. When data changes its value, the elements that are bound to the data reflect the changes automatically and when the element value is changed, the underlying data will also be updated and reflect the change.

5.1 Data Bind to Simple Objects

Problem

As part of the application business logic, you have a simple business object with data properties. You want to bind the data properties of the business object to HTML elements on the UI.

Solution

Data binding is provided by the `WinJS.Binding` namespace. It provides the `processAll()` method, which binds the value of an object to the values of any DOM element. The DOM element will have to use the `data-win-bind` attribute and provide the property name to which it needs to be bound.

How It Works

Let's see how to perform simple data binding in your apps.

1. Open Visual Studio 2015. Select **File ➤ New Project ➤ JavaScript ➤ Windows ➤ Universal ➤ Blank App (Universal Windows)** template (see Figure 5-1).

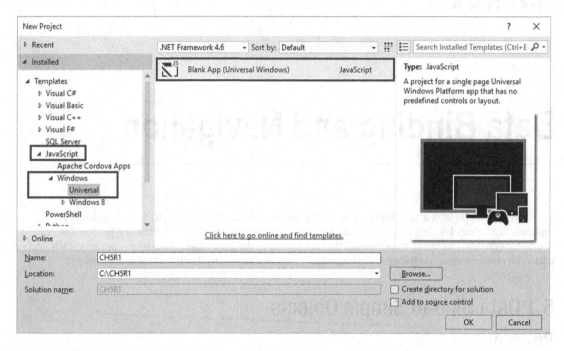

Figure 5-1. *New Project dialog*

Visual Studio creates the Universal Windows Apps blank project with all the necessary files added to the solution.

2. Open **default.js**, which is found under the js folder. Add the following lines of code inside the immediately invoked function, just after the 'use strict' directive:

```
(function () {
        "use strict";

        //create a person object
        var person = {
                name: "John Doe",
                age: 36,
                designation: "Technical Evangelist",
                city: "Boston",
        };

        var app = WinJS.Application;
        var activation = Windows.ApplicationModel.Activation;

        app.onactivated = function (args) {
                if (args.detail.kind === activation.ActivationKind.launch) {
                        if (args.detail.previousExecutionState !== activation.
                        ApplicationExecutionState.terminated) {
                        } else {
                        }
```

```
                    args.setPromise(WinJS.UI.processAll());
            }
        };

        app.oncheckpoint = function (args) {
        };

        app.start();
})();
```

Let's bind the Person object to a div element in the HTML.

3. Open **default.html**, which is found in the root of the project. Replace the contents of <body> with the following:

```
<div id="container">
    <h3>Name:</h3>
    <h2><span data-win-bind="innerText: name"></span></h2>
    <h3>Age:</h3>
    <h2><span data-win-bind="innerText: age"></span></h2>
    <h3>Designation:</h3>
    <h2><span data-win-bind="innerText: designation"></span></h2>
   <h3>City:</h3>
     <h2><span data-win-bind="innerText: city"></span> </h2>
</div>
```

You have a span element and you have a defined data-win-bind attribute for data binding. You are binding the innerText property of the span element with data property of the Person object you created in default.js.

4. Next, you need to modify the onactivated function and add the data binding call. Modify app.onactivated, as shown here:

```
app.onactivated = function (args) {
        if (args.detail.kind === activation.ActivationKind.launch) {
            if (args.detail.previousExecutionState !== activation.
            ApplicationExecutionState.terminated) {
                // TODO: This application has been newly launched. Initialize
                // your application here.
            } else {
                // TODO: This application has been reactivated from suspension.
                // Restore application state here.
            }
            var container = document.querySelector('#container');
            var prmise = WinJS.UI.processAll().then(function () {
                WinJS.Binding.processAll(container, person)
            })
            args.setPromise(prmise);
        }
    };
```

5.   Build and run the app by pressing **F5** in Visual Studio. Figure 5-2 shows the
      output on a Windows Mobile screen.

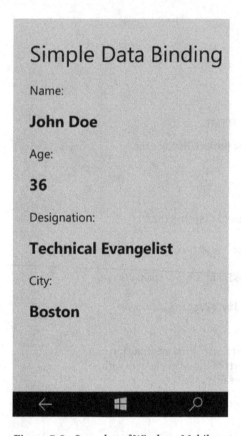

Figure 5-2. *Snapshot of Windows Mobile output*

As you can see, you have the values of the Person object (defined in `default.js`) bound to HTML
elements. This is possible because of the `WinJS.Binding` namespace. If you remember, you called the `WinJS.`
`Binding.processAll()` method inside the onactivated function. The `processAll()` method binds the value
of an object to the values of a DOM element that has the `data-win-bind` attribute. In the demo code, you had
set the `data-win-bind` attribute on `div` elements that output name, age, designation, and city information.

5.2 Data Bind Style Attributes of DOM Elements

Problem

HTML elements can be styled by using CSS definitions. At runtime, the style attributes need to be bound to
the data properties of the underlying business object data properties.

Solution

Apart from providing data binding to properties of the DOM element, the WinJS data binding framework provides options to bind style attributes of DOM elements too. The style attributes can be bound to the data property of the bound object in the data-win-bind attribute.

How It Works

1. Open Visual Studio 2015. Select **File ➤ New Project ➤ JavaScript ➤ Windows ➤ Universal ➤ Blank App (Universal Windows)** template. This creates a Universal Windows app template (see Figure 5-3).

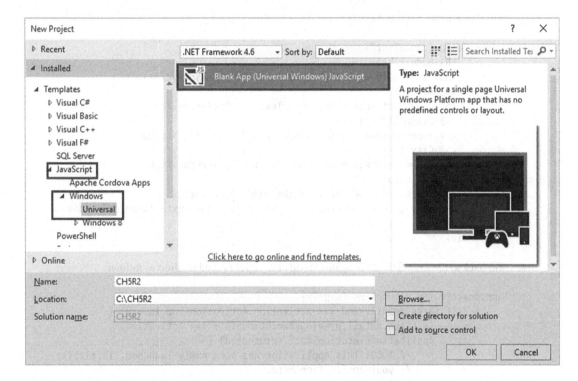

Figure 5-3. *New Project dialog*

2. Open **default.js** in the js folder. Add the following code inside the immediately invoked function after the 'use strict' directive:

```
(function () {
    "use strict";

    //create person object
    var person = {
        name: "John Doe",
        age: 36,
        designation: "Technical Evangelist",
```

```
        city: "Boston",
        favcolor: "orange"
    };

    //Other app set-up code
})();
```

You have added a favcolor property to the Person object. Let's bind the favcolor to a div element's background-color style property.

3.   Open **default.html**, which is found in the root of the project. Replace the <body> content with the following:

```
<h1>Data Bind Attributes</h1>
    <br />
    <div id="container">
        <h3>Name:</h3>
        <h2><span data-win-bind="innerText: name"></span></h2>
        <h3>Age:</h3>
        <h2><span data-win-bind="innerText: age"></span></h2>
        <h3>Designation:</h3>
        <h2><span data-win-bind="innerText: designation"></span></h2>
        <h3>City:</h3>
        <h2><span data-win-bind="innerText: city"></span> </h2>
        <h3>Fav Color:</h3>
        <div data-win-bind="style.background: favcolor" >
            <div class="favcolor" data-win-bind="innerText: favcolor"></div>
        </div>
    </div>
```

4.   Go back to the default.js file again. Modify the onactivated method as follows:

```
app.onactivated = function (args) {
        if (args.detail.kind === activation.ActivationKind.launch) {
            if (args.detail.previousExecutionState !== activation.
            ApplicationExecutionState.terminated) {
                // TODO: This application has been newly launched. Initialize
                // your application here.
            } else {
                // TODO: This application has been reactivated from suspension.
                // Restore application state here.
            }
            var container = document.querySelector("#container");
            var prmise = WinJS.UI.processAll().then(function () {
                WinJS.Binding.processAll(container, person)
            })
            args.setPromise(prmise);
        }
    };
```

You just call the WinJS Binding processAll() as usual on the container that needs to be data bound.

5. Next, build and run the app by pressing **F5** in Visual Studio. The output on a Windows Mobile screen is shown in Figure 5-4.

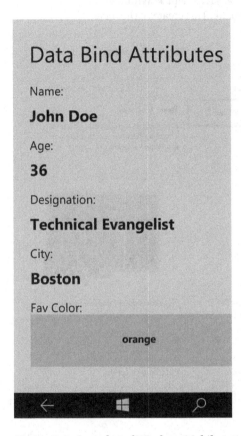

Figure 5-4. *Snapshot of Windows Mobile output*

5.3 Use Templates for Data Binding

Problem

Simple data binding can bind to only one data item at a time. When you have a list of data items, a simple data binding method won't suffice.

Solution

With simple data binding, you bind a data item to a DOM element and the element displays the values of the data properties. In order to work with a list of items and to allow users to change the data item they want to see, you need a template. The data template acts as a blueprint, and at runtime, it binds to the data item provided and renders the markup on a specified DOM element.

How It Works

1. Open Visual Studio 2015. Select **File ➤ New Project ➤ JavaScript ➤ Windows Universal ➤ Blank App (Universal Windows)** template. This creates a Universal Windows app template (see Figure 5-5).

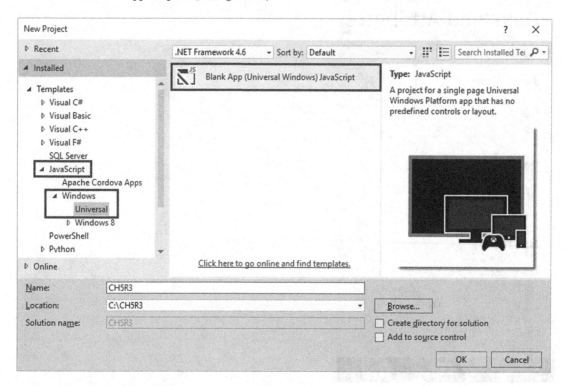

Figure 5-5. *New Project dialog*

2. Open **default.js** in js folder. Inside the immediately invoked function, let's declare a Person object with a couple of properties. This time you will use WinJS.Binding.define to declare the Person object. Using define will make all the properties bindable. Here is the code snippet for a Person object:

```
(function () {
    "use strict";

    var Person = WinJS.Binding.define({
        name: "",
        color: "",
        birthday: "",
        petname:"",
        dessert:""
    });

    //other app code ...

})();
```

3. Open **default.html**, found in root of the project. Replace the content of the
    <body> tag with the following code:

```
<h1>Data Binding Template</h1>
<div id="templateDiv" data-win-control="WinJS.Binding.Template">
    <div class="templateItem" data-win-bind="style.background: color"
    style="color:white">
        <ol>
            <li><span>Name :</span><span data-win-bind="textContent: name"></
            span></li>
            <li><span>Birthday:</span><span data-win-bind="textContent:
            birthday"></span></li>
            <li><span>Pet's name: </span><span data-win-bind="textContent:
            petname"></span></li>
            <li><span>Dessert: </span><span data-win-bind="textContent:
            dessert"></span></li>
        </ol>
    </div>
</div>

<div id="renderDiv"></div>
```

You have defined a div with the id templateDiv and then added a data-win-
control attribute with a WinJS.Binding.Template value. This defines the
template that can be used for data binding. You then have a div with the id
renderDiv. At runtime, you data bind the template with data and render the
output to the renderDiv DOM element.

4. For the purpose of this recipe, let's create three Person objects and add a drop-
    down list so that you can select the person whose details needs to be shown.
    Inside the body tag, add the following code right after the "renderDiv" element:

```
<fieldset id="templateControlObject">
    <legend>Pick a name:</legend>
    <select id="templateControlObjectSelector">
        <option value="0">Show John Doe</option>
        <option value="1">Show Jane Dow</option>
        <option value="2">Show Jake Doe</option>
    </select>
</fieldset>
```

5. Back in default.js file, right after the Person object definition, create an array of
    three Person objects, as follows:

```
(function () {
    "use strict";

    var Person = WinJS.Binding.define({
        name: "",
        color: "",
        birthday: "",
```

```
                petname:"",
                dessert:""
        })

        var people = [
            new Person({ name: "John Doe", color: "red", birthday: "2/2/2002",
            petname: "Spot", dessert: "chocolate cake" }),
            new Person({ name: "Jane Doe", color: "green", birthday: "3/3/2003",
            petname: "Xena", dessert: "cherry pie" }),
            new Person({ name: "Jake Doe", color: "blue", birthday: "2/2/2002",
            petname: "Pablo", dessert: "ice cream" }),
        ];

        //Other app code ...

    })();
```

6. Next, add a listener to the change event of the drop-down list in the onactivated method in default.js. Here is the code snippet:

```
app.onactivated = function (args) {

    // Other activation code ...

    var selector = document.querySelector("#templateControlObjectSelector");
        selector.addEventListener("change", handleChange, false);

    args.setPromise(WinJS.UI.processAll());
}
```

7. Let's create the event handler for the drop-down list change event. Select the div, which contains the template and the div where you want to render the markup. Call render on the template control. Create a handleChange function in default.js with the following code:

```
(function () {

    //Other app code...

    function handleChange(evt) {
        var templateElement = document.querySelector("#templateDiv");
        var renderElement = document.querySelector("#renderDiv");
        renderElement.innerHTML = "";

        var selected = evt.target.selectedIndex;
        var templateControl = templateElement.winControl;
        templateElement.winControl.render(people[selected], renderElement);
    }
})();
```

8. Build and run the app by pressing **F5** in Visual Studio. When you select an item in the drop-down list, the appropriate data is shown in the div above it. Figure 5-6 shows the output on a Windows Mobile screen.

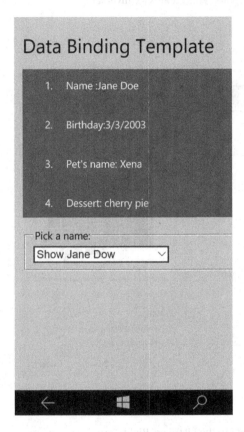

Figure 5-6. *Data binding template output on Windows Mobile screen*

5.4 Data Bind WinJS Controls

Problem

You have a list of items and you would like to data bind the list to a WinJS control, such as ListView.

Solution

With WinJS data binding, you can bind any WinJS control to a data source. For displaying each individual item, you will provide a data template. At runtime, the list gets data bound to the control and each item is rendered according to the template defined.

How It Works

1. Open Visual Studio 2015. Select **File ➤ New Project ➤ JavaScript ➤ Windows ➤ Universal ➤ Blank App (Universal Windows)** template. This creates a Universal Windows app template (see Figure 5-7).

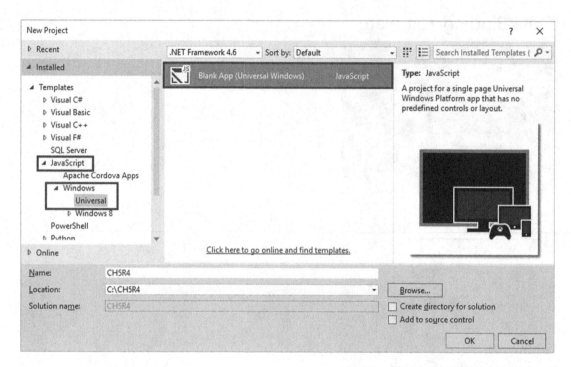

Figure 5-7. *New Project dialog*

2. Let's create a new JavaScript file that will provide data to the ListView. Right-click the js folder. Select **Add ➤ New Item**. In the New Item dialog, select the JavaScript file and name it **data.js**. Add the following code to the data.js file:

```
(function () {
    var flavors = [
        { title: "Basic banana", text: "Low-fat frozen yogurt" },
        { title: "Banana blast", text: "Ice cream" },
        { title: "Brilliant banana", text: "Frozen custard" },
        { title: "Orange surprise", text: "Sherbet" },
        { title: "Original orange", text: "Sherbet" },
        { title: "Vanilla", text: "Ice cream" },
        { title: "Very vanilla", text: "Frozen custard" },
        { title: "Marvelous mint", text: "Gelato" },
        { title: "Succulent strawberry", text: "Sorbet" }
    ];
```

```
        var flavorList = new WinJS.Binding.List(flavors);
        WinJS.Namespace.define("DataExample", {
            flavorList: flavorList
        });
    })();
```

3. Add a reference to the data.js file in your default.html, which is found at the root of the project.

```
<head>
    <!-- Other file references ... -->
    <!-- Your data file. -->
    <script src="/js/data.js"></script>
</head>
```

4. In default.html, you will now create a ListView and bind it to the data source you have created in the data.js file. Also define an item template for the list view items. Add the following code to default.html.

```
<h1>ListView Data Binding</h1>
<div id="flavorItemTemplate" data-win-control="WinJS.Binding.Template">
    <div id="templateContainer">
        <div id="itemContainer">
            <h4 data-win-bind="innerText: title"></h4>
            <h6 data-win-bind="innerText: text"></h6>
        </div>
    </div>
</div>
<div id="basicListView" data-win-control="WinJS.UI.ListView"
    data-win-options="{itemDataSource : DataExample.flavorList.dataSource,
                       itemTemplate:select('#flavorItemTemplate'),
                       selectionMode: 'none',
                       layout:{type:WinJS.UI.ListLayout}}">
</div>
```

Create the list view by setting the data-win-control attribute with a WinJS.UI.ListView value. Use the data-win-options attribute to set control options like item data source, item template, and the layout of the list view.

5. Next, you need to add a little bit of style to the list view and the list view items. Open default.css in Windows and Windows Mobile projects, and add the following style sheet definition:

```
#basicListView{
    height: 100%;
    margin-top: 10px;
    margin-right: 20px;
}
```

```
#templateContainer{
    display: -ms-grid;
    -ms-grid-columns: 1fr;
    min-height: 150px;
}

#itemContainer{
    background-color:lightgray;
    width:100%;
    padding:10px;
}
```

6. Build and run the app by pressing **F5** in Visual Studio. Figure 5-8 shows the output on a Windows Mobile screen.

Figure 5-8. *ListView Data Binding Output on a Windows Mobile Screen*

5.5 Navigational Structures in UWP Apps

Problem

You want to split your application into multiple pages/screens to handle specific functionalities. You want to know what navigation structures should be followed to provide the best experience for moving between the pages/screens.

Solution

A real-world application rarely has just one page/screen, but is made up of many pages/screens. Each page/screen is responsible for a specific functionality. It is always better to divide your app into functionalities and assign a dedicated page/screen for handling that functionality. The navigation in UWP apps are based on navigational structures, elements, and system-level features. By providing the right navigation in your app, you are enabling an intuitive user experience for moving from one page to another or from this content to that content.

Each page in your app will contain or cater to a specific set of content or functionality. For example, a contact management app will have a screen for listing the contacts, a screen for creating a contact, a screen for updating the contact, or a screen for deleting the contact. The navigation structure of the app is defined by how you organize different screens of the application. Figure 5-9 illustrates the different navigation structure that can be employed in an UWP app.

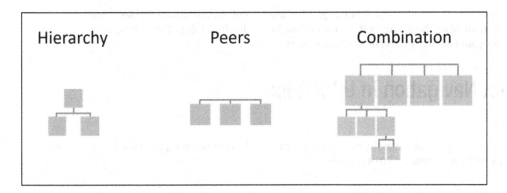

Figure 5-9. Navigation structures

The hierarchy navigation structure is a tree-like structure. Each child page has only one parent. To reach a child, you travel through the parent.

Peer is a navigation structure where pages exist side by side. You can travel from one page to another in any order.

The combination navigation structure uses both hierarchy and peer structures. Groups of pages are organized as peers or as hierarchies.

5.6 Navigational Elements in UWP Apps

Problem

You understand the navigational structures. You want to know what elements are available to achieve the navigation structure for your app.

Solution

A user can get to the content he wants to see with the help of many navigation elements. In some cases, the navigation elements indicate to users where the content is within the app. The navigational elements can be used as content or commanding elements. Hence, it is advised to use the navigational element that best suits your navigational structure. The following are some of the navigation elements available for UWP apps:

- *Pivot*: This control is used to display a persistent list of links to pages at the same level. This control can be used when you have a Peers navigation structure.

- *SplitView*: This control is used to display a list of links to top-level pages in an app. This can be used in a scenario where you need a Peers navigation structure.

- *Hub*: This control is used to display previews/summaries of child pages. Navigation to child pages is through links or section headers available in the page itself. This control is used when you have a Hierarchy navigation structure.

- *ListView*: This control is used to display a master list of item summaries. Selecting an item displays the details of the selected item in the details section. This can be used for your Hierarchy navigation structure scenarios.

5.7 Pivot Navigation in UWP Apps

Problem

In your app, you have identified that the navigational structure for navigation is peer-based. You want to implement the navigation using a Pivot control.

Solution

The Pivot control is used for navigation when you have frequently accessed distinct content categories. Pivot is made up of two or more content panes and each pane has a corresponding category header. The headers will persist on-screen and a selection state is clearly shown visible, which makes it easy for users to know which category they have selected. Users can swipe left or right on the header and doing so will allow them to navigate to an adjacent header. They can also swipe left or right on the content.

How It Works

1. Open Visual Studio 2015. Select **File ➤ New Project ➤ JavaScript ➤ Windows ➤ Universal ➤ Blank App (Windows Universal)** template. This creates a Universal Windows app project (see Figure 5-10).

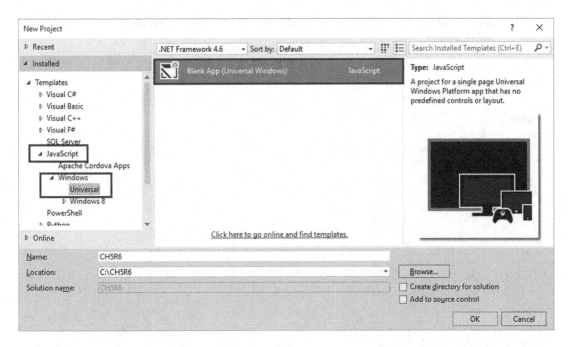

Figure 5-10. *New Project dialog*

2. Open **default.html**, which is found in the root of the project. Replace the content of the body with the following content:

```
<div data-win-control="WinJS.UI.Pivot" data-win-options="{ title: 'PIVOT
Navigation', selectedIndex: 0 }">
        <div data-win-control="WinJS.UI.PivotItem" data-win-options="{ 'header':
        'one'}">
            <p> Content - Item One </p>
        </div>
        <div data-win-control="WinJS.UI.PivotItem" data-win-options="{ 'header':
        'two'}">
            <p> Content - Item Two </p>
        </div>
        <div data-win-control="WinJS.UI.PivotItem" data-win-options="{ 'header':
        'three'}">
            <p> Content - Item Three </p>
        </div>
    </div>
```

You have placed a div and set the data-win-control attribute to a value of WinJS.UI.Pivot. This converts the div to a Pivot control. You then pass options to the Pivot control using the data-win-options attribute. You are setting the title of the Pivot and the item that will be selected. The items of the pivot control are placed as a div with the data-win-control attribute set to a value of WinJS. UI.PivotItem. Each pivot item has a header. Set the header value using the data-win-options attribute. You can place as many items that your app calls for.

3. Next, press **F5** and run the app. Figure 5-11 is a screenshot from the Windows Mobile output.

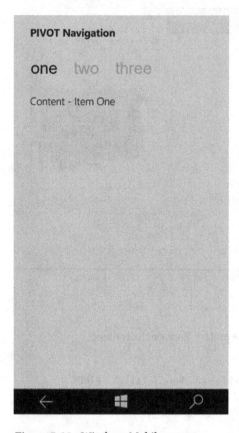

Figure 5-11. *Windows Mobile output*

As you can see, there are three pivot items. You can either click the header of the pivot items or swipe left to right to navigate to adjacent content/items.

5.8 SplitView Navigation in UWP Apps

Problem

In your app, you have identified that the navigational structure for navigation is peer-based. You want to provide a menu with links to the top-level page. You want to implement the navigation using the SplitView control.

Solution

The SplitView control contains one pane and a content area. The pane can expand or collapse, whereas the content area is always visible. The pane can also remain in an open state and has the flexibility to present itself from either the left side or the right side of the app. Usually, navigation links are placed in this pane.

How It Works

1. Open Visual Studio 2015. Select **File ➤ New Project ➤ JavaScript ➤ Windows ➤ Universal ➤ Blank App (Windows Universal)** template. This creates a Universal Windows app project (see Figure 5-12).

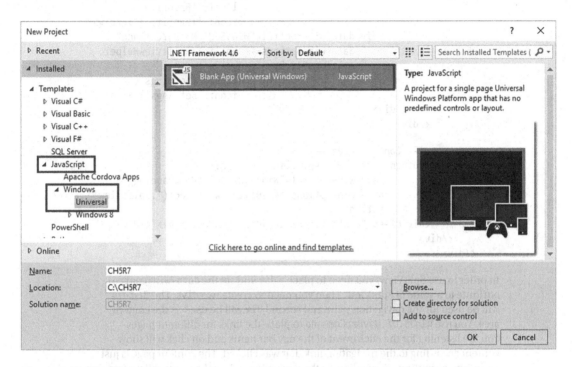

Figure 5-12. *New Project dialog*

2. Open **default.html**, which is found in the root of the project. Replace the content of the body with the following code snippet:

```
<div id="app">
    <div class="splitView"
        data-win-control="WinJS.UI.SplitView"
        data-win-options="{closedDisplayMode:'none',
        openedDisplayMode:'overlay'}">
        <!-- Pane area -->
        <div>
            <div class="header">
                <button class="win-splitviewpanetoggle"
                        data-win-control="WinJS.UI.SplitViewPaneToggle"
                        data-win-options="{ splitView:
                        select('.splitView') }"></button>
                <div class="title">Menu</div>
            </div>

            <div id='navBar' class="nav-commands">
                <div data-win-control="WinJS.UI.NavBarCommand"
```

```
                              data-win-options="{ onclick:SplitViewHelper.homeClick,
                                        label: 'Home',
                                        icon: 'home'}"></div>
               <div data-win-control="WinJS.UI.NavBarCommand"
                    data-win-options="{ onclick:SplitViewHelper.favClick,
                                        label: 'Favorite',
                                        icon: 'favorite'}"></div>
               <div data-win-control="WinJS.UI.NavBarCommand"
                    data-win-options="{ onclick:SplitViewHelper.
                    settingsClick,
                                        label: 'Settings',
                                        icon: 'settings'}"></div>
          </div>
        </div>

        <!-- Content area -->
        <button class="win-splitviewpanetoggle"
                data-win-control="WinJS.UI.SplitViewPaneToggle"
                data-win-options="{ splitView: select('.splitView') }"></
                button>
        <div class="contenttext"><h2>Page Content </h2> </div>
    </div>
  </div>
```

In order to use SplitView, you need to place a div and set the data-win-control attribute to a value of SplitView. Then you need to create two divs. The first div will be used for the navigation pane and second div will be used as the content area. You use WinJS.UI.NavBarCommand to place the links for different pages. You are listening for the click event of the nav bar items and on click will show content according to the navigation link that was clicked. The content page is just a div, and at runtime, depending on the navigation link clicked, you will update the content accordingly.

3. Next open **default.js**, found in the js folder. Replace the app.activated handler with the following code snippet:

```
app.onactivated = function (args) {
          if (args.detail.kind === activation.ActivationKind.launch) {
                  if (args.detail.previousExecutionState !== activation.
                  ApplicationExecutionState.terminated) {
                  } else {
                  }
                  args.setPromise(
              WinJS.UI.processAll().done(function () {
                  SplitViewHelper.splitView = document.querySelector(".
                  splitView").winControl;
                  new WinJS.UI._WinKeyboard(SplitViewHelper.splitView.
                  paneElement); // Temporary workaround: Draw keyboard
                  focus visuals on NavBarCommands
              })
          );
        }
    };
```

4. Next, after the IIFE (immediately invoked function expression) declaration, place the following code snippet. You are creating a small helper classto handle the navigation click event.

```
(function () {
        "use strict";

        //other app related code ommitted for brevity

})();
WinJS.Namespace.define("SplitViewHelper", {
    splitView: null,

    homeClick: WinJS.UI.eventHandler(function (ev) {
        document.querySelector('.contenttext').innerHTML = "<h2>SplitView Content
        area</h2>";
    }),
    favClick: WinJS.UI.eventHandler(function (ev) {
        document.querySelector('.contenttext').innerHTML = "<h2>Favorites!</h2>";
    }),
    settingsClick: WinJS.UI.eventHandler(function (ev) {
        document.querySelector('.contenttext').innerHTML = "<h2>Settings!</h2>";
    }),
});
```

You are replacing the inner HTML of the content div in this example. If you want to load a new page altogether, you can do so by making use of WinJS.UI.Pages.render('<URI>',<Content Host Elementn>);.

5. Now, press **F5** and run the app. Figures 5-13 and 5-14 show output on a Windows Mobile.

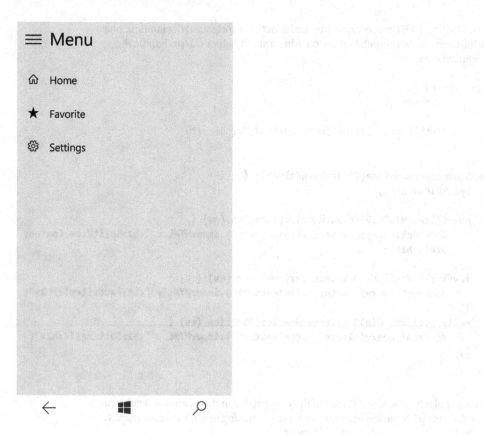

Figure 5-13. *Navigation pane*

Figure 5-14. Content area

5.9 Hub Navigation in UWP Apps

Problem

You have identified that the navigational structure for your Universal Windows platform app is hierarchical in nature. You want to use Hub as the navigational element in your app.

Solution

The Hub control is for navigation where the app's content can be separated into distinct, related sections or categories with varying detail levels. This is a common pattern used in scenarios such as relational information, which needs to be traversed in a preferred sequence. The hierarchical pattern of navigation is suitable for applications that provide a variety of experiences and content with organization and structure.

How It Works

1. Open Visual Studio 2015. Select **File ➤ New Project ➤ JavaScript ➤ Windows ➤ Universal ➤ Blank App (Windows Universal)** template. This creates a Universal Windows app project (see Figure 5-15).

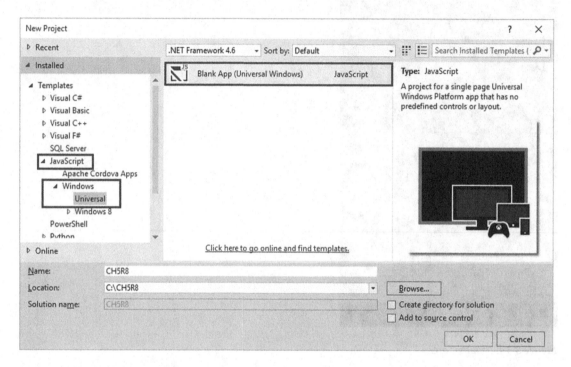

Figure 5-15. *New Project dialog*

2. Open **default.html**, found in the root of the project. Replace the contents after the <body> tag with the following code snippet:

```
<div data-win-control="WinJS.UI.Hub">
    <div class="section1" data-win-control="WinJS.UI.HubSection"
        data-win-options="{header: 'Images', isHeaderStatic: true}">
        <div class="imagesFlexBox">
            <img class="imageItem" src="/images/circle_image1.jpg" />
            <img class="imageItem" src="/images/circle_image3.jpg" />
            <img class="imageItem" src="/images/circle_image2.jpg" />
            <img class="imageItem" src="/images/circle_image1.jpg" />
            <img class="imageItem" src="/images/circle_image3.jpg" />
            <img class="imageItem" src="/images/circle_image2.jpg" />
            <img class="imageItem" src="/images/circle_image1.jpg" />
            <img class="imageItem" src="/images/circle_image3.jpg" />
            <img class="imageItem" src="/images/circle_image2.jpg" />
        </div>
    </div>
```

```
<div id="list" class="section2" data-win-control="WinJS.UI.HubSection"
    data-win-options="{header: 'ListView', isHeaderStatic: true}">
    <div id="listView"
        class="win-selectionstylefilled"
        data-win-control="WinJS.UI.ListView"
        data-win-options="{
        itemDataSource: HubExample.data.dataSource,
        itemTemplate: smallListIconTextTemplate,
        selectionMode: 'none',
        tapBehavior: 'none',
        swipeBehavior: 'none'
    }">
    </div>
    </div>
</div>
<div id="smallListIconTextTemplate" data-win-control="WinJS.Binding.
Template">
    <div class="smallListIconTextItem">
        <img src="#" class="smallListIconTextItem-Image"
            data-win-bind="src: picture" />
        <div class="smallListIconTextItem-Detail">
            <h4 data-win-bind="innerText: title"></h4>
            <h6 data-win-bind="innerText: text"></h6>
        </div>
    </div>
</div>
```

To create a Hub control, set the data-win-control attribute to a value of WinJS.
UI.Hub on a div. To create sections inside the Hub, create a div and set its data-win-control attribute to WinJS.UI.HubSection. Set the header of the sections using the data-win-options attribute. Set the header property on the section.

3. Section 2 in the preceding code makes use of a ListView. So let's create a data source for the list view. Open the **default.js** file in the js folder. Inside the immediately invoked function expression and after 'use strict' statement, copy and paste the following code snippet:

```
var myData = new WinJS.Binding.List([
    { title: "Fire Hydrant", text: "Red", picture: "/images/circle_list1.jpg" },
    { title: "Fire Hydrant", text: "Yellow", picture: "/images/circle_list2.jpg" },
    { title: "Pothole Cover", text: "Gray", picture: "/images/circle_list3.jpg" },
    { title: "Sprinkler", text: "Yellow", picture: "/images/circle_list4.jpg" },
    { title: "Electrical Charger", text: "Yellow", picture:
    "/images/circle_list5.jpg" },
    { title: "Knob", text: "Red", picture: "/images/circle_list6.jpg" },
    { title: "Fire Hydrant", text: "Red", picture: "/images/circle_list1.jpg" },
    { title: "Fire Hydrant", text: "Yellow", picture: "/images/circle_list2.jpg" },
    { title: "Pothole Cover", text: "Gray", picture: "/images/circle_list3.jpg" },
    { title: "Fire Hydrant", text: "Red", picture: "/images/circle_list1.jpg" },
    { title: "Fire Hydrant", text: "Yellow", picture: "/images/circle_list2.jpg" },
    { title: "Pothole Cover", text: "Gray", picture: "/images/circle_list3.jpg" }
]);
```

```
        WinJS.Namespace.define("HubExample", {
    data: myData
});
```

4. To run the app, press **F5** in Visual Studio. Figure 5-16 shows output on a Windows Mobile device.

Figure 5-16. *Hub navigation output*

5.10 Master/Detail Navigation Using ListView in UWP Apps

Problem

You have identified that the navigational structure for your Universal Windows Platform app is hierarchical in nature. You want to use a Master/Detail navigation pattern. You have identified ListView as the navigational element.

Solution

ListView is a control that displays a list of data items in a vertical stack. You can data bind a data source to the list view and provide a template for rendering each item.

How It Works

1. Open Visual Studio 2015. Select **File ➤ New Project ➤ JavaScript ➤ Windows ➤ Universal ➤ Blank App (Windows Universal)** template. This creates a Universal Windows app project (see Figure 5-17).

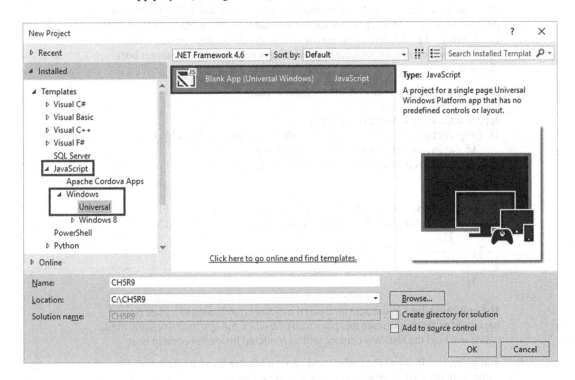

Figure 5-17. *New Project dialog*

2. Open **default.html**, which is found in the root of the project. Replace the contents of the body with the following code snippet:

```
<h1>ListView Navigation</h1>
<div id="contentHost"></div>
```

You have a div with id contentHost. Use this as a placeholder to show different pages at runtime; that is, render the master and details page inside this content host div element.

3. Next, open **default.js**, found in the js folder. Add the following code snippet just before the app.onactivated function definition:

```
WinJS.Navigation.addEventListener("navigating", function (args) {
        var url = args.detail.location;
        var host = document.getElementById("contentHost");
        host.winControl && host.winControl.unload && host.winControl.unload();
```

```
        WinJS.Utilities.empty(host);
        args.detail.setPromise(WinJS.UI.Pages.render(url, host, args.detail.
        state));
    });
```

Through this code, you are listening to a navigation event that will occur on the page. You have provided a handler for the navigation event. In the event handler, you intercept the navigation call, get the URL of the destination page, get the content host element, and render the destination page inside the content host element.

4. Next, modify the app.onactivated method, as follows:

```
app.onactivated = function (args) {
if (args.detail.kind === activation.ActivationKind.launch) {
    if (args.detail.previousExecutionState !==
activation.ApplicationExecutionState.terminated) {
    } else {
    }
    args.setPromise( WinJS.UI.processAll().then(function () {
            return WinJS.Navigation.navigate("/master.html");
        })
    );
}
    };
```

The only thing done in the activated event handler is navigating to a page named master.html (you will create this page next). So when the app loads, master.html, which will hold the ListView control, will be rendered inside the content host.

5. Add a new HTML file to the project and name it **master.html**. Replace the contents of the master.html with the following snippet:

```
<!DOCTYPE html>
<html>
<head>
    <title></title>
    <link href="/css/default.css" rel="stylesheet" />

    <!-- WinJS references -->
    <link href="WinJS/css/ui-dark.css" rel="stylesheet" />
    <script src="WinJS/js/base.js"></script>
    <script src="WinJS/js/ui.js"></script>

    <script src="js/data.js"></script>
    <script src="js/master.js"></script>
</head>
<body >
    <div class="smallListIconTextTemplate"
        data-win-control="WinJS.Binding.Template"
        style="display: none">
        <div class="smallListIconTextItem">
```

```
            <img src="#" class="smallListIconTextItem-Image"
                data-win-bind="src: picture" />
            <div class="smallListIconTextItem-Detail">
                <h4 class="win-h4" data-win-bind="textContent: title"></h4>
                <h6 class="win-h6" data-win-bind="textContent: text"></h6>
            </div>
        </div>
    </div>

    <div class="listView win-selectionstylefilled"
        data-win-control="WinJS.UI.ListView"
        data-win-options="{
                itemDataSource: ListViewExample.data.dataSource,
                itemTemplate: select('.smallListIconTextTemplate'),
                tapBehavior: WinJS.UI.TapBehavior.directSelect,
                layout: { type: WinJS.UI.ListLayout }
            }">
    </div>
</body>
</html>
```

What you have done in master.html is place a list view, provide a data source to the list view, and provide an item template for rendering each item. The template displays an image, title, and text from the data item that will be bound at runtime.

6. Next, create a new JavaScript file in the js folder and name it **master.js**. Add the following code snippet to the JavaScript file:

```
(function () {
    'use strict';
    WinJS.UI.Pages.define("/master.html", {
        ready: function (element, options) {
            var that = this;
            element.addEventListener("iteminvoked", function (evt) {
                evt.detail.itemPromise.then(function (item) {
                    WinJS.Application.sessionState.selectedItem = item.data;
                    WinJS.Navigation.navigate("/detail.html");
                });
            });
        }
    })
})();
```

Let's go over the code for a moment. You have created a logic file for master.html with this new JavaScript file. Define page members with the WinJS.UI.Pages. define() method. You have provided a ready method that will be called when the page is loaded. And you are adding event listener for ListView item tap. When the item is tapped, store the selected item in an application session state and then navigate to detail.html.

7. Next, create a new JavaScript file named **data.js** inside the js folder. This file provides the data source for the ListView in master.html. Paste the following code snippet in data.js:

```
var myData = new WinJS.Binding.List([
{ title: "Lemon", text: "Sorbet", picture: "/images/60Lemon.png" },
{ title: "Mint", text: "Gelato", picture: "/images/60Mint.png" },
{ title: "Orange", text: "Sorbet", picture: "/images/60Orange.png" },
]);
WinJS.Namespace.define("ListViewExample", {
        data : myData
});
```

8. Now let's create the details page. Add a new HTML file to the root of the project and name it **detail.html**. Paste the following code snippet to the newly created file:

```
<!DOCTYPE html>
<html>
<head>
    <title></title>
    <link href="/css/default.css" rel="stylesheet" />
    <!-- WinJS references -->
    <link href="WinJS/css/ui-dark.css" rel="stylesheet" />
    <script src="WinJS/js/base.js"></script>
    <script src="WinJS/js/ui.js"></script>
    <script src="/js/detail.js"></script>
</head>
<body>
    <div>
        <button data-win-control="WinJS.UI.BackButton"></button>
        <h3>Item Details </h3>
        <h2><span data-win-bind="innerText: title"></span></h2>
        <img data-win-bind="src: picture" />
        <h2><span data-win-bind="innerText: text"></span></h2>
    </div>
</body>
</html>
```

In this page, just output the details of the selected item in the list view. Notice that you are using data binding expressions to show the title, text, and image of the data item.

9. Now you need to create the logic file for detail.html. Add a new JavaScript file named **detail.js** inside the js folder. Paste the following code snippet to the newly created file:

```
(function () {
    'use strict';
    WinJS.UI.Pages.define("/detail.html", {
        processed: function (element, options) {
            var that = this;
```

```
        WinJS.Binding.processAll(element, WinJS.Application.sessionState.
selectedItem);
        }
    })
})();
```

When the page loads, just call the `Binding.processAll()` on the page and provide the selected item as the data item that needs to be bound to the elements.

10. You are done with all the code required for master/detail navigation. Now press **F5** and run the app. Figures 5-18 and 5-19 show the output from a Windows Mobile device.

Figure 5-18. *Master screen*

Figure 5-19. *Details screen*

CHAPTER 6

■ ■ ■

Adapting the UI for Different Screens

With the Universal Windows Platform (UWP), you have the benefit of running your app on any device in the Windows family. The device family includes phones, tablets, laptops, the Xbox, and so forth. There are different screen sizes in the device family. The platform does the magic behind the scenes and makes sure that your app's user interface is functional across all devices. Since the platform handles things for you under the hood, you aren't required to do any customization to your app to support different screen sizes. But there may be situations where you want to provide a specific UI for a specific screen size. For example, when your app runs on a phone, you could want a single-column layout; whereas when the same app runs on a tablet or PC, you want a two-column layout. This chapter looks at how to adapt your UI for different screen sizes.

If UWP apps can run on any Windows 10 device family with any screen size, why should you, as an app developer, worry about a tailor-made UI for a specific screen size?

As stated earlier, the platform takes care of making sure that your app's UI is functional across all screen sizes, but you may still have situations where you want to customize per the screen that your app is running on. The following points are worth noting. They provide insights on why you would want to customize.

- *Make effective use of available space and reduce navigation*. When an app's UI is designed to look good on a small screen, the app will be usable on PCs too. But there will probably be some wasted space. A better design would be to show more content when the screen size is above a certain size. Having more content on a bigger screen size reduces the amount of navigation that a user otherwise performs.

- *Device capability*. Different devices have different capabilities. By customizing your app for a specific device, you can take better advantage of the capabilities available on this specific device and you can then enable/disable features around this.

- *Input optimization*. The Control library in the UWP works well with all input types, including touch, pen, keyboard, and mouse. But you can optimize the input for a specific device. For example, navigation is usually provided at the bottom of a screen for a phone-based app; whereas a PC user expects the navigation to be available at the top of the screen.

6.1 Design Breakpoints for Different Screens

Problem

Since you need to support various screen sizes under the Windows 10 device family, you would like to know the specific widths to target in your apps.

Solution

Breakpoint is the terminology used in CSS (Cascading Style Sheets) to denote the size or width of a screen, against which you write the style rules. There are a great many device targets and screen sizes available in Windows 10 device families. But you don't have to optimize your UI for each of these device targets or screen sizes. Instead, you should design for key screen widths. These key screen widths are also known as breakpoints. Let's look at the breakpoints that you should be concerned with.

- *Small: 320epx.*

  These device targets/screens have an effective pixel width of 320. The typical screen size is 4 to 6 inches. Typically, these devices are phones.

- *Medium: 720epx.*

  These device targets/screens have an effective pixel width of 720. The typical screen size is 6 to 12 inches. Typically, these devices are tablets and phones with a large screen.

- *Large: 1024epx.*

  These device targets/screens have an effective pixel width of 1024 and higher. The typical screen size is 13 inches and higher. Typically, these devices are PCs, laptops, Surface Hubs, and so forth.

6.2 Adaptive UI Technique: Reposition

Problem

You would like your app to support all device targets/screen sizes. You would like to make your UI adaptive and you want to reposition certain portions of your screen based on the screen size that your app is running on.

Solution

One of the techniques to make your app's user interface adapt to different screen sizes involves CSS media queries, which are outside the scope of this book, and hence, you won't be delving deeply into it. But you can read and learn more about media queries at W3C Schools online at `http://www.w3schools.com/cssref/css3_pr_mediaquery.asp`. You will write a media query rule to target the size of a screen. The rule will have styles defined to reposition UI elements according to the screen the app is running on.

How It Works

1. Open Visual Studio 2015. Select **File ➤ New Project ➤ JavaScript ➤ Windows ➤ Universal ➤ Blank App (Universal Windows)** template. This creates a universal Windows app template (see Figure 6-1).

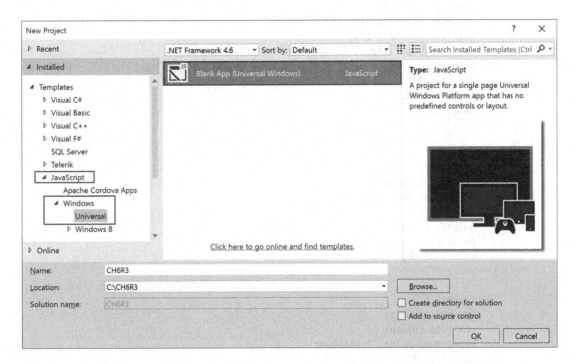

Figure 6-1. *New Project dialog*

2. Open the **default.html**, which is found at the root of the project. After the <body> tag, add the following content:

```
<div class="appGrid">
        <div class="sectionA">
            <h1>A</h1>
        </div>
        <div class="sectionB">
            <h1>B</h1>
        </div>
</div>
```

You have created a bunch of divs. The outer div (appGrid) acts as a container. Next, you have two sections that are displayed as part of the app. On a small screen, you want to show sectionA and sectionB one on top of the other. When running on medium and large screens, place sectionA and sectionB next to each other.

3. Next, you create the necessary styles for the app. Open **default.css**, which is found in the css folder. Replace the contents of default.css with the following style rules.

```
.appGrid {
    display: -ms-grid;
    -ms-grid-columns: 2fr 1fr;
    grid-columns: 2fr 1fr;
    -ms-grid-rows: 1fr;
    grid-rows: 1fr;
    width: 100%;
    height: 100%;
    margin:24px;
}

.sectionA {
    -ms-grid-row: 1;
    -ms-grid-column: 1;
    background-color: lightgray;
    width: 100%;
    height: 100%;
    padding: 10px;
    color: black;
}

.sectionB {
    -ms-grid-row: 1;
    -ms-grid-column: 2;
    background-color: lightblue;
    width: 100%;
    height: 100%;
    padding: 10px;
    color: black;

}
```

Let's go through the code once. You have just defined three rules. One of the rules is for the outer grid. You are using a grid-based display with two columns and one row. Section A is placed in column 1 and Section B is placed in column 2. Since there is no media query applied yet, these rules are applied all the time.

4. Now you define a media query for handling the UI when the max width of the screen is 320. When you are running the app on a small screen, you want the layout to be narrow—only one column and two rows. Section A is placed in row 1 and Section B is placed in row 2. You place the CSS rule in the same CSS file (default.css). Here is the code snippet for the media query:

```
@media (max-width:320px){
    .appGrid {
        display: -ms-grid;
        -ms-grid-columns: 1fr;
        grid-columns: 1fr;
```

```
        -ms-grid-rows: 2fr 1fr;
        grid-rows: 2fr 1fr;
        width: 100%;
        height: 100%;
        margin:12px;
    }

    .sectionA {
        -ms-grid-row: 1;
        -ms-grid-column: 1;
        background-color: lightgray;
        width: 100%;
        height: 100%;
    }

    .sectionB {
        -ms-grid-row: 2;
        -ms-grid-column: 1;
        background-color: lightblue;
        width: 100%;
        height: 100%;
    }
}
```

This shows that when the screen size is 320px and lower, a new style rule is picked up. As part of the style rule, the app grid is now one column and two rows. This repositioned the placement of Section A and Section B.

5. Next, press F5 and run the app. You can run the app in a Windows 10 Mobile emulator or you can run it on a local machine. Figures 6-2 and 6-3 show the output from a phone and a PC.

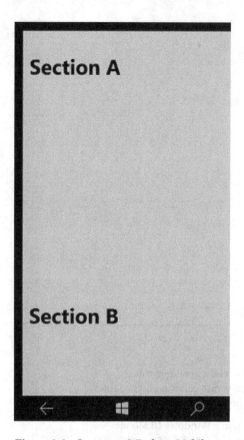

Figure 6-2. *Output on Windows Mobile*

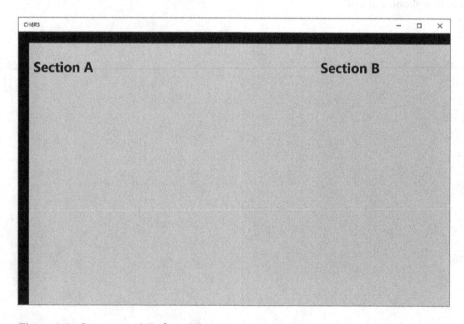

Figure 6-3. *Output on a Windows PC*

6.3 Adaptive UI Technique: Fluid Layouts

Problem

You have created a layout in which you want to show the number of items in a list view. But you want the list view to adapt to narrow screens and medium or large screens. You want the list view items to be responsive based on screen size.

Solution

The ListView control in UWP is used in scenarios where you have a number of items to display. As the name implies, a list view renders a list on the screen, with each item bound to a data item. Each item of the list view can be customized by providing a template. ListView also has a concept called Layout. Layout defines how the items should be spread out on the screen. It supports two layouts out of the box: ListLayout and GridLayout. ListLayout is used for single-column/multiple rows renderings. GridLayout renders grid-based layouts (i.e., rows and columns occupy the available space on the screen).

How It Works

1. Open **Visual Studio 2015**. Select **File ➤ New Project ➤ JavaScript ➤ Windows Universal ➤ Blank App (Universal Windows)** template. This creates a universal Windows app template (see Figure 6-4).

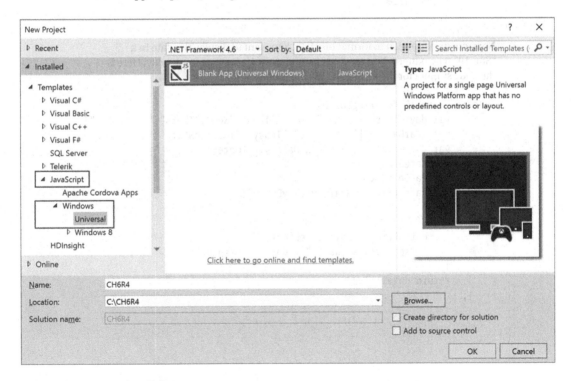

Figure 6-4. *New Project dialog*

2. Create a new file called **weatherData.js** in the js folder. Add an immediately invoked function expression. Here is the code snippet:

```
(function (undefined) {
    'use strict'
    //rest of the code here

})();
```

3. Next, create an array of weather data after the 'use strict' statement inside the function body, as shown earlier. Let's build fictitious weather data for the purpose of this recipe demo. Here is the code snippet:

```
var weatherData = [
        {
            date: formatDateString(new Date().getDate()),
            imgSrc: "images/tile-snow.png",
            hi: "32&deg;",
            low: "16&deg;",
            temp: "24&deg;",
            feelsLike: "28&deg;",
            chanceOfSnow: "88%"
        }
        //add more items here
        ];
```

4. Next, create a function to format the date. You want to display the date in a "Sun 10" type pattern. You need to customize the date string for display. Here is the code snippet for the formatDateString function:

```
function formatDateString(date) {
        var daysOfWeek = ["Sun","Mon","Tues","Wed","Thurs","Fri","Sat"];
        var nearDays = ["Yesterday","Today","Tomorrow"];
        var dayDelta = date - new Date().getDate() + 1;
        var dateString = "";
        if (dayDelta < 3) {
            dateString = nearDays[dayDelta];
        }
        else {
            dateString = daysOfWeek[date % 7] +
            " <span class='day'>" + date + "</span>";
        }
        return dateString;
    };
```

5. You need to expose this weatherData array so that you can consume it in default.html and bind it to the list view. Create a namespace and expose the weatherData, as shown here:

```
var weatherDataList = new WinJS.Binding.List(weatherData);
WinJS.Namespace.define("FluidApp.Data", {
        weatherData : weatherDataList
})
```

You have created a namespace called FluidApp.Data and exposed weatherData as a public property, which can be bound to any win control.

6. You need to add a reference to weatherData.js. Add the following script tag in head section of default.html. Add this before the default.js script file reference:

```
<script src="/js/weatherData.js"></script>
```

7. Next, you need to create the UI. In default.html, remove the default contents, which are found inside the <body> tag. Add the following template, which is used for displaying each item of the list view:

```
<div id="weatherTemplate" class="dayTemplate" data-win-
control="WinJS.Binding.Template">
<div class="dayGrid">
    <div class="win-type-x-large dayDate"
                data-win-bind="innerHTML: date">
    </div>
    <div class="dayImg">
        <img data-win-bind="src: imgSrc" />
    </div>
    <div class="win-type-x-large dayHighLow">
        <span class="dayHigh" data-win-bind="innerHTML: hi"></span>
        <span>/</span>
        <span class="dayLow" data-win-bind="innerHTML: low"></span>
    </div>
    <div class="dayFeelsLike">
        <span>Feels like </span>
        <span data-win-bind="innerHTML: feelsLike"></span>
    </div>
    <div class="dayChanceOfSnow">
        <span>Chance of snow is </span>
        <span data-win-bind="innerHTML: chanceOfSnow"></span>
    </div>
</div>
</div>
```

8. Next, let's add the ListView control. Paste the following code snippet after the template that you created in the previous step:

```
<div id="weatherListView" class="weatherListView"
        data-win-control="WinJS.UI.ListView"
        data-win-options="{
```

123

```
        itemDataSource:FluidApp.Data.weatherData.dataSource,
        itemTemplate:select('#weatherTemplate'),
      layout:WinJS.UI.GridLayout}"></div>
```

You have created a list view and provided weatherData as the item data source.
You have also provided the item template. You have set the layout of the list view
to GridLayout by default. You will change this layout property of the list view
based on the screen resize.

9. Open default.js, which is found in the js folder. Modify the app.onactivated
   function with the following code snippet:

```
app.onactivated = function (args) {
            if (args.detail.kind === activation.ActivationKind.launch) {
                  if (args.detail.previousExecutionState !== activation.
                  ApplicationExecutionState.terminated) {
                  } else {
                  }
                  args.setPromise(WinJS.UI.processAll().then
                  (function ready() {
                        var listView = document.querySelector
                        ("#weatherListView");
                        var listViewLayout = new WinJS.UI.GridLayout();
                        if (document.body.clientWidth <= 320) {
                              listViewLayout = new WinJS.UI.ListLayout();
                        }
                  listView.layout = listViewLayout;
            window.addEventListener("resize", resizeListView, false)
                  }));
            }
      };
```

Let's go over the code here. Once the UI processing is done, you grab the list view
first. You then check the width of the screen that you are currently running on.
If the width is less than or equal to 320 (i.e., you are on a small screen), you just
change the layout of the list view accordingly. If you are on a small screen, you
use ListLayout, but when not on a small screen, you set it to GridLayout. You also
register an event listener to resize the window. Next, let's look at what the resize
event handler does.

10. After the app.onactivated function, create a new function, resizeListView, and
    paste the following code snippet:

```
function resizeListView() {
      var listview = document.querySelector("#weatherListView").winControl;
      if (document.body.clientWidth <= 320) {
            if (!(listview.layout instanceof WinJS.UI.ListLayout)) {
                  listview.layout = new WinJS.UI.ListLayout();
            }
      }
```

```
        else {
            if (listview.layout instanceof WinJS.UI.ListLayout) {
                listview.layout = new WinJS.UI.GridLayout();
            }
        }
    }
}
```

11. Now run the app on a mobile device or on a PC to see the output. Press **F5** to run the app. The screenshot shown in Figure 6-5 is on Windows 10 Mobile and the one shown in Figure 6-6 is on a Windows 10 PC.

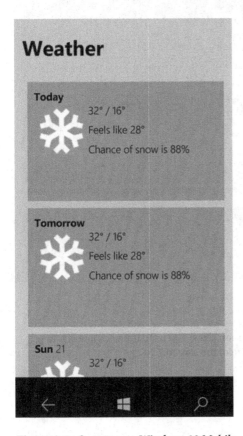

Figure 6-5. Output on a Windows 10 Mobile

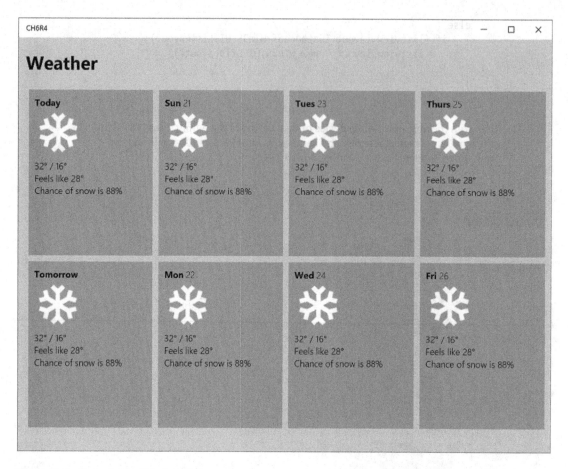

Figure 6-6. *Output on a Windows PC*

What you have just achieved is a tailored UI for different screen sizes. You used the ListView layout techniques to display a grid or a list layout, depending on the size of the screen.

■ ■ ■

CHAPTER 7

Application Lifecycle and Navigation

This chapter introduces the Universal Windows app events and lifecycle, covering the standard set of events that are raised when you start a Windows app and how to handle those events. The chapter covers how developers handle the suspension and termination of the app. It also covers how to save and restore the data during those events, which help developers provide a better user experience.

The chapter also covers the navigation model and explains how to build a single-page app that can contain multiple virtual HTML pages.

7.1 Application States and Events

Problem

You need to identify and subscribe to various events in your app when users start, close, or resume the app.

Solution

Use the `default.js` file in your Universal Windows app project to subscribe to and handle various events in the application lifecycle.

How It Works

Create a new Universal Windows project using the Universal Windows template, which can be found under the **JavaScript ➤ Windows ➤ Universal** node of the New Project dialog in Microsoft Visual Studio 2015. This creates a single project in the Visual Studio Solution along with the necessary files in it to start with.

From the project's js folder, open the **default.js** file from the Visual Studio Solution Explorer. You see two important events that are subscribed by default.

- `app.onactivated`
- `app.oncheckpoint`

The code for these events looks like the one shown next.

```
app.onactivated = function (args)
{
            if (args.detail.kind === activation.ActivationKind.launch)
        {
                if (args.detail.previousExecutionState !== activation.
                ApplicationExecutionState.terminated) {

                } else {

                }
                args.setPromise(WinJS.UI.processAll());
        }
    };

app.oncheckpoint = function (args)
{

};
```

As a developer, you should be handling these events to describe how the application should save and restore data when various execution states are triggered.

In Universal Windows apps, there are three app execution states:

- Not Running
- Running
- Suspended

Figure 7-1 demonstrates the lifecycle of a Universal Windows app.

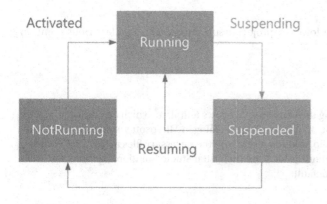

Figure 7-1. *Application states and events*

When a Universal Windows app is launched, the WinJS app fires the following events in the order shown next.

1. WinJS.Application.loaded

2. WinJS.Application.activated

3. WinJS.Application.ready

4. WinJS.Application.unload

When your app is about to be suspended, the WinJS.Application.checkpoint event is triggered. Table 7-1 provides the list of application events.

Table 7-1. *List of Application Events*

Event Name	Description
WinJS.Application.loaded	This event is triggered by the DOMContentLoaded event once the HTML document is completely loaded.
WinJS.Application.activated	This event is triggered when your application is activated.
WinJS.Application.ready	This event is triggered once the loaded and activated events execution is complete.
WinJS.Application.unload	This event is triggered by the beforeunload event before a page is unloaded.
WinJS.Application.checkpoint	This event is triggered when your application is suspended.

The developers should handle the activated event and checkpoint event to add their custom logic to save and restore the state of the app, and hence, you would see these two events included by default when creating a new project.

The other events can be subscribed using the WinJS.Application.addEventListener method.

Open the default.js file and add the following code snippet just above the onactivated event line.

```
WinJS.Application.addEventListener("loaded", function(event) {
    console.log("loaded event");
});
WinJS.Application.addEventListener("ready", function (event) {
    console.log("ready event");
});
```

Additionally, add console.log ("activated"); inside the onactivated event.

When you run the app on Windows desktop using the Local Machine option, you see the events raised in the specified order, as shown in the Figure 7-2.

```
eval code (3) (1,7)
loaded event
default.js (9,9)
activated
default.js (15,9)
ready event
default.js (12,9)
```

Figure 7-2. *Application events in the JavaScript console window*

■ **Note** The events are not raised until the WinJS.Application.start event is invoked. This method is invoked in the default.js file.

The Windows app must first be installed on the device to be activated. This can generally happen by installing the app from the Windows Store or using Visual Studio to build and deploy the universal application during development.

The Windows app is activated when the user taps on the app tile from the Start screen or from the apps list. At this stage, the application is in the NotRunning state, considering the following conditions:

- The app was launched for the first time.

- The app is not running because it crashed.

- The app was suspended and later terminated by the system.

The app can be activated several ways. The ActivationKind enumeration can be used to find out how the app was activated and to determine the exact reason for the app's activation.

For example, the app can be activated when the user taps on the application tile. The ActivationKind value is launched in this scenario. Similarly, when the activation of the app is done from the search contract, the ActivationKind value is searched.

The following code snippet shows how to handle this within the onactivated event.

```
if (args.detail.kind === activation.ActivationKind.launch) {
        console.log("launch activation kind");
}
else
if (args.detail.kind === activation.ActivationKind.Search) {
        console.log("search activation kind");
}
```

Table 7-2 shows some of the most common activation methods and their enumeration values.

Table 7-2. *Activation Methods*

Enum Member	Value	Description
launch	0	This value is received when the user launches the app or taps the tile from the app list.
search	1	This value is received when the user wants to search with the app using the search contract.
shareTarget	2	This value is received when the application was activated using the share contract.
file	3	This value is received when another app within the device launched a file where the file type is registered by the app to handle.
protocol	4	This value is received when another app launches a URI whose scheme name is registered to be handled by the app.
fileOpenPicker	5	This value is received when the user picks the files that are provided by this app.
fileSavePicker	6	This value is received when the user tries to save a file and selects the app as the location.
cachedFileUpdater	7	This value is received when the user tries to save a file that the app provides content management for.
contactPicker	8	This value is received when the user to pick contacts.
device	9	The app handles AutoPlay.
voiceCommand	16	This value is received when the app is activated because of the voice command.
toastNotification	1010	This value is received when the app is activated after a user taps on a toast notification or on the action inside the toast notification.

7.2 Handling the Unhandled Exception in Your App

Problem

Your app encounters a crash and the user is immediately taken to the Windows Start screen without any information. You need to handle this scenario to provide a better user experience.

Solution

You can handle the WinJS.Application.error event in the default.js file to log the error and display a message to the user.

How It Works

When there is an unhandled exception in your Universal Windows app, the MSApp.terminateApp function is invoked, and after which the application closes without any information to the user.

In this recipe, let's handle the WinJS.Application.error event and display a message to the user when the unhandled exception occurs in the app.

Create a new Universal Windows project using the Universal Windows template, which can be found under the **JavaScript ➤ Windows ➤ Universal** node of the New Project dialog in Microsoft Visual Studio 2015. This creates a single project in the Visual Studio Solution along with the necessary files in it to start with.

Open the default.js file from the js folder and replace it with the following code snippet.

```
(function () {
        "use strict";

        var app = WinJS.Application;
        var activation = Windows.ApplicationModel.Activation;
    WinJS.Application.addEventListener("error", function(eventArgs) {
        var errorMessage = new Windows.UI.Popups.MessageDialog("There was an error in the
        app. Kindly contact the app publisher");
        errorMessage.showAsync();
        return true;
    });

    app.onactivated = function (args) {

        args.setPromise(WinJS.UI.processAll());
        throw new WinJS.ErrorFromName();
    };
        app.start();
})();
```

This code snippet throws an exception from the onactivated event. The WinJS.Application. addEventListener function is used to add a listener to the error event to handle the unhandled exception and display a message to the user.

Run the app on Windows desktop using the Local Machine option in Visual Studio 2015. You see the message displayed in Figure 7-3.

Figure 7-3. Displaying a message on an unhandled exception in the app

---

■ **Note** The error handler function returns true. The value true is used to indicate that the error is handled, and hence the app should not be terminated.

7.3 Handling the Termination and Resuming of the App

Problem

You need to identify the previous execution state of the app so that you restore it when launching.

Solution

You can use the detail.previousExecutionState property of the activated event's parameter to identify the state of the app. This property determines if the app was launched as a new app, or if it was previously closed by the user, or if the user is launching the app after it was suspended or terminated.

How It Works

The previous ExecutionState contains the value indicating the previous state of the application. You can use this value in the activated event to load the previous state values or the initial state values based on this value.

Create a new Universal Windows project using the Universal Windows template, which is found under the **JavaScript ➤ Windows ➤ Universal** node of the New Project dialog in Microsoft Visual Studio 2015. This creates a single project in the Visual Studio Solution along with the necessary files in it to start with.

Open the default.js file from the js folder and replace the onactivated event with the following code snippet.

```
app.onactivated = function (args) {
        if (args.detail.kind === activation.ActivationKind.launch) {
            if (args.detail.previousExecutionState === activation.
            ApplicationExecutionState.notRunning) {

                console.log("Previous state is not running");
            }
            if (args.detail.previousExecutionState === activation.
            ApplicationExecutionState.closedByUser) {
                console.log("Previous state is closed by the user");
            }
                if (args.detail.previousExecutionState === activation.
                ApplicationExecutionState.terminated) {
                    console.log("Previous state is terminated");
                }
                args.setPromise(WinJS.UI.processAll());
        }
    };
```

This code handles the onactivated event where the args.detail.previousExecutionState is used to find the previous state of the app. The ApplicationExecutionState enum is used to check the state of the app.

When you run the app, you see the previous state displayed in the JavaScript console window, as shown in Figure 7-4.

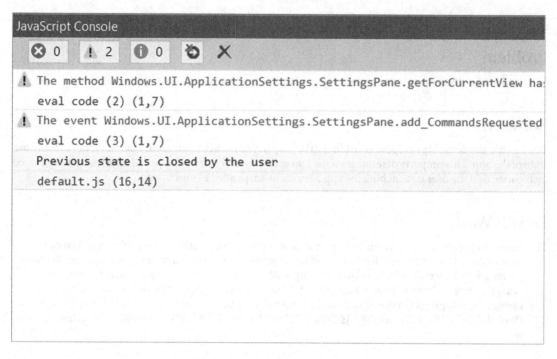

Figure 7-4. *PreviousExecutionState displayed in the JavaScript console window*

The ApplicationExecutionState enumeration contains the values, as shown in Table 7-3.

Table 7-3. *ApplicationExecutionState and Enumeration Values*

State	Description
notRunning	This app's previous state is "notRunning" when the user launches the app for the first time, closes the app, and launches the app within 10 seconds, or when the app crashes.
running	The app's previous state is "running" if the app is already running and the user launches the app using the contracts or a secondary tile.
suspended	The app's previous state is "suspended" if the app is suspended and later activated via the secondary tile or contracts.
terminated	The app's previous state is "terminated" if the app was previously terminated by the operating system.
closedByUser	The app's previous state is "closedByUser" if the app was closed by the user and not restarted within 10 seconds. The app could be closed by using the Alt+ F4 shortcut key or by using the close gesture.

7.4 Using SessionState to Store the State

Problem

You need to store the state of the app across the application lifecycle so that the value can be restored on the app activation.

Solution

Use the `WinJS.Application.sessionState` to store data to an app's state, which can be used to restore the app after it is suspended or terminated.

How It Works

The `WinJS.Application.sessionState` object is used to store app information to restore the app's state after the app is suspended or terminated.

When the app is suspended and then launched back, it does not lose its state. But when the app is suspended and later the operating system terminates the app due to memory or another reason, the application's state is lost. The app will start from scratch when launched again.

The `WinJS.Application.sessionState` helps overcome this issue.

Let's demonstrate the usage of the SessionState with some code.

1. Create a new Universal Windows project using the Universal Windows template, which can be found under the **JavaScript** ➤ **Windows** ➤ **Universal** node of the New Project dialog in Microsoft Visual Studio 2015. This creates a single project in the Visual Studio Solution along with the necessary files in it to start.

2. Open the **default.html** page from Visual Studio Solution Explorer and replace it with the following code snippet.

```
<!DOCTYPE html>
<html>
<head>
    <meta charset="utf-8" />
    <title>Recipe7.4</title>
    <!-- WinJS references -->
    <link href="WinJS/css/ui-light.css" rel="stylesheet" />
    <script src="WinJS/js/base.js"></script>
    <script src="WinJS/js/ui.js"></script>
    <!-- Recipe7.4 references -->
    <link href="/css/default.css" rel="stylesheet" />
    <script src="/js/default.js"></script>
</head>
<body class="win-type-body" style="margin: 20px">
<div>
    <input id="txt1"/>
    <input id="txt2"/>
</div>
</body>
</html>
```

The preceding code snippet adds two input controls on the page so that the user can enter data.

3. Open the **default.js** file from the js folder and replace the onactivated and oncheckpoint events with the following code snippet.

```
app.onactivated = function (args) {
        if (args.detail.kind === activation.ActivationKind.launch) {
            if (args.detail.previousExecutionState === Windows.
            ApplicationModel.Activation.ApplicationExecutionState.
            notRunning) {
                console.log("setting the initial values");
                document.getElementById("txt1").value = '';
                document.getElementById("txt2").value = '';
            }
            if (args.detail.previousExecutionState === Windows.
            ApplicationModel.Activation.ApplicationExecutionState.
            closedByUser) {
                console.log("setting the initial values");
                document.getElementById("txt1").value = '';
                document.getElementById("txt2").value = '';
            }
            if (args.detail.previousExecutionState === Windows.
            ApplicationModel.Activation.ApplicationExecutionState.
            terminated) {
                console.log("setting the previous state values");
                document.getElementById("txt1").value = WinJS.
                Application.sessionState.txt1;
                document.getElementById("txt2").value = WinJS.
                Application.sessionState.txt2;
            }

            args.setPromise(WinJS.UI.processAll());
        }
    };
    app.oncheckpoint = function (args) {
        WinJS.Application.sessionState.txt1 = document.
        getElementById("txt1").value;
        WinJS.Application.sessionState.txt2 = document.
        getElementById("txt2").value;
};
```

The code snippet handles the onactivated and the oncheckpoint events. The oncheckpoint event is triggered when the app is suspended. At this stage, the value entered by the user in the two text boxes are saved in the sessionState.

If the previous state of the application was terminated, when the app is reactivated, the value from the sessionState is restored and updated to the text boxes on the page. If the previous state is notRunning or closedByUser, then the default values are restored.

When you run the app that is already suspended and terminated, you see the application data restored in the page, as shown in Figure 7-5.

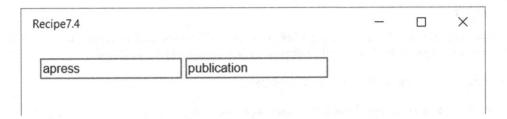

Figure 7-5. Page displaying the data restored from the sessionState

You can test the application state and simulate the suspended and terminated events from Visual Studio 2015. To do this, you need to use the **Lifecycle Events** drop-down list in the Debug Location toolbar, as shown in Figure 7-6.

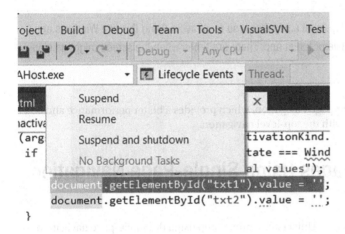

Figure 7-6. Tool to test the Application Lifecycle events from Visual Studio

The Suspend and Resume lifecycle events can be simulated by clicking the **Suspend** option to suspend the app when it is running, and then clicking the **Resume** option to resume the app. On clicking the Suspend option, the onCheckpoint event is raised. The suspension and termination events can be simulated by clicking the **Suspend and shutdown** button. At this time, the onCheckpoint event is raised and your app terminates. When you run the app again, the previousExecutionState contains the value terminated.

7.5 Navigate Between Pages Using Hyperlinks

Problem

You need to navigate between pages within your Universal Windows app in one of the simplest ways.

Solution

One of the simplest ways to navigate between pages within your app with HTML is to use hyperlinks.

How It Works

Assuming that you have `default.html` and `newpage.html` files in your app, if you want to navigate to `newpage.html` from the `default.html`, adding the following code in `default.html` will do this.

```
<p><a href="newpage.html">Navigate to page 2</a></p>
```

The `href` in the code is a relative link that refers to `newpage.html`. This is a HTML page that is part of your Universal Windows app and should be in the root of the project.

Alternatively, you can use the new package content URI scheme called ms-appx if you want to specify the URI of the local file that is part of your application.

The preceding code can be rewritten as follows:

```
<p><a href="ms-appx:///newpage.html">Navigate to New page</a></p>
```

■ **Note** Although this recipe performs the top-level navigation, you must avoid doing this in a Windows app. This is ideal for a web page but *not* for a mobile or tablet app. There are times when the screen might go blank when the app loads the next page.

Microsoft recommends using the single-page navigation, which provides a better performance and a more app-like experience when compared with the top-level navigation.

7.6 Navigate Between Pages Using Single-Page Navigation

Problem

You need to navigate between pages within your Universal Windows app using the single-page navigation model.

Solution

One of the simplest solutions to implement the single-page navigation in a Universal Windows app is to use the necessary files that perform the navigation logic from the Windows 8.1 Navigation App template in to the Windows 10 project.

■ **Note** At the time of writing, Windows 10 does not provide an equivalent navigation template like the one in Windows 8.1.

How It Works

Visual Studio 2015 does not provide a navigation template for the UWP apps. It only provides the Blank App template. Fortunately, VS 2015 also includes the templates for the Windows 8.1 app and one of the templates that does a lot of navigation logic. Let's include the necessary files from the Windows 8.1 project to the Universal Windows app.

Launch Visual Studio 2015 and create a new Windows 8.1 project using the Navigation App template, as shown in Figure 7-7.

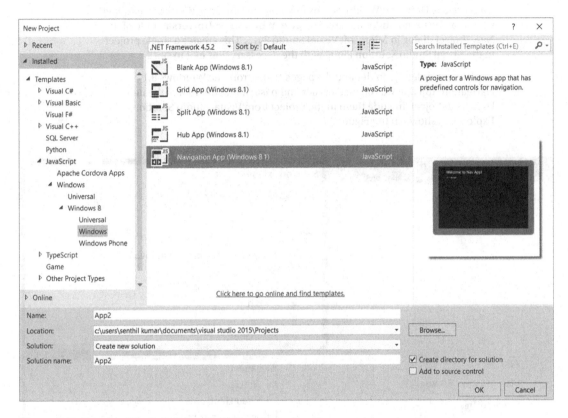

Figure 7-7. *Creating Windows 8.1 project using Navigation App*

This template adds the `navigator.js` file as well as updates the `default.js` with the navigation logic. These files can be found under the `js` folder of the project.

The template also creates a folder called `pages` and includes a `home` subfolder with three files: `home.css`, `home.html`, and `home.js`.

The `pages` folder contains all the page controls, which are like the pages in your Windows app. The `pagecontrol home.html` file is loaded by default when you start the Navigation App template. This is set in the `default.html` page.

All the details of loading the page controls are handled by the `PageControlNavigator`, which is part of the `navigator.js` file.

The next step is to create a new Universal Windows app and update it to include the files from the project created with the Windows 8.1 Navigation template.

1   Create a new Universal Windows Project using the Universal Windows template, which can be found under the **JavaScript ➤ Windows ➤ Universal** node of the New Project dialog in Microsoft Visual Studio 2015. This creates a single project in the Visual Studio Solution along with the necessary files in it to start.

2. Copy the complete js folder and the pages folder from the Windows 8.1 Navigation App that was created earlier and paste it into the root of the new Universal Project. Include them in the project from Visual Studio Solution Explorer, as shown in the Figure 7-8.

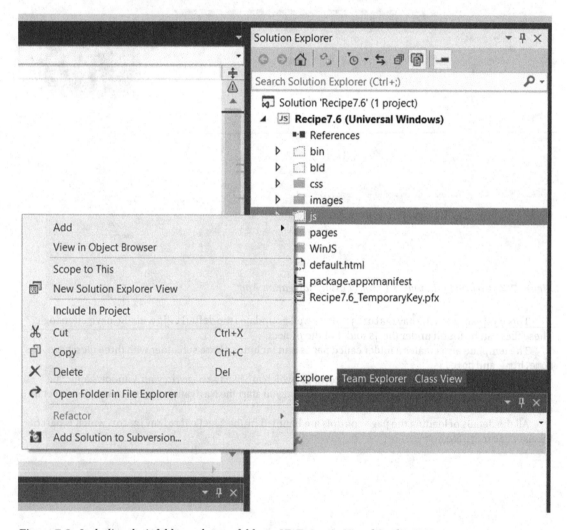

Figure 7-8. Including the js folder and pages folder to UWP App in Visual Studio 2015

Now, you are all set to modify the Universal Windows app to perform the navigation between pages.

Open the default.html page from Visual Studio Solution Explorer and replace the body section with the following code.

```
<div id="contenthost" data-win-control="Application.PageControlNavigator" data-win-
options="{home: '/pages/home/home.html'}"></div>
```

Also, include the reference to the navigator.js in the default.html page.

```
<script src="/js/navigator.js"></script>
```

The default.html page acts like a shell for loading different page controls from the pages folder. By default, it loads the home.html page from the pages/home folder.

The PageControlNavigator control has an id with a content host value that acts as host for the content loaded up from the page controls.

The next step is to add a new page control to the project so that the user can navigate from the home.html file to the new page control.

Microsoft Visual Studio provides the Page Control item template, which allows the developers to easily create page control.

Right-click the pages folder in Visual Studio Solution Explorer and select **Add ➤ New item** from the context menu. In the **Add New Item** dialog, select **Page Control** and provide the name **page2.html**. Click **Add** button.

This adds three files to the project:

- page1.html

- page1.css

- page1.js

The content of the page1.html is shown next.

```
<!DOCTYPE html>
<html>
<head>
    <meta charset="utf-8" />
    <title>page1</title>

    <link href="page1.css" rel="stylesheet" />
    <script src="page1.js"></script>
</head>
<body>
    <div class="page1 fragment">
        <header class="page-header" aria-label="Header content" role="banner">
            <button class="back-button" data-win-control="WinJS.UI.BackButton"></button>
            <h1 class="titlearea win-type-ellipsis">
                <span class="pagetitle">Welcome to page1</span>
            </h1>
        </header>
```

```
        <section class="page-section" aria-label="Main content" role="main">
            <p>The content of page 2</p>
        </section>
    </div>
</body>
</html>
```

The content of page1.js file looks like this:

```
// For an introduction to the Page Control template, see the following documentation:
// http://go.microsoft.com/fwlink/?LinkId=232511
(function () {
    "use strict";

    WinJS.UI.Pages.define("/pages/page1.html", {
        // This function is called whenever a user navigates to this page. It
        // populates the page elements with the app's data.
        ready: function (element, options) {
        },

        unload: function () {
        },

        updateLayout: function (element) {
        }
    });
})();
```

You will only modify the body tag of page1.html to show that the navigation to page 1 is successful.

Now, you have two HTML pages within the Universal app. The first page is home.html and the second page is page1.html. How to navigate between the two pages?

You can navigate between pages using the WinJS.Navigate.navigate() method.

Let's modify the home.html to include a hyperlink to navigate to page 1 by adding the following code snippet.

```
<a id="lnkPage2"> Navigate to Page 2</a>
```

Note that the hyperlink has the id attribute but not the href attribute.

Open the home.js file and replace it with the following code snippet.

```
(function () {
    "use strict";

    WinJS.UI.Pages.define("/pages/home/home.html", {
        // This function is called whenever a user navigates to this page. It
        // populates the page elements with the app's data.
        ready: function (element, options) {
            var page2link = document.getElementById('lnkPage2');
```

```
        page2link.addEventListener('click', function(eventargs) {
            eventargs.preventDefault();
            WinJS.Navigation.navigate("/pages/page1.html");
        });
    }
  });
})();
```

The code sets up the click event handler for the hyperlink in the ready event of the page. The click event handler first invokes the preventDefault function to prevent the normal link navigation, and then invokes the WinJS.Navigation.navigate method to navigate to page1.html.

When you run the app on Windows desktop using the Local Machine option, you see the homepage displayed with a hyperlink, as shown in the Figure 7-9.

Figure 7-9. *home.html page with a hyperlink to navigate to page 2*

When you click the **Navigate to Page 2** link, the user is taken to page 2, as shown in Figure 7-10. When you look at page2.html, notice the Back button, which takes you back to the previous page.

Figure 7-10. *Page1.html with the Back button*

Table 7-4 shows some of the methods that are available in the WinJS.Navigation class.

Table 7-4. *WinJS.Navigation Class*

Method Name	Description
WinJS.Navigation.back()	This method navigates the user back to the previous page in the history.
WinJS.Navigation.forward()	This method enables the developers to navigate forward in the history.
WinJS.Navigation.navigate()	This method enables the developers to navigate to the specified page.

■ ■ ■

CHAPTER 8

Globalization and Localization

There are opportunities to market your Windows app in nearly 240 Windows marketplaces. The target audiences vary in culture, region, and language. Your app's users may be located anywhere in the world. They may speak different languages—or even multiple languages. As an application developer, it is necessary for you to adapt your application for several languages, markets, cultures, and regions. *Globalization* means making your application culture, language, and region aware. *Localization* is the ability to localize certain aspects of your app to the culture in which it is running; for example, date, number, or currency formats, and so forth. In this chapter, you will see recipes on how to globalize and localize your apps.

8.1 Using Resource Strings

Problem

When your app is used in a non-English culture, the text does not adapt to the new culture and language; instead, the user sees English text.

Solution

In order to globalize applications, it is necessary to use a resource string in place of static text. For example, any label text in the application should not be hard-coded as a static text. Instead, a resource file should be created for the culture/language you need to support. Add strings that will translate text into the corresponding language. Also use resource strings for label text, rather than hard-coding it.

How It Works

Let's look at the usage of resource strings in applications, as well as how to add them.

1. Open Visual Studio 2015. Select File ➤ New Project ➤ JavaScript ➤ Windows ➤ Universal and select Blank App (Universal Windows) template. This will create a universal app with the necessary files that can run on machines powered by Windows 10.

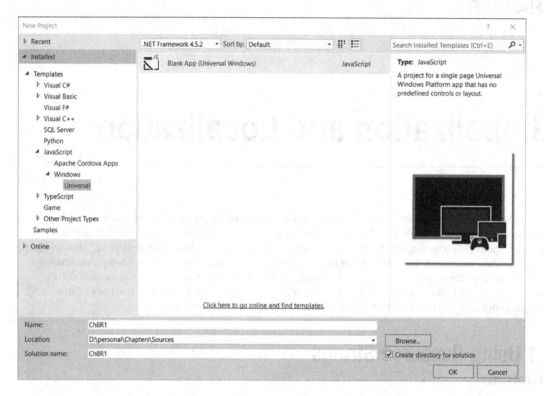

Figure 8-1. Choosing the Blank App (Universal Windows) template in the New Project window

2. Open the package.appxmanifest file from the project in Visual Studio solution explorer. Go to the Application tab and check that the default language is set to en-US. When a new project is created, the language is set to en-US by default (see Figure 8-2).

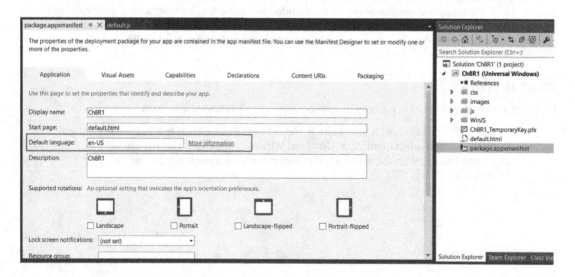

Figure 8-2. Default language settings in the application manifest

3. Create a resource folder, as follows:

    a. In the Solution Explorer, select the Universal Windows project and right-click on it. Select Add ➤ New Folder from the context menu.

    b. Name the new folder **strings**. You will create different culture/language resource files inside this folder (see Figure 8-3).

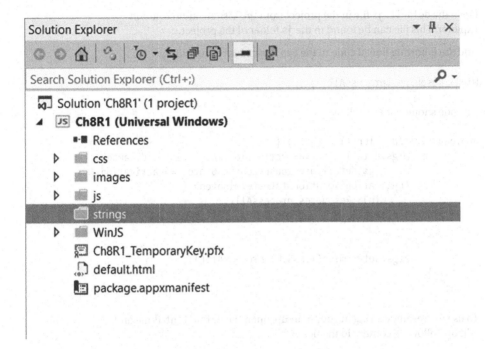

Figure 8-3. *Strings folder in the Windows project*

4. Create a subfolder and an English resource file, as follows:

    a. Create a folder named **en-US** in the `strings` folder (created in step 3).

    b. Right-click the en-US folder and select Add ➤ New Item.

    c. Select Text File from the template and give the name `resources.resjson` for the file. It is recommended to use this default name when naming the resource file.

    d. Replace the content of the file with the following content:

```
{
"greeting"          : "Hello World!",
"_greeting.comment" : "Hello World Text comment",

"farewell"          : "Goodbye",
"_farewell.comment" : "A farewell comment."
}
```

The resource file is nothing but a JSON file with key value pairs. Here, "greeting" and "farewell" identify the strings that will be displayed. The other keys— "_greeting.comment" and "_farewell.comment" are comments that describe the strings itself. It's a good practice to have meaningful comments for all of your strings.

5. Use string resource identifiers to do the following:

   a. Open the default.js file in the project from the Visual Studio solution explorer. This file can be found in the js folder of the project.

   b. Add the following line of code to the app.onactivated function:

      WinJS.Resources.processAll();

   The completed code should look as follows:

```
app.onactivated = function (args) {
        if (args.detail.kind === activation.ActivationKind.launch) {
            if (args.detail.previousExecutionState !== activation.
            ApplicationExecutionState.terminated) {
                WinJS.Resources.processAll();
            } else {

            }
            args.setPromise(WinJS.UI.processAll());
        }
};
```

   c. To use the resource string in your markup, open the default.html file and add the following content in the body:

```
<h2>
<span data-win-res="{textContent: 'greeting'}"></span></h2>
<h2>
<span data-win-res="{textContent: 'farewell'}"></span>
</h2>
```

6. Add additional language resource files:

   a. In the strings folder of the project, add a folder named **de-DE**. This is for German culture.

   b. Add a resource file in the de-DE folder. Name the resource file **resources. resjson**. Replace the content of the file with the following code:

```
{
        "greeting"          : "Hallo Welt!",
        "_greeting.comment" : " Hello World Text comment.",

        "farewell"          : "Auf Wiedersehen",
        "_farewell.comment" : "A farewell comment."
}
```

c. Add another folder in the `strings` folder of the project and name it **fr-FR**. This is for French culture.

d. Add a resource file in the `fr-FR` folder. This resource file name should also be `resources.resjson`. Replace the content of the file with the following code:

```
{
        "greeting"          : "Salut tout le monde",
        "_greeting.comment" : "Hello World Text comment.",

        "farewell"          : "Au revoir",
        "_farewell.comment" : "A farewell comment."
}
```

7. Run the app, as follows:

a. Build and run the app by pressing F5.

b. Greeting and farewell messages are displayed in a user's preferred language, set on the device. Figure 8-4 shows the output on a Windows screen run using the Local Machine option.

Hello World!

Goodbye

Figure 8-4. *English culture resource strings display*

c. Change the language setting on the device and run the app again. Figure 8-5 shows the same text displayed with the language set to French on the device.

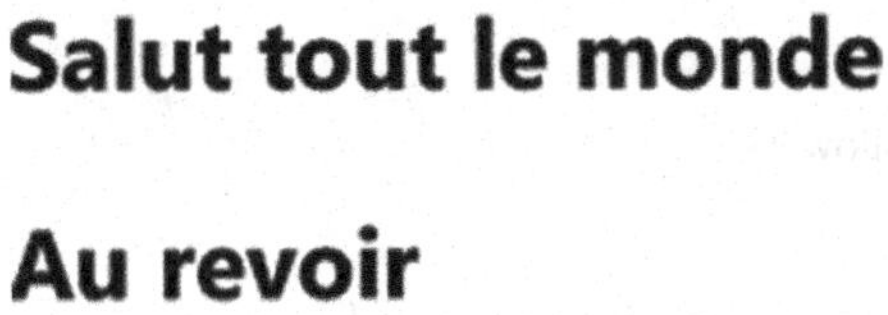

Salut tout le monde

Au revoir

Figure 8-5. *French culture resource strings display.*

Note that you have to restart the device when changing the language settings on Windows Mobile.

8.2 Formatting Date, Time, Number, and Currency

Problem

Date, Time, Number, and Currency show English-culture settings when the language is changed to a non-English culture/language.

Solution

Static text content in the application can be localized by making use of resource strings. But if your application has to show date, time, numbers, or currencies, you cannot make use of the resource strings. Instead you will need to use the `WinJS.Globalization` namespace, which provides the capabilities of DateTime, Number, and Currency formatting helper methods.

How It Works

Format Date and Time

The following steps explain how to format the date and the time.

1. Use `DateTimeFormatter` in the `Windows.Globalization.DateTimeFormatting` namespace. Create a `DateTimeFormatter` instance with a template format. For a list of template formats, you can check the MSDN documentation at http://msdn.microsoft.com/en-us/library/windows/apps/windows. globalization.datetimeformatting.datetimeformatter.aspx.

2. Add the following markup to `default.html` file inside the body element:

```
<h1>Formatting Demo</h1>
<br />
<h3>Long Date:</h3>
<h3 id="spnDate"></h3>
<br />
<h3>Long Time:</h3>
<h3 id="spnTime"></h3>
```

3. Modify the onactivated method in `default.js` as follows:

```
app.onactivated = function (args) {
        if (args.detail.kind === activation.ActivationKind.launch) {
            if (args.detail.previousExecutionState !== activation.
            ApplicationExecutionState.terminated) {

                var lang = Windows.System.UserProfile.GlobalizationPreferences.
                languages[0];

                var shortDateFmt = new Windows.Globalization.DateTimeFormatting.
                DateTimeFormatter("longdate", [lang]);
                var shortTimeFmt = new Windows.Globalization.DateTimeFormatting.
                DateTimeFormatter("longtime",[lang]);
```

```
            var currentDateTime = new Date();
            var shortDate = shortDateFmt.format(currentDateTime);
            var shortTime = shortTimeFmt.format(currentDateTime);

            document.getElementById("spnDate").innerHTML = shortDate;
            document.getElementById("spnTime").innerHTML = shortTime;
        } else {
            // TODO: This application has been reactivated from suspension.
            // Restore application state here.
        }
        args.setPromise(WinJS.UI.processAll());
    }
};
```

4.   Run the app and verify the output (see Figure 8-6 and Figure 8-7).

Formatting Demo

Long Date:

26 November 2015

Long Time:

19:39:30

Figure 8-6. *Formatted output for English culture*

Formatting Demo

Long Date:

jeudi 26 novembre 2015

Long Time:

19:33:07

Figure 8-7. *Formatted output for French culture*

Figure 8-6 shows the date formatted for English culture and Figure 8-7 shows the date formatted for French culture.

Format Numbers and Currencies

The following steps explain how to format numbers and currencies:

1. NumberFormatting should be used to display decimal and percentage numbers and currencies.

2. Add the following markup in default.html and append to the body:

   ```
   <h3>Number Format:</h3>
   <h3 id="spnCurrency"></h3>
   ```

3. Modify the onactivated method in default.js and append the following code:

   ```
   var userCurrency = Windows.System.UserProfile
                        .GlobalizationPreferences.currencies;
   var number = 23456.78
   var currFmt = new Windows.Globalization.NumberFormatting
   ```

```
            .CurrencyFormatter(userCurrency[0],[lang]);
var formattedCurrency = currFmt.format(number);
document.getElementById("spnCurrency").innerHTML =
    formattedCurrency;
```

4. Run the app by pressing F5. Change the language settings on your phone or tablet to see the number and currency formatting in action (see Figure 8-8 and Figure 8-9).

Formatting Demo

Long Date:

26 November 2015

Long Time:

19:42:18

Number Format:

$ 23456.78

Figure 8-8. *Date and currency formatted output in English culture*

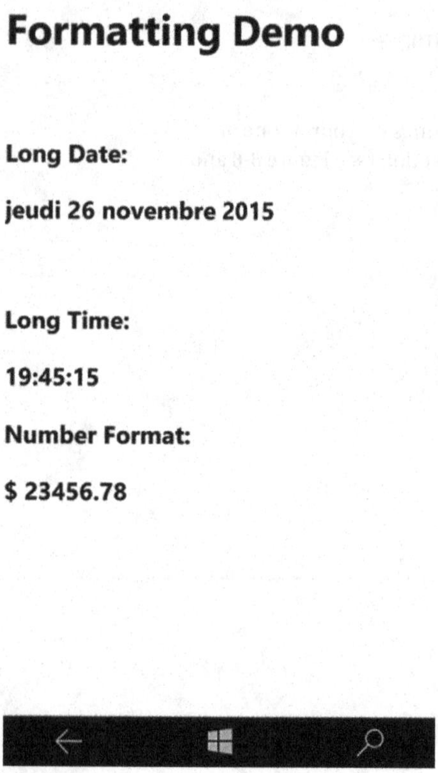

Formatting Demo

Long Date:

jeudi 26 novembre 2015

Long Time:

19:45:15

Number Format:

$ 23456.78

Figure 8-9. *Date and currency formatted output in French culture*

8.3 Localizing WinJS Controls

Problem

WinJS controls do not show a localized string when a culture or language is changed.

Solution

Usually, a controls property like label or title is set in the markup. It is somewhat like hard-coding the string value. Hence, when a culture or language is changed, the controls do not adapt, and show the hard coded strings as is. By using resource files, it is possible to bind WinJS control properties to localized strings. WinJS provides flexibility to directly bind a controls property to a resource key from the resource file.

How It Works

The following steps explain how to localize WinJS controls:

1. Open Visual Studio 2015. Select File ➤ New Project ➤ JavaScript ➤ Windows ➤ Blank App (Universal Windows). This will create a universal app which is a single project that can run on devices powered by Windows 10.

2. Add resource files to the project (see Recipe 8.1 on how to add resource files).

3. Add the following string keys:

```
{
"ShowMoreTilesTitle"            : "Show more Tiles",
"_ShowMoreTilesTitle.comment"   : "show more tiles toggle title",

"VibrateOnCallTitle"            : "Vibrate on Call",
"_VibrateOnCallTitle.comment"   : "vibrate on call toggle title",

"ShowArtistTitle"               : "Show artist when playing music",
"_ShowArtistTitle.comment"      : "Show artist when playing music
                          toggle title",

"ToggleOn"          : "Yes",
"_ToggleOn.comment" : "show more tiles toggle on label",

"ToggleOff"          : "No",
"_ToggleOff.comment" : "show more tiles toggle off label"
}
```

Similarly, I have also added strings for other languages.

4. Add the following code to the `default.js` onactivated method:

```
WinJS.UI.processAll().then(function(){
    WinJS.Resources.processAll();
});
```

You need to call `processAll()` on the `WinJS.Resource` class because you will be referring to the resource strings in the markup.

5. Add the following markup to `default.html` inside the body element:

```
<div>
<h1>Controls Localization</h1>
<br />
<div class="toggle" data-win-control="WinJS.UI.ToggleSwitch"
    data-win-res="{winControl: {labelOn:'ToggleOn',
                                labelOff:'ToggleOff',
                                title:'ShowMoreTilesTitle'}}"
    data-win-options="">
</div>
<br />
```

```
<div class="toggle" data-win-control="WinJS.UI.ToggleSwitch"
    data-win-res="{winControl: {labelOn:'ToggleOn',
                                labelOff:'ToggleOff',
                                title:'VibrateOnCallTitle'}}"
    data-win-options="">
</div>
<br />
<div class="toggle" data-win-control="WinJS.UI.ToggleSwitch"
    data-win-res="{winControl: {labelOn:'ToggleOn',
                                labelOff:'ToggleOff',
                                title:'ShowArtistTitle'}}"
    data-win-options="">
</div>
</div>
```

Notice that you use data-win-res and refer the resource strings by their key names, and assign it to a property of the control. Usually, it is of the following pattern:

```
data-win-res="{winControl: {propertyName1:'resourceID1',
                            propertyName2:'resourceID2'}}"
```

6. Press F5 and run the app. Initially, you will see an English string used by the control. Change the Language in the device and then run the app again. Now it will pick up the appropriate resource file and use the appropriate resource strings (see Figure 8-9 and Figure 8-10).

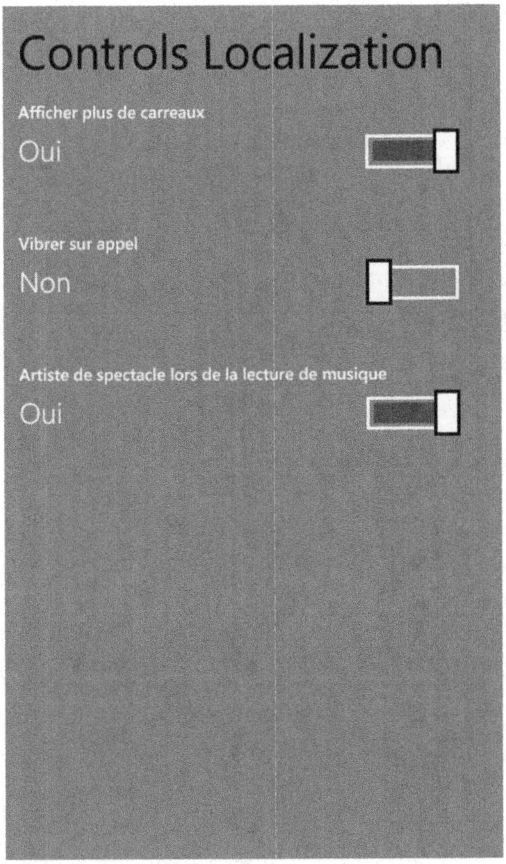

Figure 8-10. *Formatted output in French culture*

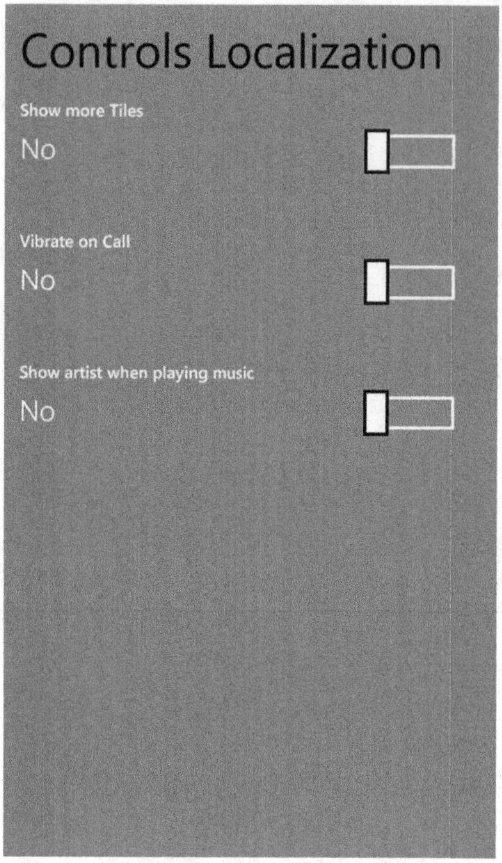

Figure 8-11. *Formatted output in English culture*

■ ■ ■

CHAPTER 9

Data Storage and App Data

This chapter provides an overview of the data storage techniques to store app data in a Windows 10 app. You will learn about app settings, how to store and retrieve app settings as app data, and working with app data folders.

So what is app data? Well, the data that is specific to a particular app is known as *app data*. Generally, app data is the user's preferences, the app's configuration, the app's state, and so forth, which are alterable.

When you install an app on a device, the app creates app data on it. But what happens when you remove or uninstall the app from the device? Well, when an app is uninstalled, the app data is removed from the device. So it is recommended not to store the user's data (such as the user's pictures) as app data.

The other type of data that your app creates is user data. User data is created by the user, such as documents, pictures, video files, audio files, and so forth.

9.1 How to Create and Delete a Local App Data Settings Container

Problem

You need to create and delete a local app data store container in the app data store of your Windows 10 app.

Solution

Use the `Windows.Storage.ApplicationData.current.LocalSettings.createContainer` to create the local app settings container in the local app data store.

How It Works

The container allows you to organize your app data settings; for example, you can create a container called `Greeting_Data_Container` to store all the greetings for your app. Create another container, called `UserPreference_Container`, to store all the user preferences settings for your app users. You can add a container to the local settings and the roaming settings. A container can also have another container in it. Universal Windows apps allow you to create up to 32 nested levels of containers.

1. Create a new project using the **Windows Universal (Blank App)** template in Microsoft Visual Studio 2015. This creates a Windows Universal app, which can be run on PCs, tablets, and Windows Phones running Windows 10.

2. Open the **default.html** page from the project in Visual Studio Solution Explorer.

3. Define an HTML tag for a button within the `<body>` tag of default.html.

```
<div id="titleBarContent" style="width: 100%;height:30px; background:border-box
darkblue; overflow: hidden; z-index: 3">
        <i>App Settings Admin Screen</i>
    </div>
<span> Click on the button to Create a local app data settings container</span>
        <input type="button" value="Local Data Demo" id="btnLocalData" />
        <h3><span id="msgspan"></span></h3>
```

The complete `default.html` code will look like this:

```
<!DOCTYPE html>
<html>
<head>
    <meta charset="utf-8" />
    <title>Recipe9.1</title>

    <!-- WinJS references -->
    <link href="WinJS/css/ui-dark.css" rel="stylesheet" />
    <script src="WinJS/js/base.js"></script>
    <script src="WinJS/js/ui.js"></script>

    <!-- Recipe9.1 references -->
    <link href="/css/default.css" rel="stylesheet" />
    <script src="/js/default.js"></script>
</head>
<body class="win-type-body">
    <div id="titleBarContent" style="width: 100%;height:30px; background:border-
    box darkblue; overflow: hidden; z-index: 3">
        <i>App Settings Admin Screen</i>
    </div>
        <span> Click on the button to Create a local app data settings
        container</span>
        <input type="button" value="Local Data Demo" id="btnCreateContainer" />
        <h3><span id="msgspan"></span></h3>

</body>
</html>
```

4. Right-click the project's **js** folder in Solution Explorer and add a **js** file in the project's js folder by using the **Add ➤ New JavaScript file**. Provide a name for the file. In this example, let's name the file **DatastorageDemo.js**.

5. Refer to this file in `default.html` by adding the following code to the `<head>` tag:

```
<script src="js/DatastorageDemo.js"></script>
```

6. Add the following code to the newly created js file:

```
(function () {
    "use strict";
    function GetControl() {
        WinJS.UI.processAll().done(function () {
    var localSettingsButton = document.getElementById("btnCreateContainer");
    localSettingsButton.addEventListener("click", btnCreateContainerClick, false);
        });
    }

    document.addEventListener("DOMContentLoaded", GetControl);


})();
```

This code gets the button element and binds an event listener to the button, which is fired when user clicks the button. Now, add an event method or function using the following code snippet in the DatastorageDemo.js file.

```
function btnCreateContainerClick(mouseEvent) {

    var applicationData = Windows.Storage.ApplicationData.current;
    var localSettings = applicationData.localSettings;

    // Creating a local settings container

    var localSettingscontainer = localSettings.createContainer("App_GreetingDataContainer",
Windows.Storage.ApplicationDataCreateDisposition.Always);

document.getElementById("msgspan").innerText = "Container Created, the name of the container
is :" + localSettingscontainer.name;

    }
```

This code declares a variable named applicationData. It is assigned Windows.Storage.ApplicationData.current, which allows you to access the app data store. The app data store can store app settings and files. The next line then retrieves the localSettings from the ApplicationData to a variable localSettings.

It then calls the createContainer method to create a settings container. The preceding example creates a settings container, App_greetingData. The createContainer method takes two parameters: the name of the settings container and Windows.Storage.ApplicationDataCreateDisposition.Always, which indicates to always check if the container exists or not. If it exists, return the specified container; else, create a new one.

You can also delete a container using the localSettingscontainer.deleteContainer("<<name>>") method. The deleteContainer method deletes the container from the app data store.

The delete code snippet checks whether a container exists by using the hasKey function, and then it uses the deleteContainer function to delete the container by passing the container key.

The complete code for DataStorageDemo.js is given here:

```
(function () {
    "use strict";
    function GetControl() {
        WinJS.UI.processAll().done(function () {
            var localSettingsButton = document.getElementById("btnCreateContainer");
            localSettingsButton.addEventListener("click", btnCreateContainerClick, false);
        });
    }

    document.addEventListener("DOMContentLoaded", GetControl);

})();

function btnCreateContainerClick(mouseEvent) {

    var applicationData = Windows.Storage.ApplicationData.current;
    var localSettings = applicationData.localSettings;

    // Creating a local settings container

    var localSettingscontainer = localSettings.createContainer("App_GreetingDataContainer",
Windows.Storage.ApplicationDataCreateDisposition.Always);

    document.getElementById("msgspan").innerText = "Container Created, the name of the
container is :" + localSettingscontainer.name;

}
```

Now, let's build the app and run it in Windows 10.

Figure 9-1 demonstrates the appearance of a button and an h2 tag. When you click the local data demo button, it executes the btnSaveClick method, which creates the container and displays a message with the name of the container.

Figure 9-1. Creating a local app data settings container

9.2 How to Create and Read Local App Data Settings

Problem

You need to create local app data settings in the app data settings container in the app data store.

Solution

Use `ApplicationDataContainer.values` to create local app data settings in the app data settings container in the local app data store in your Windows 10 app.

How It Works

App settings are the personalized data or customization settings in your app. User preferences—such as whether the user wants to enable or disable location services—is an app setting. Universal Windows app development exposes APIs, which allows you to store and retrieve app settings as app data in the app data store.

The app store consists of two different settings locations: local settings and roaming settings.

1. Create a new project using the Windows Universal (Blank App) template in Microsoft Visual Studio 2015.

2. Open the **default.html** page from the project in Visual Studio Solution Explorer.

3. Define HTML tags for two text boxes, a button, and a `<span>` tag within the `<body>` tag of `default.html`.

```
<div id="titleBarContent" style="width: 100%;height:30px; background:border-box
darkblue; overflow: hidden; z-index: 3">
  <i>App Settings Admin Screen (Use this Screen to configure app Settings)</i>
</div>
    <br />
    <i>Welcome Greeting in English</i> <input type="text" value=""
id="txtWelcomeGreetingseng" /><br />
    <i>Welcome Greeting in French</i><input type="text" value=""
id="txtWelcomeGreetingsfr" /><br />
    <input type="button" value="Create Local App Data Demo" id="btnLocalData" />
```

The complete `default.html` contains should look like this:

```
<!DOCTYPE html>
<html>
<head>
    <meta charset="utf-8" />
    <title>Recipe9.2</title>

    <!-- WinJS references -->
    <link href="WinJS/css/ui-dark.css" rel="stylesheet" />
    <script src="WinJS/js/base.js"></script>
    <script src="WinJS/js/ui.js"></script>
```

```
    <!-- Recipe9.2 references -->
    <link href="/css/default.css" rel="stylesheet" />
    <script src="/js/default.js"></script>
</head>
<body class="win-type-body">
    <div id="titleBarContent" style="width: 100%;height:30px; background:border-
    box darkblue; overflow: hidden; z-index: 3">
        <i>App Settings Admin Screen (Use this Screen to configure app
        Settings)</i>
    </div>
    <br />
    <i>Welcome Greeting in English</i> <input type="text" value=""
    id="txtWelcomeGreetingseng" /><br />
    <i>Welcome Greeting in French</i><input type="text" value=""
    id="txtWelcomeGreetingsfr" /><br />
    <input type="button" value="Create Local App Data Demo" id="btnLocalData" />
</body>
</html>
```

4.   Right-click the project's **js** folder in Solution Explorer and select **Add ➤ New
     JavaScript file**. Provide a name for the file. In this example, let's name the file
     DataStorageDemo.js.

```
(function () {
    "use strict";
    function GetControl() {
        WinJS.UI.processAll().done(function () {
            var submitbutton = document.getElementById("btnLocalData");
            submitbutton.addEventListener("click", btnLocalDataClick, false);
        });

    GetCurrentSettingValues();

    }

    document.addEventListener("DOMContentLoaded", GetControl);

})();
```

5.   Now, add a function to retrieve the current greeting settings from the container:

```
function GetCurrentSettingValues() {
    var applicationData = Windows.Storage.ApplicationData.current;
    var localSettings = applicationData.localSettings;

    // Creating a local settings container
    var containerExists = localSettings.containers.hasKey("App_
    GreetingDatalocalContainer");
    if (containerExists) {
```

```
        document.getElementById("txtWelcomeGreetingseng").value = localSettings.
        containers.lookup("App_GreetingDatalocalContainer").values["App_Heading_
        English"];
        document.getElementById("txtWelcomeGreetingsfr").value = localSettings.
        containers.lookup("App_GreetingDatalocalContainer").values["App_Heading_
        French"];


    }
  }
```

This code is executed on load of the app; it retrieves the local greetings settings from the container. When you run this app for the first time, you will not see any values populated, but when you run it the next time, it will show settings stored in the container.

Now, add an event method or a function using the following code snippet in the DataStorageDemo.js file:

```
function btnLocalDataClick(mouseEvent) {

  var applicationData = Windows.Storage.ApplicationData.current;
  var localSettings = applicationData.localSettings;

  // Creating a local settings container

  var localSettingscontainer = localSettings.createContainer("App_
  GreetingDatalocalContainer", Windows.Storage.ApplicationDataCreateDisposition.Always);

  if (!localSettingscontainer.values.hasKey("App_Heading_English")) {
      localSettingscontainer.values["App_Heading_English"] = document.getElementById("txtWel
      comeGreetingseng").value;
    }
  if (!localSettingscontainer.values.hasKey("App_Heading_French")) {
        localSettingscontainer.values["App_Heading_French"] = document.getElementById("txtW
        elcomeGreetingsfr").value;
      }
    } //end of function btnLocalDataClick
```

This code creates applicationData and localSettings variables to reference the localSettings. After that, it creates a container named App_GreetingDatalocalContainer using the createContainer function. It then uses the localSettingscontainer.values.hasKey("App_Heading_English") to ensure that the setting named App_Heading_English exists in the localSettings container of application data. If the setting doesn't exist, then it creates one by using the localSettingscontainer.["name"] function. It also assigns a string value from the text box to it by using the following line of code:

```
localSettingscontainer.values["App_Heading_English"] = document.getElementById
("txtWelcomeGreetingseng").value;
```

It does same thing for the app heading in French.

When you run the application on the Windows 10, you see the screen shown in Figure 9-2.

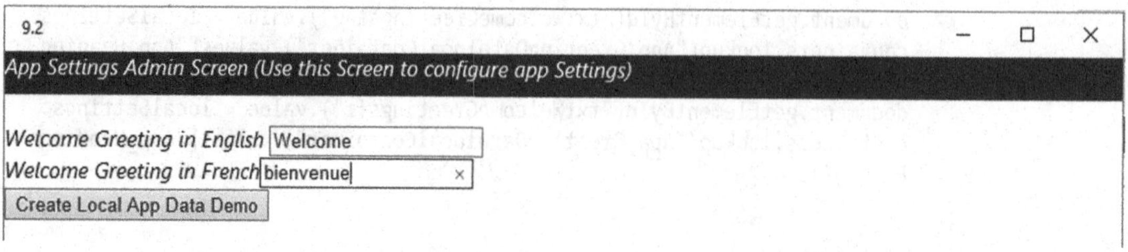

Figure 9-2. *Creating local app data settings for the greetings settings*

9.3 How to Create and Retrieve Local Composite Settings

Problem

You need to create and read local composite values in the app data store in your Windows 10 app.

Solution

Use the `ApplicationDataCompositeValue` class to create and read local composite values.

How It Works

The `Windows.Storage.ApplicationDataCompositeValue` class allows you to create composite settings that can be stored in local settings or roaming settings. The composite value class allows you to store name value pairs as app data in the app data store. Let's say you want to store book information as

```
book["ISBN"] = 12345;
book["BookTitle"] = "Windows 10 Development";
```

To store composite information, you can use the code shown here:

```
var applicationData = Windows.Storage.ApplicationData.current;

var localSettings = applicationData.localSettings;
// Create a BookInfo Composite setting

var bookInfo = new Windows.Storage.ApplicationDataCompositeValue();
bookInfo["ISBN"] = 12345;
bookInfo["Title"] = "Windows 10 Development";

localSettings.values["AppLocalSettings"] = bookInfo;
```

To read data from a composite setting, you can use the code shown here:

```
var bookInfo = localSettings.values["AppLocalSettings"];

if (bookInfo)
{
    var ISBN = bookInfo["ISBN"];
    var Title = bookInfo["Title"]
}
```

9.4 How to Create a Roaming App Data Store Container

Problem

You need to create a roaming app data store container in the app data store of your Windows 10 app.

Solution

Use roamingSettings.createContainer to create the roaming app settings container in the app data store.

How It Works

It's very similar to what you saw in the local settings in the app data store, but instead of using Windows. Storage.ApplicationData.current.LocalSettings, you use Windows.Storage.ApplicationData. current.roamingSettings.

1. Create a new project using the Windows Universal (Blank App) template in Microsoft Visual Studio 2015.

2. Open the **default.html** page from the project in Visual Studio Solution Explorer. Add the following HTML markup within the body tag of default.html:

```
<body class="win-type-body" style="background-color:goldenrod">
<div id="titleBarContent" style="width: 100%;height:30px; background:border-box
darkblue; overflow: hidden; z-index: 3">
        <i>User Preferences Settings Screen (These settings will be available
        across devices)</i>
    </div>
    <br />

    <input type="button" value="Save User Preference" id="btnUserPreferenceRoamin
    gData" />
    <br />
    <span id="spantoDisplayRoamingData" style="color:white"></span>
</body>
```

3. Right-click the project's **js** folder in the Solution Explorer and select **Add ➤ New JavaScript file**. Provide the name for the file. In this example, let's name the file **DatastorageDemo.js**.

```
(function () {
    "use strict";
    function GetControl() {
        WinJS.UI.processAll().done(function () {
            var submitbutton = document.getElementById("btnUserPreferenceRoamingD
            ata");
            submitbutton.addEventListener("click",
            btnCreateRoamingContainerClick, false);
        });
    }
```

```
        document.addEventListener("DOMContentLoaded", GetControl);

    })();
```

4. Now, add an event method or function using the following code snippet in the
    Datastoragedemo.js file:

```
function btnCreateRoamingContainerClick(mouseEvent) {

var ApplicationData = Windows.Storage.ApplicationData.current;
var roamingSettings = ApplicationData.roamingSettings;

// Creating a local settings container

if (!roamingSettings.containers.hasKey("UserPreference_RoamingProfile")) {
var roamingSettingscontainer = roamingSettings.createContainer("UserPreference_
RoamingProfile", Windows.Storage.ApplicationDataCreateDisposition.Always);
document.getElementById("spantoDisplayRoamingData").innerText
=roamingSettingscontainer.name +" User Preference Roaming App Data Container
Created!!";
    }
}
```

This code declares a variable named ApplicationData. It is assigned the Windows.Storage.
ApplicationData.current, which denotes a container for app settings in the app data store. The next
line then retrieves the roamingSettings from the ApplicationData and stores it in the roamingSettings
variable.

It then calls the roamingSettings.containers.hasKey function to check if the container exists.
If it doesn't exist, then it uses createContainer method to create a settings container. The preceding
example creates a settings container, App_GreetingDataRoamingContainer, and stores it in the
roamingSettingscontainer. The createContainer method takes two parameters: the name of the settings
container and Windows.Storage.ApplicationDataCreateDisposition.Always, which directs that it always
check if a container exists or not; if it exists, return the specified container; else, create a new one.

When you run the application on a Windows 10 emulator or Windows Mobile, it should look like what's
shown in Figure 9-3.

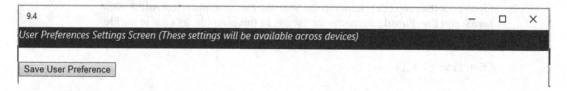

Figure 9-3. *The form to save user preference settings using roaming app data settings*

Great. In the preceding code snippet, you learned both the createContainer and deleteContainer
methods of the roamingSettings object.

9.5 How to Create and Read Roaming App Data Settings

Problem

You need to create and read roaming app data settings in the roaming app data settings container in the app data store in your Windows 10 app.

Solution

Use `ApplicationDataContainer.values` to create roaming app data settings in the app data settings container in the app data store in your Windows 10 app.

How It Works

1. Create a new project using the **Windows Universal (Blank App)** template in Microsoft Visual Studio 2015.

2. Open the **default.html** page from the project in Visual Studio Solution Explorer.

3. Add a form control to the body section of the page. The form control has a few div controls to display the title bar, input control for email, and a toggle switch control for mobile data and location services.

```
<body class="win-type-body">
    <div id="titleBarContent" style="width: 100%;height:30px; background:border-
    box darkblue; overflow: hidden; z-index: 3">
        <i>User Preferences Settings Screen (These settings will be available
        across devices)</i>
    </div>
    <br />
    <form id="form1">
        <fieldset class="formSection">
            <legend class="formSectionHeading">User Preferenses</legend>
            <div class="twoColumnFormContainer">
                <div id="UserMobileData" data-win-control="WinJS.UI.ToggleSwitch"
                data-win-options="{title :'Use Mobile Data',labelOff: 'Disabled',
                belOn:'Enabled',hecked: true}">
                </div>
                <br />
                <div id="LocationServices" data-win-control="WinJS.
                UI.ToggleSwitch" data-win-options="{title :'Location
                Services',labelOff: 'Disabled',belOn:'Enabled',hecked: true}">
                </div>
                <br />
                <div id="msg" style="color:red"></div>
                <br />
                <div class="buttons">

                        <button type="submit" id="btnSubmit"
                        class="horizontalButtonLayout win-button">
                            Submit
                        </button>
```

```
                </div>
            </div>
        </fieldset>
    </form>

        <br />
    </body>
```

4. Right-click the project in Solution Explorer and select **Add ➤ New JavaScript file** and provide the name for the file. In this example, let's name the file **DataStorageDemo.js**.

5. Add the following code to the DataStorageDemo.js file:

```
(function () {
    "use strict";
    function GetControl() {
        WinJS.UI.processAll().done(function () {
            var submitbutton = document.getElementById("btnSubmit");
            submitbutton.addEventListener("click",
            btnCreateRoamingContainerClick, false);
        });
    }

    document.addEventListener("DOMContentLoaded", GetControl);

})();
```

The preceding code added an event receiver to the btnSubmit button. Now add a btnCreateRoamingContainerClick function, which is triggered when the user clicks the Submit button on the user's preference form control.

```
function btnCreateRoamingContainerClick(mouseEvent) {
        var ApplicationData = Windows.Storage.ApplicationData.current;
        var roamingSettings = ApplicationData.roamingSettings;
        // Creating a local settings container
if (roamingSettings.containers.hasKey("UserPreference_RoamingProfile")) {
 var roamingSettingscontainer = roamingSettings.createContainer("UserPreference_
 RoamingProfile", Windows.Storage.ApplicationDataCreateDisposition.Always);

var toggleMobileDataButton = document.getElementById("UserMobileData").winControl;
  if (toggleMobileDataButton.checked) {
    roamingSettingscontainer.values["UseMobileData"] = "Yes";
    }
  else {
    roamingSettingscontainer.values["UseMobileData"] = "No";
  }

 var toggleLocationDataButton = document.getElementById("LocationServices").winControl;
    if (toggleLocationDataButton.checked) {
        roamingSettingscontainer.values["LocationServices"] = "Yes";
      }
```

```
        else {
                roamingSettingscontainer.values["LocationServices"] = "No";
        }
        document.getElementById("msg").innerText = "Data Saved!!";
    }
}//end of function btnCreateRoamingContainerClick
```

This code declares a variable named `ApplicationData`. It is assigned `Windows.Storage.ApplicationData.current`, which denotes a container for app settings in the app data store. The next line retrieves the `roamingSettings` from `ApplicationData` and stores it in the `roamingSettings` variable.

It then calls the `roamingSettings.containers.hasKey` function to check if the container exists. If it does not exist, it uses the `createContainer` method to create a settings container. The preceding example creates a settings container, `App_GreetingDataRoamingContainer`, and stores it in the `roamingSettingscontainer`. The `createContainer` method takes two parameters: the name of the settings container and the `Windows.Storage.ApplicationDataCreateDisposition.Always`, which directs that it always check if a container exists or not. If it exists, return the specified container; else, create a new one.

The next line of code checks the value of the toggle switch control, based on whether it is selected or not. If toggle switch is selected "yes", it stores the roaming data app settings using the `roamingSettingscontainer.values["UseMobileData"]` function, which uses the `container.value` method to set the value. It also does the same thing for the location service toggle switch.

The complete code in the `DataStorageDemo.js` file looks like this:

```
(function () {
    "use strict";
    function GetControl() {
        WinJS.UI.processAll().done(function () {
            var submitbutton = document.getElementById("btnSubmit");
            submitbutton.addEventListener("click", btnCreateRoamingContainerClick, false);
        });
    }

    document.addEventListener("DOMContentLoaded", GetControl);

    function btnCreateRoamingContainerClick(mouseEvent) {
        var ApplicationData = Windows.Storage.ApplicationData.current;
        var roamingSettings = ApplicationData.roamingSettings;
        // Creating a local settings container
        if (roamingSettings.containers.hasKey("UserPreference_RoamingProfile")) {
            var roamingSettingscontainer = roamingSettings.createContainer("UserPreference_
            RoamingProfile", Windows.Storage.ApplicationDataCreateDisposition.Always);

            var toggleMobileDataButton = document.getElementById("UserMobileData").
            winControl;
            if (toggleMobileDataButton.checked) {
                roamingSettingscontainer.values["UseMobileData"] = "Yes";
            }
            else {
                roamingSettingscontainer.values["UseMobileData"] = "No";
            }
```

```
        var toggleLocationDataButton = document.getElementById("LocationServices").
        winControl;
        if (toggleLocationDataButton.checked) {
            roamingSettingscontainer.values["LocationServices"] = "Yes";
        }
        else {
            roamingSettingscontainer.values["LocationServices"] = "No";
        }
        document.getElementById("msg").innerText = "Data Saved!!";
    }
}//end of function btnCreateRoamingContainerClick

})();
```

That's it. The roaming data will be available on all the devices on which this Win 10 app will be accessed by the user.

When you run the application on a Windows 10 emulator or Windows Mobile, it will look like what's shown in Figure 9-4.

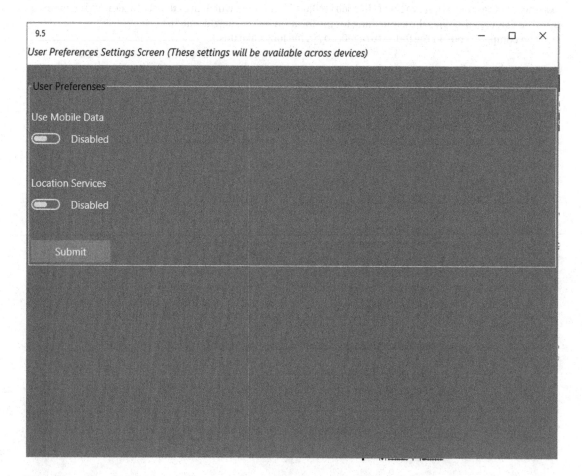

Figure 9-4. *Form to save user preference settings using roaming app data settings*

9.6 How to Register the Data Change Event

Problem

You need to register and implement a data change event handler.

Solution

You can use the `ApplicationData.DataChanged` event to register the data change event for roaming data.

How It Works

When roaming data are changed on one of device, the Universal Windows app replicates the roaming data to cloud and then it synchronizes the roaming data to other devices where app is installed by users. Let's say after the synchronization you want to ensure that app data is updated which is based on roaming data. For example, you storing user preferences in roaming data and when user preferences are changed, you want to change the settings on user's devices as per the new preference. Well, Universal Windows app allows you to register an event, which will be executed after the app data has just finished syncing from the cloud.

You can use `ApplicationData.DataChanged` event to register an event. So let's implement this.

1. Create a new project using the **Windows Universal (Blank App)** template in Microsoft Visual Studio 2015. This creates a Windows Universal app that can run on Windows tablets and Windows Phone running Windows 10.

2. Open the **default.html** page from the project in Visual Studio Solution Explorer.

3. Define an HTML `div` tag for the app title bar.

```
<body class="win-type-body">
    <div id="titleBarContent" style="width: 100%;height:30px; background:border-
    box darkblue; overflow: hidden; z-index: 3">
        <i>Custom title bar</i>
    </div>
</body>
```

The complete `default.html` code will look like this:

```
<!DOCTYPE html>
<html>
<head>
    <meta charset="utf-8" />
    <title>_9.7</title>

    <!-- WinJS references -->
    <link href="WinJS/css/ui-dark.css" rel="stylesheet" />
    <script src="WinJS/js/base.js"></script>
    <script src="WinJS/js/ui.js"></script>

    <!-- _9.7 references -->
    <link href="/css/default.css" rel="stylesheet" />
    <script src="/js/default.js"></script>
    <script src="/js/DatastorageDemo.js"></script>
</head>
```

173

```
<body class="win-type-body">
    <div id="titleBarContent" style="width: 100%;height:30px; background:border-
    box darkblue; overflow: hidden; z-index: 3">
        <i>Custom title bar</i>
    </div>

</body>

</html>
```

Right-click the project in the Solution Explorer and select **Add ➤ New JavaScript file**. Provide a name for the file. In this example, let's name the file **DatastorageDemo.js**.

Add the following code in the js file. The code first registers a data changed event with the applicationData object.

```
(function () {
    "use strict";
    function GetControl() {
        WinJS.UI.processAll().done(function () {

        });
    }
    document.addEventListener("DOMContentLoaded", GetControl);
    var applicationData = Windows.Storage.ApplicationData.current;
    applicationData.addEventListener("datachanged", datachangeHandler);

function datachangeHandler(eventArgs) {
        var applicationData = Windows.Storage.ApplicationData.current;
        var roamingSettings = applicationData.roamingSettings;
        // Creating a roaming settings container
        var roamingSettingscontainer = roamingSettings.containers ("App_
        GreetingDataContainer");

        //Read the Data again
        document.getElementById("titleBarContent").innerText = roamingSettingscontainer.
        values["App_Heading_English"];
    }
})();
```

This code also defines the data changed event handler in the same js file. The datachangeHandler event retrieves the roaming container from the applicationData object by using the loopup function. It then reads the roaming settings named App_Heading_English and assigns that to the div tab for the title bar.

9.7 How to Create, Write, and Read a Local File

Problem

You need to create a file, write to a file, and read from a file in the app data store in your Windows 10 app.

Solution

Use the `Windows.Storage.StorageFile` class for file handling.

How It Works

The `Windows.Storage.StorageFile` class provides necessary methods for file handling in a Universal Windows app. The file you create can be stored in folders, libraries (picture library) and Universal Windows apps support network locations, such as OneDrive and so forth.

Local Folder

As you know, a Universal Windows app can run on many devices: Windows Mobile, PCs running Windows 10, the Microsoft Surface tablet, and so forth. So when you deploy your app in the Windows Store, your app users can download and run you app on one or more devices. So how do you manage app settings specific to your app on a particular device? Well, you can use a local folder for that. The local folder can be used to store local app data on a particular device. The local folder data is available for the device on which it is stored. It can't be synchronized with other devices. A Universal Windows app stores app data in the app package's `LocalState`.

Roaming Folder

Now let's say you want to store user preferences for your app and you want to ensure that same user preference is available on all devices for a particular user. Well, you can achieve this by using the roaming folder for that. It stores the app data in the app package's `RoamingState`. The app data stored in a roaming folder is synchronized between devices when app users run apps on multiple devices.

Temporary Folder

The third type of location is the temporary folder, which allows you to store app data for a short duration. App data stored in a temporary folder is deleted once the data is not in use. So always use this folder to store data that is less important. A Universal Windows app stores app data in the app package's `TemporaryState`.

The `StorageFolder` class exposes many methods for creating files, reading content from a file, and writing content to a file. Let's look at each of the methods.

The `createFileAsync` method creates a new file on the specified location. If a file already exists, it will overwrite the file.

The syntax for using the function is given here:

```
storageFolder.createFileAsync(desiredName).done(function CreationSuccess(newFileObj))
{
 /* Success call back */

}, CreationFailed(error))
{
 Failed call back */
});
```

As you see, the createFileAsync method has to be defined using a success callback function and a failed callback function.

The complete code to create a file in the local folder is given here:

```
function btnDataToFileClick(mouseEvent) {

    var ApplicationData = Windows.Storage.ApplicationData.current;
    var localFolder = ApplicationData.localFolder;

    var newFilePromise = localFolder.createFileAsync("MyFile.txt");
    newFilePromise.done(
        function (file) {
            // WinJS.log("The file MyFile.txt was created.", "sample", "status");
            WinJS.log && WinJS.log("The file MyFile.txt was created.", "sample", "status");

        },
        function (error) {

        });

}
```

When you run this application on your Windows 10 local device, a file named MyFile.txt is created in the local folder, as shown in Figure 9-5.

Figure 9-5. *A file created in local folder*

The local folder location is C:\Users\<<UserName>>\AppData\Local\Packages\5342d954-ee4c-413c-8ed8-41b3befa6afc_khbmmdtkmdajr\LocalState. This file is empty, as we haven't written into this file yet.

Great. Now let's write code to write content to the file. For that, we first add a text area box in the default.html file. The default.html's body tag looks like this:

```
<body class="win-type-body" style="background-color:goldenrod">
    <div id="titleBarContent" style="width: 100%;height:30px; background:border-box
    darkblue; overflow: hidden; z-index: 3">
        <i>File Handling Demo</i>
    </div>
    <br />
        <input type="button" value="Save Data to File" id="btnCreateAFile" />
        <textarea rows="10" cols="100" id="textarea" class="win-textarea"></textarea>
        <input type="button" value="Save Data to File" id="btnDataToFile" />

</body>
```

This code adds a text area to the default.html file, along with buttons named btnDataToFile and btnCreateaFile.

Right-click the project's **js** file in Solution Explorer and select **Add ➤ New JavaScript file**. Provide a name for the file. In this example, let's name the file **DatastorageDemo.js**.

```
(function () {
    "use strict";
    function GetControl() {
        WinJS.UI.processAll().done(function () {
            var submitbutton = document.getElementById("btnCreateAFile");
            submitbutton.addEventListener("click", btnCreateAFileClick, false);

            var submitbutton = document.getElementById("btnDataToFile");
            submitbutton.addEventListener("click", btnDataToFileClick, false);
        });
    }

    document.addEventListener("DOMContentLoaded", GetControl);

})();
```

This code adds event receivers to both button controls. Now add an event code in the **DatastorageDemo.js** file.

```
function btnCreateAFileClick(mouseEvent) {

    var ApplicationData = Windows.Storage.ApplicationData.current;
    var LocalFolder = ApplicationData.localFolder;

    var newFilePromise = LocalFolder.createFileAsync("MyFile.txt");
    newFilePromise.done(
        function (file) {
            // WinJS.log("The file MyFile.txt was created.", "sample", "status");
            WinJS.log && WinJS.log("The file MyFile.txt was created.", "sample", "status");
```

```
    },
    function (error) {

    });
}
```

This code is to create a new file on the local folder. You will not add another event to the DataStorageDemo.js file for the btnDataToFile's click event.

```
function btnDataToFileClick(mouseEvent) {

    var ApplicationData = Windows.Storage.ApplicationData.current;
    var LocalFolder = ApplicationData.localFolder;

    // Open sample file.
    var FilePromise = LocalFolder.getFileAsync("MyFile.txt");
    FilePromise.then(function (file) {
        // If file found …
        if (file) {
            // Write to file.
            var txtarea = document.getElementById("textarea").innerText;
            Windows.Storage.FileIO.writeTextAsync(file, txtarea).then(function (contents) {
                WinJS.log && WinJS.log("The text was wrttien to file MyFile.txt.", "sample",
                "status");
            });
        }
    }, function (error) {
        // Handle error.
    });
}
```

This code gets the file by using the getFileAsync method of the local folder. If file exists, then it next uses the Windows.Storage.FileIO.writeTextAsync.writeTextAsync method to write content to the file.

When you run this app using a local device in Visual Studio, you see the default screen, as shown in Figure 9-6.

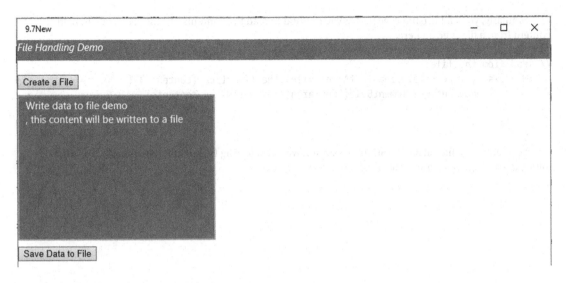

Figure 9-6. *File handling demo's default screen*

The **Create a File** button creates a file in the local folder of the device where you are running your app. Once the file is created, type some text to the text area. Clicking **Save Data to File** saves data to the file. When you open the file in the in Notepad, you see the content of the file, as shown in Figure 9-7.

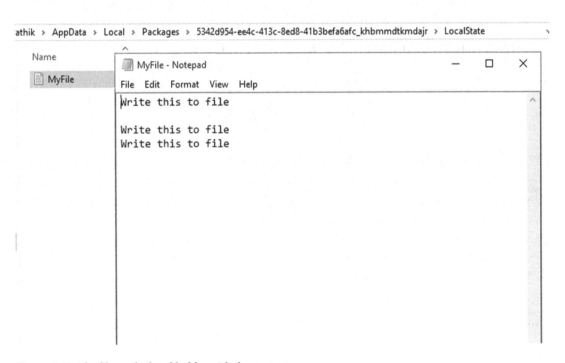

Figure 9-7. *The file on the local holder with the content*

Similarly, you can use the readTextAsync method to read the contents of a file. The code to read content from a file is given here:

```
// Read from the file.
    Windows.Storage.FileIO.readTextAsync(file).then(function (contents) {
            document.getElementById("textarea1").innerText = contents;

    });
```

You can create files at any location in a similar way by referring to the right location, such as a local folder, a roaming folder, and so forth.

CHAPTER 10

■ ■ ■

Sharing Data

This chapter covers how to share data between Universal Windows Platform apps. Sharing data enables developers to build features that allow users to share information, copy/paste, and drag and drop from one app to another app. For example, a user might want to copy some text or an image from one app and paste it into another app. Users also look for sharing information/links to social networking sites.

Windows 10 apps support sharing data in two different ways.

- A *source app* allows users to share data from the app to other apps.

- A *target app* allows users to declare an app as a target app, which can retrieve the shared data from other apps. An app that is declared a target app allows the user to select it as a destination app while sharing data.

By using the sharing data options, users can share plain text, web links, photos, and videos with other apps. In this chapter, you will learn to implement sharing data from a source app and declaring a target app.

Share Contract

In order to share data or receive data, every app needs to implement a share contract as either a source app or a target app. The data sharing involves the following three components:

- *Source app*: The source app implements a share contract as a source app to share data. This app registers the data transfer manager and fills the data package to be shared.

- *Share broker*: The share broker is the Share charm that enables the communication between the source and the target app.

- *Target app*: The target app implements the share contract as a target app to receive data shared by other apps.

10.1 Set up an Event Handler for a Share Option for a Source App

Problem

You need to set up an event handler for a share option for a source app.

Solution

You need to use the datarequested event listener of Windows.ApplicationModel.DataTransfer. DataTransferManager.

How It Works

The datarequested event listener method of the Windows.ApplicationModel.DataTransfer. DataTransferManager class is triggered when the user invokes the share. This event can be fired by a user's actions or automatically in a specific scenario; for example, when a user completes a survey and the app would like to share the result of the survey.

To register the event handler with the DataTransferManager object, you can use the following code:

```
var dataTransferManager = Windows.ApplicationModel.DataTransfer.DataTransferManager.
getForCurrentView();

dataTransferManager.addEventListener("datarequested", dataRequested_Share);
```

In the preceding code, the first thing you do is get the current page's DataTransferManager object using the DataTransferManager.getForCurrentView() function.

The next line then adds an event listener for the datarequested event to the DataTransferManager object. In the preceding code, dataRequested_Share is the listener and datarequested is an event. You can then define the receiver, as shown in the following code.

```
function dataRequested_Share () {

   // Your code for the sharing data

}
```

Let's create a Universal Windows app using the preceding code to set up the event handler for the share options for a source app.

Create a new project using the Windows Universal (Blank App) template in Microsoft Visual Studio 2015.

Right-click the project's js folder in Solution Explorer and select **Add ➤ New JavaScript file**. Provide the name for the file. In this example, let's name the file **DataSharingDemo.js**.

```
(function () {
    "use strict";
    function GetControl() {
        WinJS.UI.processAll().done(function () {

var dataTransferManager = Windows.ApplicationModel.DataTransfer.DataTransferManager.
getForCurrentView();

dataTransferManager.addEventListener("datarequested", shareDataHandler);
        });
    }
    document.addEventListener("DOMContentLoaded", GetControl);
})();

function shareDataHandler(e) {
    // Your code to share the text, image etc

}
```

The preceding code gets the current page's DataTransferManager object using the
DataTransferManager.getForCurrentView() function and then adds an event listener to it, as explained
earlier.

Now, add the DataSharingDemo.js reference to default.html, as shown here:

```
<!DOCTYPE html>
<html>
<head>
    <meta charset="utf-8" />
    <title>_10.1</title>

    <!-- WinJS references -->
    <link href="WinJS/css/ui-dark.css" rel="stylesheet" />
    <script src="WinJS/js/base.js"></script>
    <script src="WinJS/js/ui.js"></script>

    <!-- _10.1 references -->
    <link href="/css/default.css" rel="stylesheet" />
    <script src="/js/default.js"></script>
    <script src="/js/DataSharingDemo.js"></script>
</head>
<body class="win-type-body">
    <p>Content goes here</p>
</body>
</html>
```

10.2 Share Plain Text Data to Other Apps

Problem

You need to develop a feature that allows users to share plain text data to other Windows 10 apps.

Solution

Use `request.data.setText` and `request.Data.Properties.description` to share the data. The request. data.title is the mandatory field.

How It Works

In the previous recipe, you learned that the `datarequested` event listener is fired when a user starts a sharing session by using Share charm. So now we will write code in the listener to share data. The listener accepts a parameter, which is the event argument. First, you need to retrieve the request object from the event argument, as shown here:

```
function shareDataHandler(e) {
        //Start your code to share data
        var request = e.request;
}
```

You need to set properties for the request object. In order to share plain text you will need to populate the following properties:

```
request.Data.Properties.Title = "Title of the Data";
request.Data.Properties.Description = "Description of the Data";
```

Great, it looks simple, doesn't it? Let's implement this and see a live demo of sharing data between apps. Create a new project using the Windows Universal (Blank App) template in Microsoft Visual Studio 2015. First, add the following code to `default.html`. You need to replace the body tag with the following code:

```
<body class="win-type-body" style="background-color:white">
    <div>
        <p style="color:black">Enter Project Title:</p>
        <input class="text-box" id="txttitle" value="Project Title" size="40"/>
        <p style="color:black">Enter Project Description:</p>
        <input class="text-box" id="txtdesc" value="Project Desc" size="40" />
        <p style="color:black">Enter Project Weekly Summary:</p>
        <textarea id="txttext" maxlength="1000" style="width:50%">Weekly Status: Here is the
        weekly status</textarea>
        <br />
        <br />

    </div>
</body>
```

This code defines a user interface for the sharing data demo. The user interface looks like what's shown in Figure 10-1.

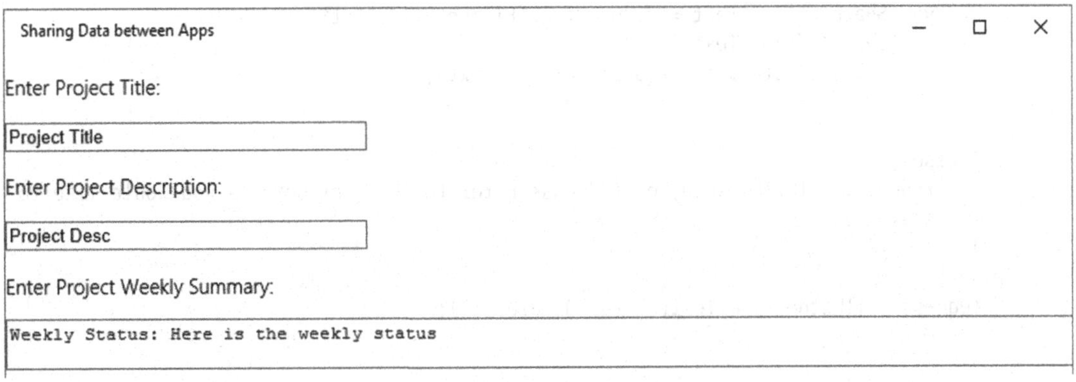

```
Sharing Data between Apps                                          —    □    ×

Enter Project Title:

Project Title

Enter Project Description:

Project Desc

Enter Project Weekly Summary:

Weekly Status: Here is the weekly status
```

Figure 10-1. *Sharing Data user interface*

Now, right-click the project's js folder in the Solution Explorer and select **Add ➤ New JavaScript file**. Provide the name for the file. In this example, let's name the file **DataSharingDemo.js**.

```
(function () {
    "use strict";
    function GetControl() {
        WinJS.UI.processAll().done(function () {

            var dataTransferManager = Windows.ApplicationModel.DataTransfer.
            DataTransferManager.getForCurrentView();
            dataTransferManager.addEventListener("datarequested", shareDataHandler);

        });
    }
    document.addEventListener("DOMContentLoaded", GetControl);
})();
```

Also add the following code to default.html to reference the DataSharingDemo.js file:

```
<script src="/js/DataSharingDemo.js"></script>
```

So you have the user interface for the data you want to share. You have also added the event listener for the datarequested event. Now the most important piece of the sharing data feature is implementing the code to populate the request object. So add the following code for the function shareDataHandler to the DataSharingDemo.js file.

```
function shareDataHandler(e) {
    var request = e.request;

    // The request.data.properties.title is mandatory
    var ShareInfoTitle = document.getElementById("txttitle").value;
    if (ShareInfoTitle !== "") {
        var ShareInfoDesc = document.getElementById("txtdesc").value;
        if (ShareInfoDesc !== "") {
            request.data.properties.title = ShareInfoTitle;
            request.data.properties.description = ShareInfoDesc;
```

185

```
                var ShareInfoFullText = document.getElementById("txttext").value;
                if (ShareInfoFullText !== "") {
                    request.data.setText(ShareInfoFullText);
                }

        } else {
            request.failWithDisplayText("Please Enter the Project Details you would like to
            share.");
        }
    } else {
        request.failWithDisplayText("Error Occured!!");
    }
}
```

The preceding code first retrieves the request object from the event argument. This function populates as follows:

```
request.data.properties.title = ShareInfoTitle;
request.data.properties.description = ShareInfoDesc;
```

Finally, add the following code:

```
request.data.setText(ShareInfoFullText);
```

This function checks if the title is empty or not, as the request's title property is mandatory. When you run the application on Windows 10, you see the screen shown in Figure 10-2.

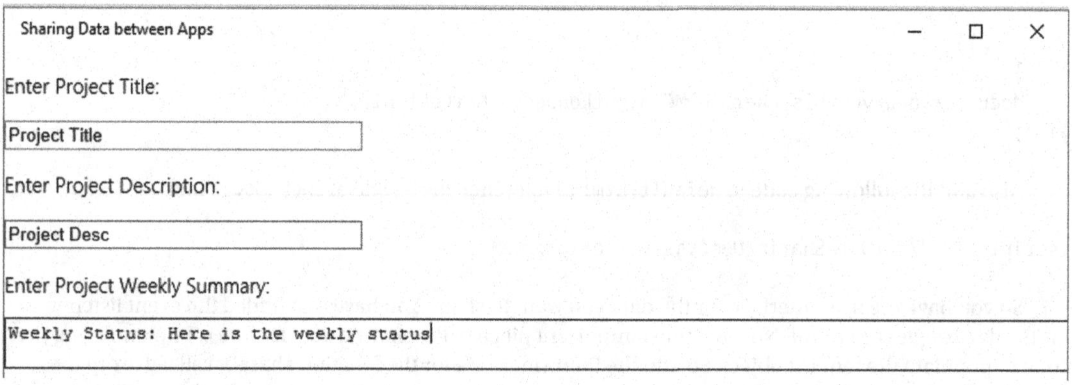

Figure 10-2. *Sharing Data demo*

Now click the Share charm or press the Windows logo key ⊞ + H. You will see the screen shown in Figure 10-3.

Figure 10-3. *The Share charm windows showing the project title as a sharing data object*

Now, click **OneNote** from the list. You are presented with a screen, as shown in Figure 10-4.

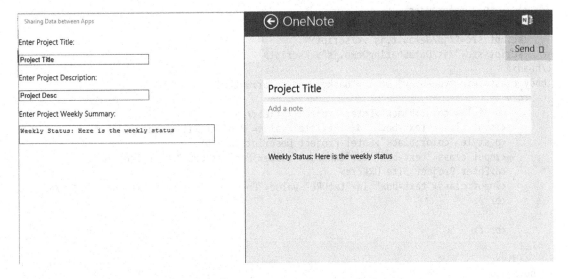

Figure 10-4. *OneNote showing the shared data from the Universal Windows app*

10.3 Share Web Links to Other Apps

Problem

You need to develop a feature that allows users to share web links with other Windows 10 apps.

Solution

Use request.data.setWebLink along with title and description fields.

How It Works

To share web links, you need to use the `request.data.setWebLink()` method of the `request` object.

Create a new project using the Windows Universal (Blank App) template in Microsoft Visual Studio 2015.

First, add the following code to `default.html`. You will need to replace the body tag with the following code:

```
<!DOCTYPE html>
<html>
<head>
    <meta charset="utf-8" />
    <title>_10.3</title>

    <!-- WinJS references -->
    <link href="WinJS/css/ui-dark.css" rel="stylesheet" />
    <script src="WinJS/js/base.js"></script>
    <script src="WinJS/js/ui.js"></script>

    <!-- _10.3 references -->
    <link href="/css/default.css" rel="stylesheet" />
    <script src="/js/default.js"></script>
    <script src="/js/DataSharingDemo.js"></script>
</head>
<body class="win-type-body" style="background-color:white">
    <div>
        <p style="color:black">Enter Project Title:</p>
        <input class="text-box" id="txttitle" value="Project Title" size="40" />
        <p style="color:black">Enter Project Description:</p>
        <input class="text-box" id="txtdesc" value="Project Desc" size="40" />
        <p>Enter Project Site URL</p>
        <input class="text-box" id="txtURL" value="Enter Project Site URL" size="40" />
        <br />

        <br />

    </div>
</body>

</html>
```

Now, right-click the project's js folder in Solution Explorer and select **Add ➤ New JavaScript file**. Provide the name for the file. In this example, let's name the file **DataSharingDemo.js**.

```
(function () {
    "use strict";
    function GetControl() {
        WinJS.UI.processAll().done(function () {
```

```
            var dataTransferManager = Windows.ApplicationModel.DataTransfer.
            DataTransferManager.getForCurrentView();
            dataTransferManager.addEventListener("datarequested", shareDataHandler);

        });
    }
    document.addEventListener("DOMContentLoaded", GetControl);
})();
```

Also add the following code to default.html to reference the DataSharingDemo.js file:

```
<script src="/js/DataSharingDemo.js"></script>
```

Add a new shareDataHandler function to DataSharingDemo.js. The complete shareDataHandler function will look as follows. The following uses the request.data.setWebLink() function to set the web links that are being shared.

```
function shareDataHandler(e) {
    var request = e.request;

    // The request.data.properties.title is mandate
    var ShareInfoTitle = document.getElementById("txttitle").value;
    if (ShareInfoTitle !== "") {
        var ShareInfoDesc = document.getElementById("txtdesc").value;
        if (ShareInfoDesc !== "") {
            request.data.properties.title = ShareInfoTitle;
            request.data.properties.description = ShareInfoDesc;

            var ShareURL = document.getElementById("txtURL").value;
            if (ShareURL !== "") {
                request.data.setWebLink(new Windows.Foundation.Uri(ShareURL));
            }

        } else {
            request.failWithDisplayText("Please Enter the Project Details you would like to
            share.");
        }
    } else {
        request.failWithDisplayText("Error Occured!!");
    }
}
```

The request.data.setWebLink() method accepts a parameter of type URI, which is why the conversion from a string to Windows.Foundation.Uri is necessary before passing it to the function.

10.4 Share an Image to Other Apps

Problem

You need to develop a feature that allows users to share an image with other Windows 10 apps.

Solution

Use request.data.setStorageItems or request.data.setBitmap along with title and description fields. You can also use both for sharing an image, as you will not know which one is supported by the target app.

How It Works

Universal Windows apps also allow you to share an image with other apps. You can allow users to select an image from the local device and then use the Share charm to share with other apps. Let's see image sharing in action.

First, add the following code to default.html. You need to replace the body tag with the following code:

```
<body class="win-type-body" style="background-color:white">
    <div>
        <p style="color:black">Enter Project Title:</p>
        <input class="text-box" id="txttitle" value="Project Title" size="40" />
        <p style="color:black">Enter Project Description:</p>
        <input class="text-box" id="txtdesc" value="Project Desc" size="40" />
        <p>Select the image to share</p>
        <button class="action" id="selectImageButton">Select image</button>
        <br />

        <br />

    </div>
<div class="imageDiv">
        <img class="imageHolder" id="imageHolder" alt="image holder" src="" />
    </div>
</body>
```

The preceding code defines a user interface for the sharing image with an image picker button. Now add the following function in the DataSharingDemo.js file.

```
(function () {
    "use strict";
    var objimgFile;
    function GetControl() {
        WinJS.UI.processAll().done(function () {
            var objimgFile = null;
            var dataTransferManager = Windows.ApplicationModel.DataTransfer.
            DataTransferManager.getForCurrentView();
            dataTransferManager.addEventListener("datarequested", shareDataHandler);
```

```
document.getElementById("selectImageButton").addEventListener("click",
selectImage, false);
```

```
    });
}
    document.addEventListener("DOMContentLoaded", GetControl);
})();
```

The preceding code adds a listener to the selectImageButton control, as shown in the bolded lines.

Apart from adding a listener, it also declares a variable called objimgFile, which holds the image object that you will use in the following function.

Add a selectImage function, which is the listener of the click event of the Select Image button. This function uses the FileOpenPicker method, which allows users to select an image from the device.

```
function selectImage() {
    var picker = new Windows.Storage.Pickers.FileOpenPicker();
    picker.fileTypeFilter.replaceAll([".jpg", ".bmp", ".gif", ".png"]);
    picker.viewMode = Windows.Storage.Pickers.PickerViewMode.thumbnail;
    picker.pickSingleFileAsync().done(function (file) {
        if (file) {
// Display the image to the user
 document.getElementById("imageHolder").src = URL.createObjectURL(file, { oneTimeOnly: true
});
// The imageFile variable will be set to shareValue when the user clicks Set
        objimgFile = file;
        }
    });
}
```

Once the picker selects the single file successfully, it calls the async method, which then sets the src property.

Now, let's add the shareDataHandler() method to the js file as follows:

```
function shareDataHandler(e) {
    var request = e.request;

    // The request.data.properties.title is mandate
    var ShareInfoTitle = document.getElementById("txttitle").value;
    if (ShareInfoTitle !== "") {
        var ShareInfoDesc = document.getElementById("txtdesc").value;
        if (ShareInfoDesc !== "") {
            request.data.properties.title = ShareInfoTitle;
            request.data.properties.description = ShareInfoDesc;


            if (objimgFile != null) {
//Create a stream variable and using randomStreamReference.createFromFile //function create
the stream for the image file object "objimgFile"
                var imageStream = Windows.Storage.Streams.RandomAccessStreamReference.
                createFromFile(objimgFile);
```

```
                request.data.setStorageItems([objimgFile]);

                // The setBitmap method requires a stream object
                request.data.setBitmap(imageStream);


            }

        } else {
            request.failWithDisplayText("Please Enter the Project Details you would like to
            share.");
        }
    } else {
        request.failWithDisplayText("Error Occured!!");
    }
}
```

The shareDataHandler function first sets the title and description of the request.data object. To set the image, it uses the stream object, as per the following code:

```
var imageStream = Windows.Storage.Streams.RandomAccessStreamReference.
createFromFile(objimgFile);
```

This line creates a stream variable, and using the createFromFile function, it creates the stream for the image file objimgFile object.

The next line calls the setStorageItems function of the request.data object by passing the image object. The objimgfile object was set to a file in the selectImage() folder.

```
request.data.setStorageItems([objimgFile]);
```

The next line in the preceding code is the setBitMap method of the request.data object, which sets the image to the data object being shared:

```
// pass the stream imageStream to the setBitMap method
request.data.setBitmap(imageStream);
```

When you run the application on Windows 10 using the Share charm feature, you see the Select Image button, as shown in Figure 10-5.

Figure 10-5. *Sharing image demo*

Click the **Select Image** button and select an image from device camera folder or photo folder. Once you select the photo, you see the image in your default.html file, as shown in Figure 10-6.

Figure 10-6. *Sharing Image demo*

Now click the Share charm or press the Windows logo key ■■ + H. When you select **OneNote** from the list, the app will share data with OneNote and you will see a screen like the one shown in Figure 10-7.

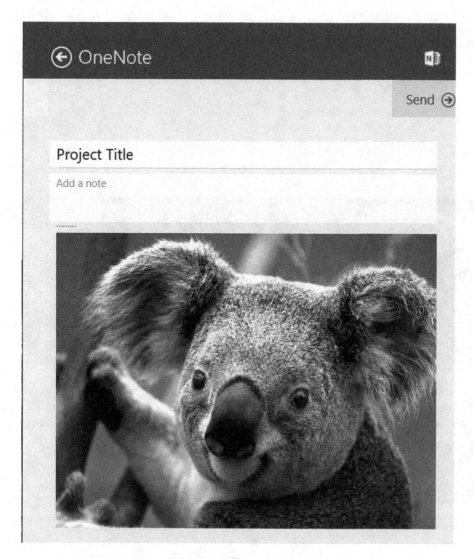

Figure 10-7. *Image shared along with project title*

10.5 Declare App As a Share Target

Problem

You need to declare an app as a share target in the list when the user uses the Share charm feature.

Solution

Configure the share target in the package.appxmanifest file, which enables the share contract as a share target app.

How It Works

Windows 10 displays a list of possible target apps when the user invokes sharing using the Share charm. A target share app is the app that can receive the data shared by other apps. You need to declare your app as a target app and implement the function to receive the data and store it in the right place or display it on the screen. For example, you have two apps: one for time management reporting, and other for project listing in an organization. What if you want to share data from time management reporting to the project listing app? The time management reporting app will become a source app and the project listing app is the target app.

When you declare an app as a target app that can receive the data shared by other apps, your app adheres to the share contract. By declaring your app as a target app, you are providing a good experience to your app's users, which enhances social connectivity with other apps.

If you want to receive data or support the share contract from other apps via a sharing option, you need to declare your app as a share target.

To declare your app a share target, follow these guidelines:

1. Open the manifest file (`package.appxmanifest`), which is available in the root folder of the project.

2. Click the **Declaration** tab.

3. From the available declarations, select **Share Target**.

4. On the right side of the screen, enter **Sharing Description**.

5. Select the data format by clicking **Add new**.

6. Define two data formats: Text and Image.

The declaration settings window should look as shown in Figure 10-8.

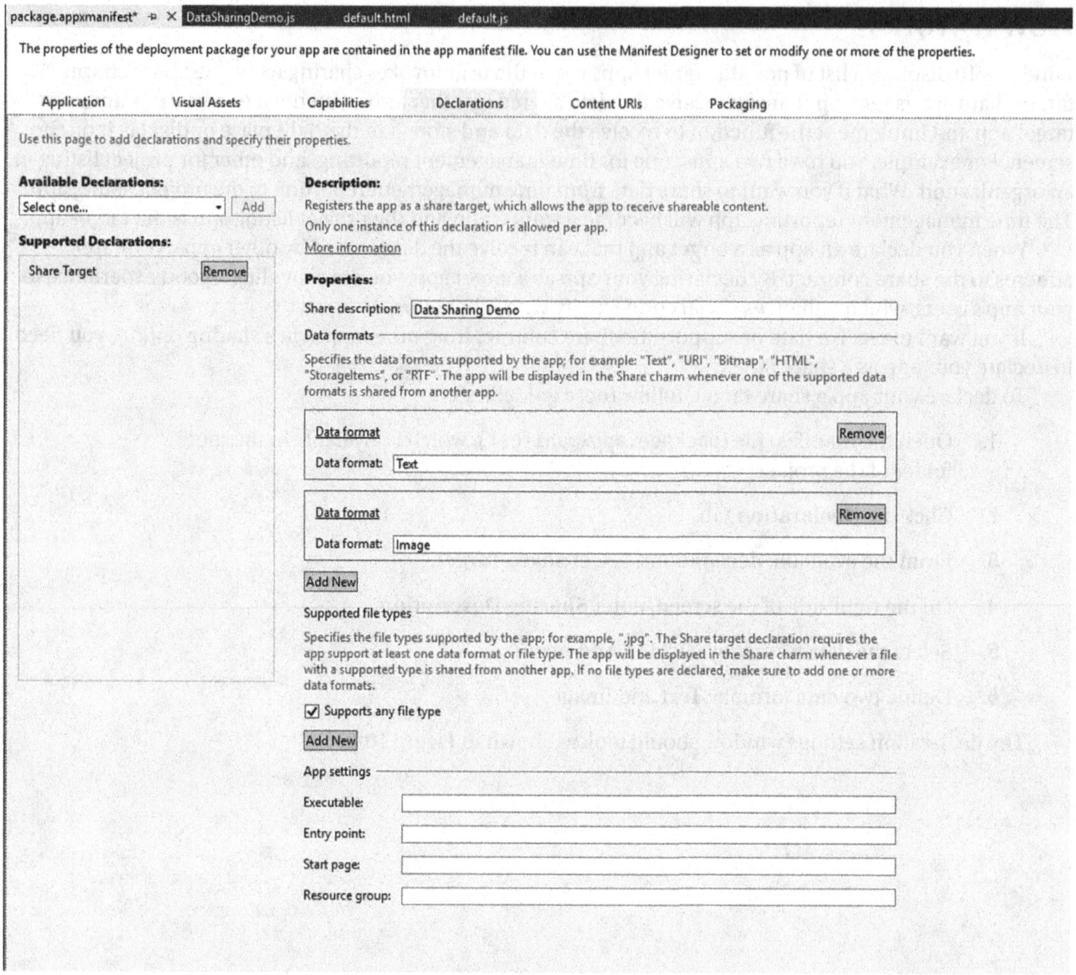

Figure 10-8. *Image shared along with project title*

When you run the application in Windows 10 and use the Share charm feature, you see that your app appears in the list, as shown in Figure 10-9.

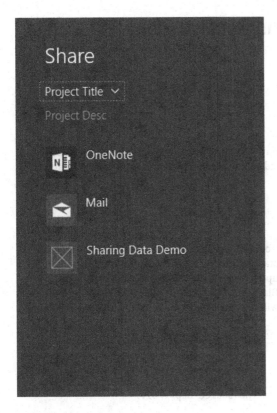

Figure 10-9. *Share Charm windows*

Let's go over the data types supported by the share contract. Table 10-1 lists the data types supported in the sharing data using the share contract.

Table 10-1. *Data Types in Share Contract*

Data Type	Description
Text	Plain text string
URI	A web link (for example, http://www.apress.com)
Image	A bitmap image
HTML	HTML content
Files	Files as storage items
Custom Data	Custom data using JSON format
Rich Text	Rich text–formatted string

10.6 Handle Share Activation and Receive Plain Text

Problem

You need to handle share activation as a share target app.

Solution

When your app appears in the list of target apps of the Share charm, users can select your app from the list to share data. The `Application.OnShareTargetActivated` event is fired when the user selects your app to share the data.

How It Works

When your app is selected for sharing data, an `Application.OnShareTargetActivated` event is triggered. Your app needs to implement this event to receive the data that the user is sharing from other apps.

Let's implement this event in a Universal Windows app to receive data from other apps.

Create a new project using the Windows Universal (Blank App) template in Microsoft Visual Studio 2015.

First, add the following code to `default.html`. You will need to replace the body tag with the following code:

```
<body class="win-type-body">
    <div>
        <br /><br />
        <div>The following Data  was received from the source app:</div>
        <br />
        <h3>Data Properties</h3>
        <strong>Title: </strong><span id="txttitle" data-win-automationId="Title">(No
        title)</span><br />
        <strong>Description: </strong><span id="txtdescription" data-win-
        automationId="Description">(No description)</span><br />
        <strong>Data: </strong><span id="txtdata" data-win-automationId="Description">(No
        data)</span><br />
    </div>
</body>
```

This code defines a user interface for the sharing data demo. The user interface looks like what's shown in Figure 10-10.

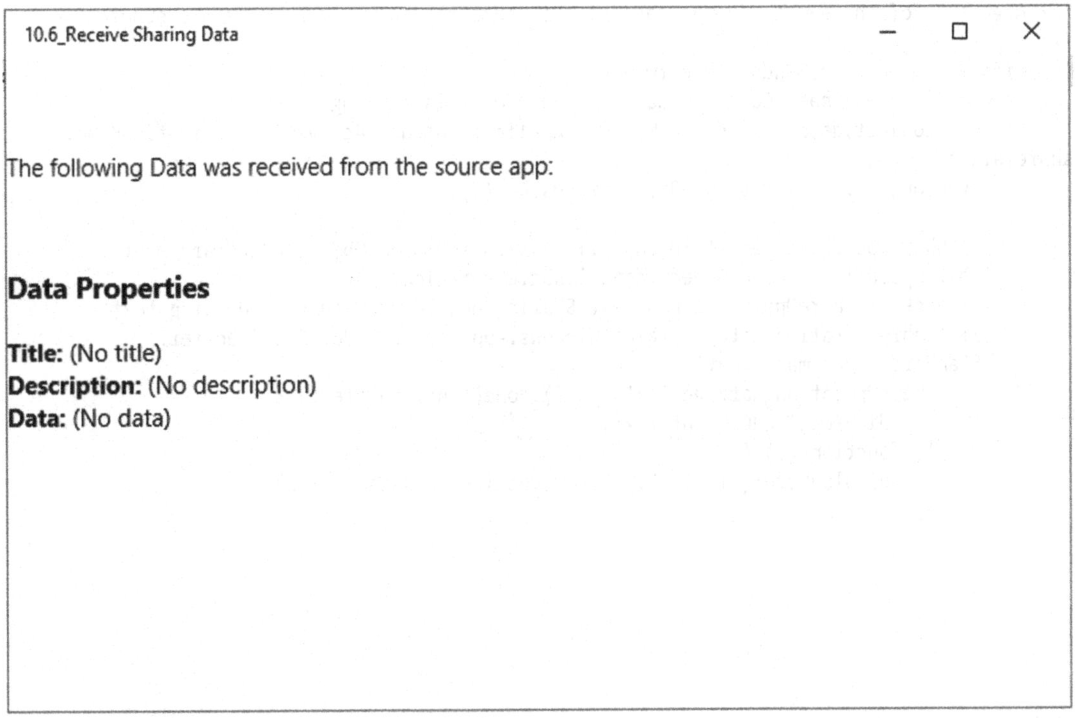

```
10.6_Receive Sharing Data                                    ─    □    ✕
```

The following Data was received from the source app:

Data Properties

Title: (No title)
Description: (No description)
Data: (No data)

Figure 10-10. Share Charm windows

Now, right-click the project in Solution Explorer and select **Add ➤ New JavaScript file**. Provide the name for the file. In this example, let's name the file **DataSharingDemo.js**.

```
(function () {
    "use strict";
    function GetControl() {
        WinJS.UI.processAll().done(function () {

            // Initialize the activation handler
            WinJS.Application.addEventListener("activated", activatedShareHandler, false);


        });
    }
    document.addEventListener("DOMContentLoaded", GetControl);
})();
```

The preceding code adds an event listener activated to the application object. The event listener function named activatedShareHandler is provided as follows; add this function to the js file.

```
/// <summary>
/// Function to handle the activation
/// </summary>
/// <param name="eventArgs">
```

```
/// Arguments of the event. In the case of the Share contract, it has the ShareOperation
/// </param>
function activatedShareHandler(eventObject) {
    // Check if the Share Contract was the cuase of this sharing
    if (eventObject.detail.kind === Windows.ApplicationModel.Activation.ActivationKind.
shareTarget) {
        eventObject.setPromise(WinJS.UI.processAll());

        // ShareOperation object in initiliaze with the eventObject event arugment
        shareOperation = eventObject.detail.shareOperation;
        //check if shareOperation has text Sharing enable or data shared using text
        if (shareOperation.data.contains(Windows.ApplicationModel.DataTransfer.
        StandardDataFormats.text)) {
            shareOperation.data.getTextAsync().done(function (text) {
                dispReceivedContent(text);
            }, function (e) {
                displayError("Text: ", "Error retrieving data: " + e);
            });
        }


}

}
```

The preceding code receives the share data of the activatedShareHandler event listener. This code first checks if the sharing is triggered with the share contract. It then creates a shareOperation object from the event argument, as shown in the following code:

```
// ShareOperation object in initiliaze with the eventObject event arugment
        shareOperation = eventObject.detail.shareOperation;
```

The code then uses the shareOperation.data.getTextAsync function to get the text asynchronously. In the success method of the async call, the received text is then passed to the dispReceivedContent() function, which then displays the text on the target app. The following is the code for the display the share content function:

```
function dispReceivedContent(content) {

    document.getElementById("txttitle").innerText = shareOperation.data.properties.title;
    document.getElementById("txtdescription").innerText = shareOperation.data.properties.
    description;
    document.getElementById("txtdata").innerText = content;
}
```

The complete code of the DataSharingDemo.js file is shown here:

```
(function () {
    "use strict";
    function GetControl() {
        WinJS.UI.processAll().done(function () {
```

```
        // Initialize the activation handler
        WinJS.Application.addEventListener("activated", activatedShareHandler, false);



    });
    }
    document.addEventListener("DOMContentLoaded", GetControl);
})();

/// <summary>
/// Function to handle the activation
/// </summary>
/// <param name="eventArgs">
/// Arguments of the event. In the case of the Share contract, it has the ShareOperation
/// </param>
function activatedShareHandler(eventObject) {
    // Check if the Share Contract was the cause of this sharing
    if (eventObject.detail.kind === Windows.ApplicationModel.Activation.ActivationKind.
    shareTarget) {
        eventObject.setPromise(WinJS.UI.processAll());

        // ShareOperation object in initiliaze with the eventObject event argument
        shareOperation = eventObject.detail.shareOperation;
        //check if shareOperation has text Sharing enable or data shared using text
        if (shareOperation.data.contains(Windows.ApplicationModel.DataTransfer.
        StandardDataFormats.text)) {
            shareOperation.data.getTextAsync().done(function (text) {
                dispReceivedContent(text);
            }, function (e) {
                displayError("Text: ", "Error retrieving data: " + e);
            });
        }



}


}


function dispReceivedContent(content) {

document.getElementById("txttitle").innerText = shareOperation.data.properties.title;
document.getElementById("txtdescription").innerText = shareOperation.data.properties.
description;
 document.getElementById("txtdata").innerText = content;
}
```

When you run a source app in Windows 10 (we are running another app that we developed in Recipe 10.2), you see the screen shown in Figure 10-11.

Figure 10-11. Share charm windows showing the target app

As shown in Figure 10-11, the app 10.6_Receive Sharing Data is listed in the app's Share charm share target list. When you select the app, you see the data (title, description, and text) that was shared from the source app, as highlighted in Figure 10-12.

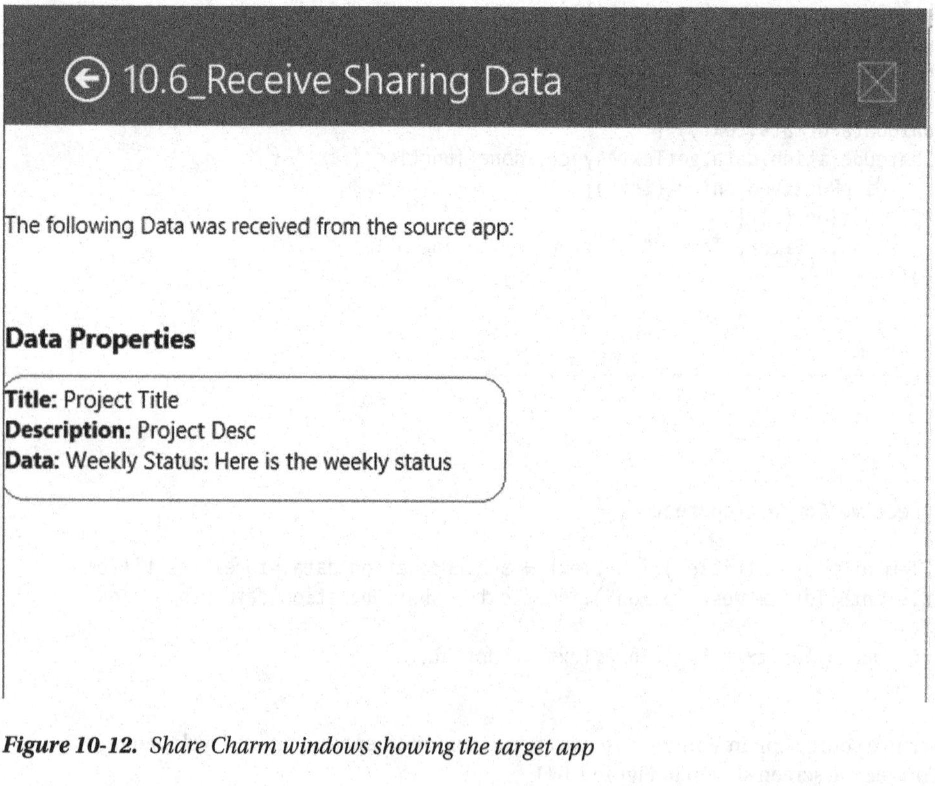

Figure 10-12. Share Charm windows showing the target app

10.7 Receive Images Shared by Other Apps

Problem

You need to develop a feature that will allow users to receive an image shared by another Windows 10 app.

Solution

Use shareOperation.data.getBitmapAsync to receive the image shared by another app.

How It Works

The source app can also share an image with the other apps as you saw in Recipe 10.4. To share a bitmap image, the source app uses the request.data.setBitmap(imageStream) method by passing the image stream to set the bitmap image to the request object being shared.

To receive the bitmap image, the target app uses the shareOperation.data.getBitmapAsync() method of the data packages view. The complete code to receive a bitmap image is shown here:

```
// ShareOperation object in initiliaze with the eventObject event arugment
shareOperation = eventObject.detail.shareOperation;

if (shareOperation.data.contains(Windows.ApplicationModel.DataTransfer.StandardDataFormats.
bitmap)) {
        shareOperation.data.getBitmapAsync().done(function (bitmapStreamReference) {
            bitmapStreamReference.openReadAsync().done(function (bitmapStream) {
            if (bitmapStream) {
    document.getElementById("imageHolder").src = URL.createObjectURL(bitmapStream, {
    oneTimeOnly: true });
                }
            }, function (e) {
                displayError("Bitmap: ", "Error reading image stream:  " + e);
            });
        }, function (e) {
            displayError("Bitmap: ", "Error retrieving data: " + e);
        });
    }
```

This code first checks if the shareOperation object contains a bitmap image. It then invokes the getBitmapAsync() method to receive the image from the request object. At the end, in the success method of the async call, another async call to bitmapStreamReference.openReadAsync() is invoked to read the stream object. openReadAsync returns the stream object. The URL.createObjectURL(bitmapStream, { oneTimeOnly: true }) line of code then creates the URL of the object, which is then assigned to the imageHolder as a source to the HTML img tag.

Let's implement this event in a Universal Windows app to receive bitmaps from other apps.

Create a new project using the Windows Universal (Blank App) template in Microsoft Visual Studio 2015.

First, add the following code to default.html. You need to replace the body tag with the following code:

```
<body class="win-type-body" style="background-color:white" >
    <div>
        <br /><br />
        <div><p style="color:black">The following Data  was received from the
        source app:</p></div>
        <br />
        <h3 style="color:black">Data Properties</h3>
        <strong style="color:black">Title: </strong><span id="txttitle" data-win-
        automationId="Title" style="color:black">(No title)</span><br />
        <strong style="color:black">Description: </strong><span id="txtdescription" data-
        win-automationId="Description" style="color:black">(No description)</span><br />
        <strong style="color:black">Data: </strong><span id="txtdata" data-win-
        automationId="Description" style="color:black">(No data)</span><br />

        <div class="imageDiv">
            <img class="imageHolder" id="imageHolder" alt="image holder" src="" />
        </div>
    </div>
</body>
```

Now, right-click the project in Solution Explorer and select **Add ➤ New JavaScript file**. Provide the name for the file. In this example, let's name the file **DataSharingDemo.js**.

```
(function () {
    "use strict";
    function GetControl() {
        WinJS.UI.processAll().done(function () {

            // Initialize the activation handler
            WinJS.Application.addEventListener("activated", activatedHandler, false);


        });
    }
    document.addEventListener("DOMContentLoaded", GetControl);
})();
```

The preceding code adds an event listener activated to the application object. The following is the event listener function named activatedShareHandler. Add this code to the js file.

```
/// <summary>
/// Function to handle the activation
/// </summary>
/// <param name="eventArgs">
/// Arguments of the event. In the case of the Share contract, it has the ShareOperation
/// </param>
function activatedShareHandler(eventObject) {
    // Check if the Share Contract was the cuase of this sharing
    if (eventObject.detail.kind === Windows.ApplicationModel.Activation.ActivationKind.
    shareTarget) {
        eventObject.setPromise(WinJS.UI.processAll());

        // ShareOperation object in initiliaze with the eventObject event arugment
        shareOperation = eventObject.detail.shareOperation;

        if (shareOperation.data.contains(Windows.ApplicationModel.DataTransfer.
        StandardDataFormats.bitmap)) {
            shareOperation.data.getBitmapAsync().done(function (bitmapStreamReference) {
                bitmapStreamReference.openReadAsync().done(function (bitmapStream) {
                    if (bitmapStream) {
                        document.getElementById("imageHolder").src = URL.
                        createObjectURL(bitmapStream, { oneTimeOnly: true });
                    }
                }, function (e) {
                    displayError("Bitmap: ", "Error reading image stream:  " + e);
                });
            }, function (e) {
                displayError("Bitmap: ", "Error retrieving data: " + e);
            });
        }

    }

}
```

Finally, declare this app as a target app by using package.appxmanifest, as shown in Figure 10-13.

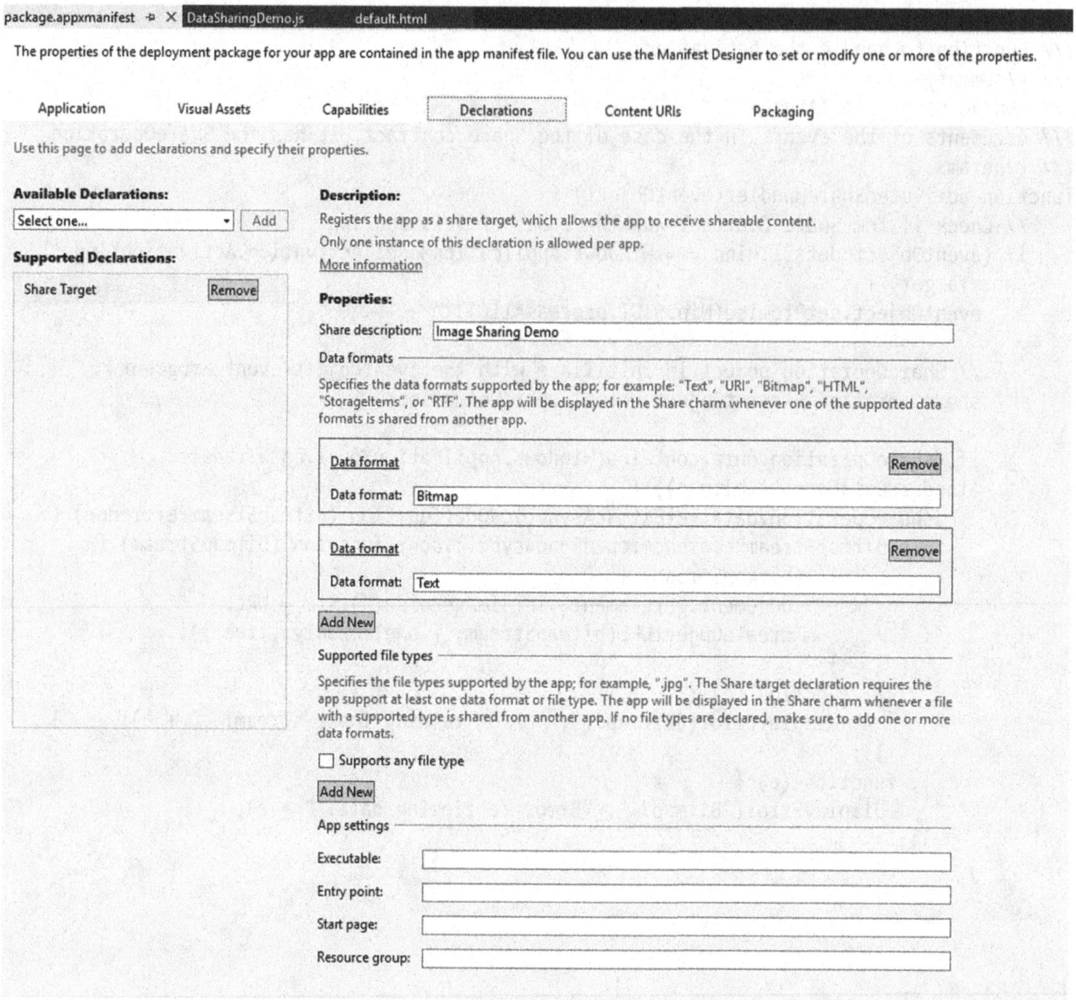

package.appxmanifest -₽ ✕ DataSharingDemo.js   default.html

The properties of the deployment package for your app are contained in the app manifest file. You can use the Manifest Designer to set or modify one or more of the properties.

| Application | Visual Assets | Capabilities | Declarations | Content URIs | Packaging |

Use this page to add declarations and specify their properties.

Available Declarations:

Select one... ▼ Add

Supported Declarations:

Share Target   Remove

Description:

Registers the app as a share target, which allows the app to receive shareable content.

Only one instance of this declaration is allowed per app.

More information

Properties:

Share description: Image Sharing Demo

Data formats

Specifies the data formats supported by the app; for example: "Text", "URI", "Bitmap", "HTML", "StorageItems", or "RTF". The app will be displayed in the Share charm whenever one of the supported data formats is shared from another app.

Data format   Remove

Data format: Bitmap

Data format   Remove

Data format: Text

Add New

Supported file types

Specifies the file types supported by the app; for example, ".jpg". The Share target declaration requires the app support at least one data format or file type. The app will be displayed in the Share charm whenever a file with a supported type is shared from another app. If no file types are declared, make sure to add one or more data formats.

☐ Supports any file type

Add New

App settings

Executable: [   ]

Entry point: [   ]

Start page: [   ]

Resource group: [   ]

Figure 10-13. *Share Charm windows showing the target app*

That's it. Now deploy the app using the project deploy menu in Visual Studio.

You do not have to run this app to receive the image, as this is the registered target app. The Share charm lists this app as a target app in the Share charm windows, and when a user selects the app from the list, a new instance is activated for this app. The activated event will be invoked, which will then receive the image shared by the source app.

10.8 Share Custom Data Type

Problem

You need to develop a feature that allows users to share a custom data format, such as a person's name and job title.

Solution

Use the `request.data.setData` function as follows:

```
request.data.setData("Schema", "ObjectName");
```

How It Works

The share contract also allows developers to build apps to share custom format data, such as for a book (book title, publisher, author name, etc.) or a person, with properties like name, job title, profile picture, and so forth.

The custom format supported in a Windows 10 Universal Windows app can be based on schema defined by `http://schema.org`, such as `http://schema.org/person` or `http://schema.org/Book`. The set data method accepts two parameters, as follows:

```
request.data.setData("http://schema.org/Person", person);
```

The first parameter is the schema format id and the second parameter is the object itself.

Let's implement sharing custom data in a Universal Windows app.

Create a new project using the Windows Universal (Blank App) template in Microsoft Visual Studio 2015.

First, add the following code in the `default.html`. You need to replace the body tag with the following code:

```
<body class="win-type-body" style="background-color:white">
    <div>
        <p style="color:black">Enter Person  Name:</p>
        <input class="text-box" id="txttitle" value="Name" size="40" />
        <p style="color:black">Enter Person Title:</p>
        <input class="text-box" id="txtjobtitle" value="Job Title" size="40" />
        <p style="color:black">Enter telephone:</p>
        <input class="text-box" id="txtphone" value="Telephone" size="40" />
        <br />
        <br />

    </div>
</body>
```

Now, right-click the project in Solution Explorer and select **Add ➤ New JavaScript file**. Provide the name for the file. In this example, let's name the file **DataSharingDemo.js**.

```
(function () {
    "use strict";
    function GetControl() {
        WinJS.UI.processAll().done(function () {

            var dataTransferManager = Windows.ApplicationModel.DataTransfer.
            DataTransferManager.getForCurrentView();
            dataTransferManager.addEventListener("datarequested", shareDataHandler);

        });
    }
    document.addEventListener("DOMContentLoaded", GetControl);
})();
```

Implement the `shareDataHandler` function by copying the following code:

```
function shareDataHandler(e) {
    var request = e.request;
    ;

    // The request.data.properties.title is mandate
    var name = document.getElementById("txttitle").value;
    var person = {
        "type": "http://schema.org/Person",
        "properties":
        {
            "name": name,
            "jobtitle": document.getElementById("txtjobtitle").value
        }
    };
    person = JSON.stringify(person);

    request.data.properties.title = name;
    request.data.properties.description = name;

    request.data.setData("http://schema.org/Person", person);
}
```

The code in the preceding function implements the sharing of the custom data. The `person` object is defined as a JSON string that sets properties like name and job title, as schema.org supports both JSON and XML format.

Now let's create another project and implement code to receive custom data.

Create a new project using the Windows Universal (Blank App) template in Microsoft Visual Studio 2015. First, add the following code to `default.html`. You need to replace the body tag with the following code.

```
<body class="win-type-body">

    <textarea class="text-box" id="txtconent" rows="4" cols="50" />
    <br />
    <br />

</body>
```

Now, right-click the project in Solution Explorer and select **Add ➤ New JavaScript file**. Provide the name for the file. In this example, let's name the file **DataSharingDemo.js**.

```
(function () {
    "use strict";
    function GetControl() {
        WinJS.UI.processAll().done(function () {

            // Initialize the activation handler
            WinJS.Application.addEventListener("activated", activatedShareHandler, false);

        });
    }
    document.addEventListener("DOMContentLoaded", GetControl);
})();
```

Implement the activatedShareHandler function by copying the following code:

```
function activatedShareHandler(eventObject) {

    if (eventObject.detail.kind === Windows.ApplicationModel.Activation.ActivationKind.
    shareTarget) {
        eventObject.setPromise(WinJS.UI.processAll());

        // ShareOperation object is initiliaze with the eventObject event argument
        shareOperation = eventObject.detail.shareOperation;

        if (shareOperation.data.contains("http://schema.org/Person")) {
            shareOperation.data.getTextAsync("http://schema.org/Person").done(function
            (customFormatString) {
                var customFormatObject = JSON.parse(customFormatString);
                if (customFormatObject) {
                    // This sample expects the custom format to be of type http://schema.
                    org/Person
                    if (customFormatObject.type === "http://schema.org/Person") {
                        customFormatString = "Type: " + customFormatObject.type;
                        if (customFormatObject.properties) {
                            customFormatString += "\nName: " + customFormatObject.
                            properties.name,
                            customFormatString += "\nNjobtitle: " + customFormatObject.
                            properties.jobtitle;
                        }
                    }
                }
```

```
            document.getElementById("txtconent").value = customFormatString;
        }, function (e) {

        });
    }
   }
}
```

This code first checks if the event is fired for the share operation. It then initializes shareOperation = eventObject.detail.shareOperation. Then it checks shareOperation.data.contains (http://schema.org/Person). If it contains a Person object, it then calls the shareOperation.data. getTextAsync method to retrieve the custom data properties. In the success method, it parses the JSON string into a variable, as shown here:

```
var customFormatObject = JSON.parse(customFormatString);
```

Finally, it reads those properties and displays it in the text area. You need to deploy this app using the Visual Studio deploy option.

Now run the app, which shares the custom data. You are presented with a screen, as shown in Figure 10-14.

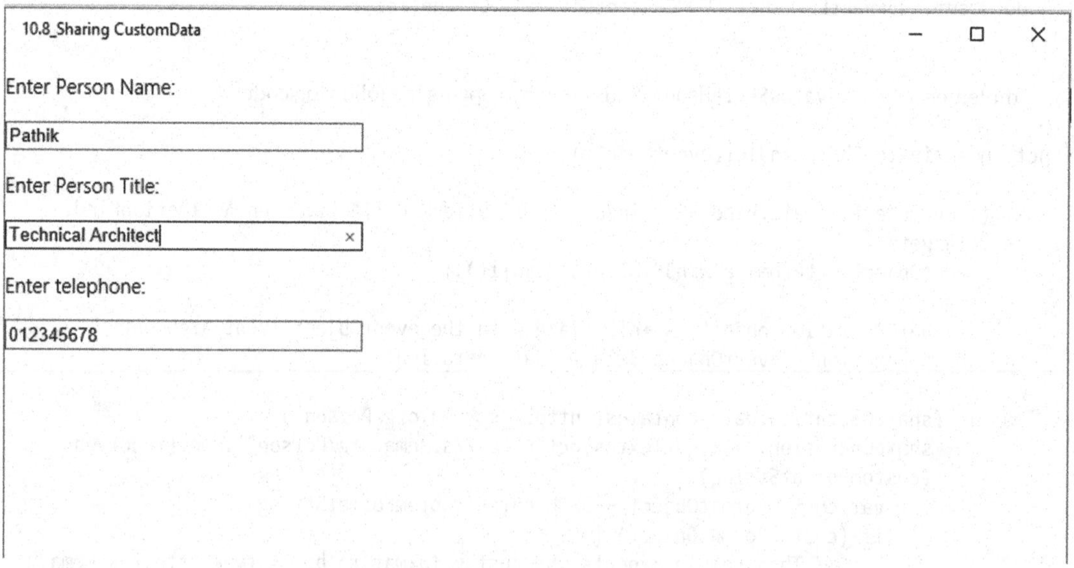

Figure 10-14. *The app UI that shares a custom data format*

Now click the Share charm or press the Windows logo key ⊞ + H. When you select 10.7B_ReceiveCustom_data app from the list, you see the screen shown in Figure 10-15.

Figure 10-15. *The receiver app for the custom data in the Share charm*

When you select the app, you are presented with the user interface of the receiver app within the Share charm windows, as shown in Figure 10-16.

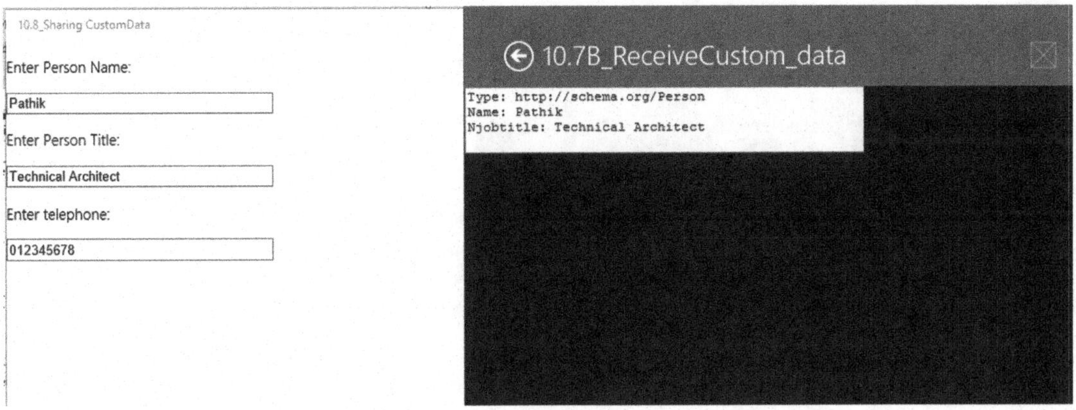

Figure 10-16. *The receiver app with the received custom data*

■ ■ ■

Background Tasks

In any application, you may have to silently perform certain tasks in the background. The Universal Windows Platform provides a Background Tasks feature that lets you run code in the background. A background task is nothing but a JavaScript file that the OS runs in the background. A *background task* is usually run against a system trigger that you can subscribe to. A background task needs to be declared in the application task. Background tasks can report progress, completion, and cancellation to apps through certain events.

11.1 System Event Triggers for Background Tasks

Problem

You have decided to implement a background task in your application. You would like to know the various system event triggers that you can subscribe to and run a background task when that trigger occurs.

Solution

System events are made available through a system-wide trigger object called SystemTrigger. When creating a new background task, you need to let the OS know which system trigger you want to subscribe to. You create a new instance of SystemTrigger and pass the trigger type in the constructor. The trigger types are defined in SystemTriggerType enumeration. Table 11-1 lists the triggers with their descriptions.

Table 11-1. *System Trigger Types*

Trigger Name	Description
InternetAvailable	The Internet becomes available
NetworkStateChange	A network change has occurred
OnlineIdConnectedStateChange	Online id associated with the account changes
SmsReceived	A new SMS message is received
TimeZoneChange	The time zone changes on the device

11.2 Create and Register a Background Task

Problem

You want to create a background task for your app and register it with the OS.

Solution

Use the `BackgroundTaskBuilder` found in the `Windows.ApplicationModel.Background` namespace to create a new background task and to register it.

How It Works

1. Open Visual Studio 2015 Community edition. Select **File ➤ New Project**. In the New Project dialog window, select **Templates ➤ JavaScript ➤ Windows ➤ Universal** from the Installed Templates section (see Figure 11-1). Select **Blank App (Universal Windows)** from the available project templates. Provide a name and location for the app and click **OK**.

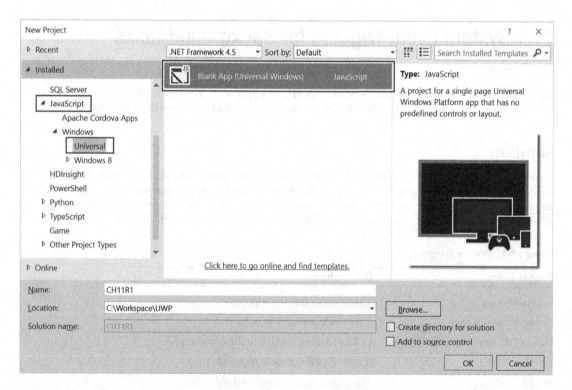

Figure 11-1. New Project dialog

2. Visual Studio prepares the project, which will look like what's shown in Figure 11-2 once done.

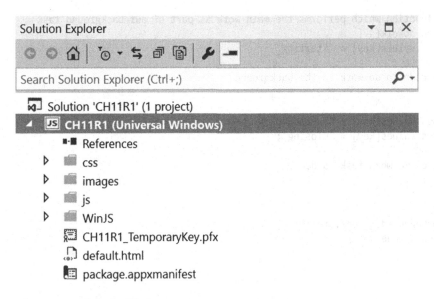

Figure 11-2. Solution Explorer

3. Create a new JavaScript file in your js folder. Let's name the file **mytask.js**. This js file contains the logic for the background work/task that you want to perform. You will use the file name of this js file to register the task, so keep note of the file name.

4. Here is the skeleton code of the mytask.js file:

```
(function () {

"use strict";

//gets the current instance of the background task
var backgroundTaskInstance = Windows.UI.WebUI.WebUIBackgroundTaskInstance.
current;

var canceled = false,
    settings = Windows.Storage.ApplicationData.current.localSettings,
    key = backgroundTaskInstance.task.name;

backgroundTaskInstance.addEventListener("canceled", OnCanceled);

//checking if the background task is cancelled by the user.
if (!canceled) {
    doWork();
}
else {
    settings.values[key] = "Canceled";
    close();
}
```

```
        //the function which performs the main work as part of our background task
        function doWork() {
            settings.values[key] = "Starting"

            //Your code to do work in the background
            //...

            settings.values[key] = "Succeeded";
            settings.values[key] = "Closing";

            //call close when task is done
            close();
        }

        function OnCanceled(sender, reason) {
            canceled = true;
        }

    })();
```

Let's go over the code. You get an instance of the background task using the WebUIBackgroundTaskInstance.current property. You then attach a canceled event handler to the cancellation of the background task. You then define a doWork() function, which does the actual work as part of the background task. You make use of the localSettings and update state of the task so that the main app can read the same and perform any updates on the UI. Notice the call to the close() function; a background task should call this function once it has finished its work. Next, you register the task that you just created.

1. In default.js, once the app has been activated, register the mytask.js background task that you just created. The following are the steps involved in registering a task.

   a. Iterate over all the tasks using the BackgroundTaskRegistration.allTasks property. It is important to check if your task is already registered or not. If you don't check for this and register blindly, the background task is registered multiple times, which may lead to unexpected results. Here is the code snippet to do this:

```
var task = null,
  taskRegistered = false,
  background = Windows.ApplicationModel.Background,
  iter = background.BackgroundTaskRegistration.allTasks.first();

while (iter.hasCurrent) {
    task = iter.current.value;
    if (task.name === exampleTaskName) {
        taskRegistered = true;
        break;
    }
    iter.moveNext();
}
```

b. If the task is not already registered, perform the registration by using the BackgroundTaskBuilder class. You need to set the system trigger on which the task should be invoked. In this example, you listen to timeZoneChange as the trigger for the background task. Here is the code snippet:

```
if (taskRegistered != true)
{
    var builder = new
    Windows.ApplicationModel.Background.BackgroundTaskBuilder();
    var trigger = new Windows.ApplicationModel.Background.SystemTrigger(
Windows.ApplicationModel.Background.SystemTriggerType.timeZoneChange, false);
    builder.name = exampleTaskName;
    builder.taskEntryPoint = "js\\mytask.js";
    builder.setTrigger(trigger);
    task = builder.register();
}
```

c. Next, you need to handle the task completion. Add a completed event handler on the task itself. Here is the code snippet:

```
task.addEventListener("completed", function (args) {
        var settings = Windows.Storage.ApplicationData.current.localSettings;
        var key = args.target.name;
    settings.values[key] = "Completed";
});
```

d. Here is the complete code snippet for registering the background task:

```
app.onactivated = function (args) {
        if (args.detail.kind === activation.ActivationKind.launch) {
                if (args.detail.previousExecutionState !==
        activation.ApplicationExecutionState.terminated) {
        var task = null,
            taskRegistered = false,
            background = Windows.ApplicationModel.Background,
            iter = background.BackgroundTaskRegistration.allTasks.first();
        while (iter.hasCurrent) {
        task = iter.current.value;
            if (task.name === exampleTaskName) {
                    taskRegistered = true;
                break;
            }
            iter.moveNext();
        }

        if (taskRegistered != true) {
        var builder = new        Windows.ApplicationModel.Background.
                                 BackgroundTaskBuilder();
        var trigger = new        Windows.ApplicationModel.Background.
                                 SystemTrigger(
```

```
                Windows.ApplicationModel.Background.SystemTriggerType.timeZoneChange, false);
                    builder.name = exampleTaskName;
                        builder.taskEntryPoint = "js\\mytask.js";
                        builder.setTrigger(trigger);
                        task = builder.register();
                }
                task.addEventListener("completed", function (args) {
                    var settings =            Windows.Storage.ApplicationData.current.
                                              localSettings;
                    var key = args.target.name;
                        settings.values[key] = "Completed";
                });

                } else {


                    }
                                args.setPromise(WinJS.UI.processAll());
                    }
                };
```

e. Next, you need to add a declaration for the background task in the
    application manifest file. Open the manifest file by double-clicking **package.
    appxmanifest**, which is in the root of the application.

f. Click the **Declarations** tab. Select **Background Tasks** from the available
    declarations drop-down list. Click the **Add** button to add a declaration.

g. In the **Supported task types** section, select **System event**.

h. In the **App settings** section, under the **Start page** entry, add **js\mytask.js** as
    the value.

i. Save the package manifest file.

With the preceding code, you have created a custom background task and registered it with the OS. You
used a system trigger event, namely a time zone change event, to run the task. Press **F5** to run the app and
then change the time zone settings of your system. The background task will be triggered as soon as the time
zone changes.

11.3 Setting Conditions for Running a Background Task

Problem

You want to create and register a custom background task. But you want the background task to be run only
when a certain condition is met; for example, user is present or user is not present, and so forth.

Solution

A background task is run only when the set trigger is fired. As seen in the previous recipe, you provide the
trigger when you create the task. If your task requires a certain condition to be met, even after the system
trigger has been fired, you can create a system condition and provide the condition to the task builder
during task registration. Conditions are provided using the SystemConditionType enumeration. Table 11-2
describes the system condition types available on the UWP.

Table 11-2. *System Condition Types*

Trigger Name	Value	Description
invalid	0	Not a valid condition type
userPresent	1	Task can run only when user is present
userNotPresent	2	Task can run only when user is not present
InternetAvailable	3	Task can run only when Internet is available
internetNotAvailable	4	Task can run only when Internet is not available
sessionConnected	5	Task can run only when user session is connected
sessionDisconnected	6	Task can run only when user session is disconnected
freeNetworkAvailable	7	Task can run only when a free network (non-metered) is available
backgroundWorkCostNotHigh	8	Task can run only when the cost to do background work is low

How It Works

Let's learn how to set a system condition on a task.

1. Create a SystemCondition object. Before registering a task, the condition to apply for the background task to run needs to be built. You need to create a SystemCondition object to represent the condition. The constructor of the SystemCondition object expects the SystemConditionType enumeration value, which is the condition that needs to be met before running the task. Here is the code snippet for providing the condition:

```
var internetConditionType = Windows.ApplicationModel.Background.
SystemConditionType.InternetAvailable;
var internetCondition = new Windows.ApplicationModel.Background.
SystemCondition(internetConditionType);
```

2. Add the SystemCondition object to background task. Once you have built the system condition, the next step is to add it to the task builder. BackgroundTaskBuilder provides an AddCondition() method that is used to set the condition. Here is the code snippet for adding the condition:

```
taskBuilder.AddCondition(internetCondition);
```

3. Next, you register the task using the Register() method of the TaskBuilder. Here is the code snippet for the task registration:

```
var task = builder.Register();
```

11.4 Monitor Background Task Progress and Completion

Problem

You have a background task that is created and registered by your app. You want to monitor the progress and completion of the task in your app.

Solution

A task that is registered with the system fires progress and completion events. Your app needs to provide event handlers and subscribe to the events exposed by the task.

How It Works

1. Handle the task completion. First, you need to create a function to attach to the Completion event of the background task. This function takes in a parameter of type BackgroundTaskCompletedEventArgs. Here is the skeleton of the function:

    ```
    function onCompleted(args){
            //code to deal with the completion of the task
    }
    ```

2. Next, you need to register the function with the background task. Here is the code snippet to do that:

    ```
    task = builder.register();
    task.addEventListener("completed",onCompleted);
    ```

3. Put any code that needs to be executed upon task completion in the onCompleted function.

4. Handle the task progress. Similar to the completion event, a task fires a progress event too. You need to write a function that can be used to attach to the progress event of the background task. By subscribing to the progress event, any time a progress event is fired by the task, the function attached to the event is called. Any progress reporting routine can be written in the function. The function takes in two parameters: an IBackgroundTaskRegistration object and a BackgroundTaskProgressEventArgs object. Here is the skeleton of the function that handles the progress event:

    ```
    function onProgress(task, args){
            //add code to perform progress related routine here
    }
    ```

5. Next, you need to register the function with the progress event of the background task. Here is the code snippet to register the function:

    ```
    task = builder.register();
    task.addEventListener("progress", onProgress);
    ```

■ ■ ■

CHAPTER 12

Location and Maps in Windows Apps

Developers who build Windows apps can utilize the capabilities of the Windows device to integrate the location and maps in their apps. In this chapter, you will look at recipes on how to use the location API in Universal Windows Runtime apps.

12.1 Get the Current Location

Problem

You don't know where you are. The Windows app needs to determine and display your current location.

Solution

Use the getGeopositionAsync method of the Geolocator class defined in the Windows.Devices. Geolocation namespace to get the current location from the devices powered by Windows 10.

How It Works

1. Create a new Universal Windows project using the Universal Windows template, which can be found under the **JavaScript ➤ Windows ➤ Universal** node of the **New Project** dialog in Microsoft Visual Studio 2015. This creates a single project in the Visual Studio Solution with the necessary files in it to start with.

2. The first step to integrate the location functionality in the app is to declare the Location capability in the package.appxmanifest file of the project. From Visual Studio Solution Explorer, double-click the **package.appxmanifest** file. In the GUI designer, click the **Capabilities** tab and select **Location**, as shown in Figure 12-1.

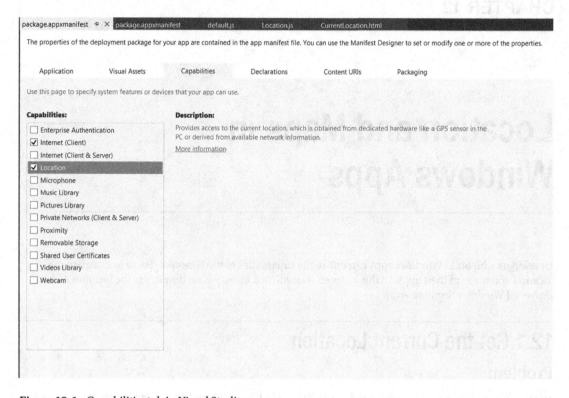

Figure 12-1. Capabilities tab in Visual Studio

3. Open the project **default.html** file and add the following code under the body tag of each file:

```
<div>
    <p>Get the Current Location</p>
    <br />
    <button id="btnLocation">Get Location</button> <br />
</div>
<br />
<div>
    <table>
        <tr>
            <td>
                Latitude
            </td>
            <td >
                <div id="latitude">
                </div>
            </td>
        </tr>
        <tr>
            <td>
                Longitude
            </td>
```

```
            <td>
                <div id="longitude">

                </div>
            </td>
        </tr>
        <tr>
            <td>
                Accuracy
            </td>
            <td>
                <div id="accuracy">
                </div>
            </td>
        </tr>
    </table>
</div>
```

4. Open **default.js (/js/default.js)** in the project and replace the code in the file
   with the following:

```
// For an introduction to the Blank template, see the following documentation:
// http://go.microsoft.com/fwlink/?LinkID=392286
(function () {
    "use strict";
    var app = WinJS.Application;
    var activation = Windows.ApplicationModel.Activation;

    app.onactivated = function (args) {
        if (args.detail.kind === activation.ActivationKind.launch) {
            if (args.detail.previousExecutionState !== activation.
            ApplicationExecutionState.terminated) {
            } else {
            }
            args.setPromise(WinJS.UI.processAll().
                done(function ()
                {
                    // Add an event handler to the button.
                    document.querySelector("#btnLocation").
                    addEventListener("click",
                        getLocation);
                }));

        }
    };
    var geolocation = null;

    function getLocation()
    {
        if (geolocation == null) {
            geolocation = new Windows.Devices.Geolocation.Geolocator();
        }
```

```
        if (geolocation != null) {
            geolocation.getGeopositionAsync().then(getPosition);
        }
    }
    function getPosition(position)
    {
        document.getElementById('latitude').innerHTML = position.coordinate.
        point.position.latitude;
        document.getElementById('longitude').innerHTML = position.coordinate.
        point.position.longitude;
        document.getElementById('accuracy').innerHTML = position.coordinate.
        accuracy;
    }

    app.oncheckpoint = function (args) {

    };

    app.start();
})();
```

The document.querySelector is used to add the click event handler for the btnLocation element. Upon click of the button, the getLocation method is called.

5. To get the current location information, create an instance of the Geolocator class defined in the Windows.Devices.Geolocation namespace and then invoke the getGeopositionAsync method of the Geolocator class. Once the location is retrieved, an action method needs to be defined to perform a certain set of actions. The getPosition method, as shown in the preceding code snippet, takes care of this. The parameter position is of type Geolocation, which can be used to get the current location information like latitude, longitude, accuracy, and so forth.

The next step is to build the project and run it in the emulator or local machine.

6. Choose the **Build** menu and select **Build Solution** from Visual Studio to build the project. Select **Mobile Emulator** from the **Run** drop-down menu in the Visual Studio standard toolbar.

7. When you run the app for the first time on Windows, you are prompted to confirm if it is OK to use your location. Click **Allow** so that the app can use the location.

8. In the application, click the **Get Location** button to display the current location's latitude and longitude, as shown in Figure 12-2.

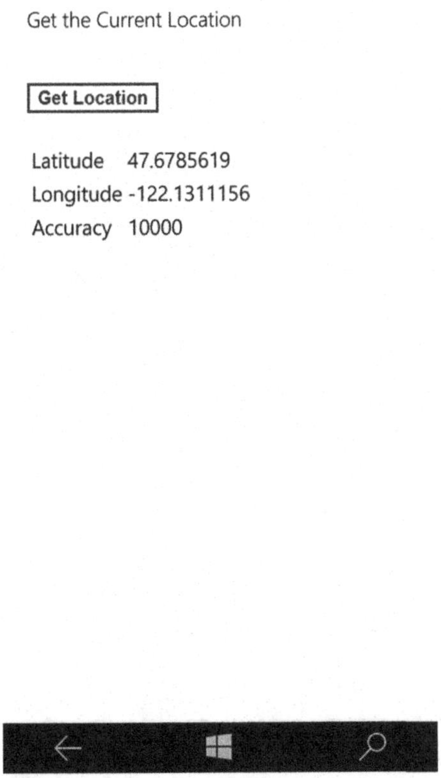

Get the Current Location

Latitude   47.6785619
Longitude -122.1311156
Accuracy   10000

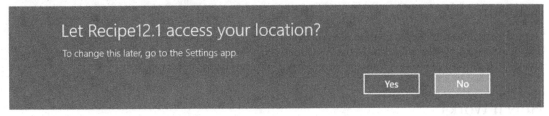

Figure 12-2. *Current location in Windows Mobile app*

9. When you click the app on the local machine, you are prompted with a message, as shown in Figure 12-3. Click the **Allow** button. This displays the current location (see Figure 12-4).

Let Recipe12.1 access your location?

Let Recipe12.1 access your location?
To change this later, go to the Settings app.

Yes   No

Figure 12-3. *Allow current location prompt in Windows desktop family app*

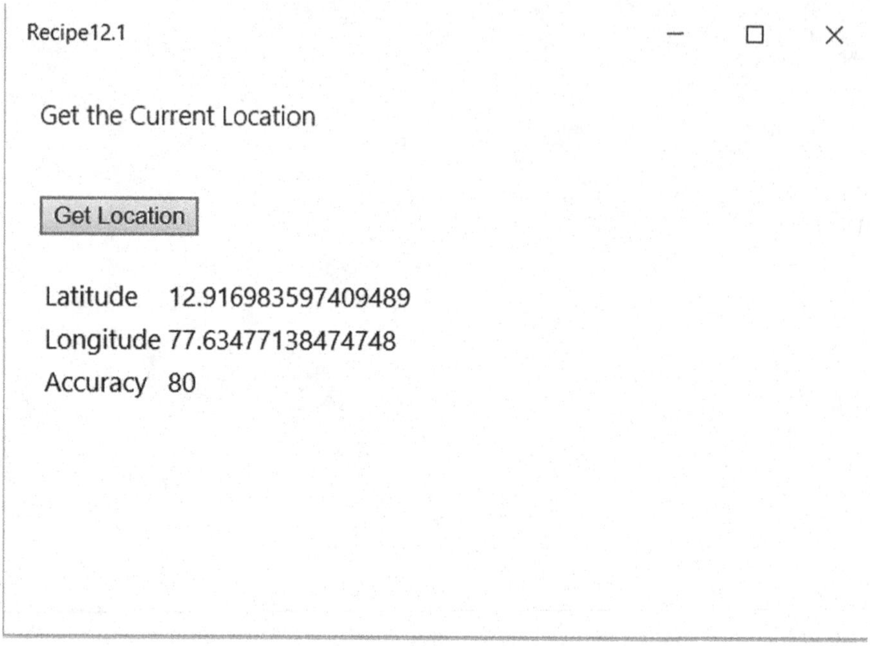

Recipe12.1   —   □   ✕

Get the Current Location

[Get Location]

Latitude   12.916983597409489
Longitude 77.63477138474748
Accuracy 80

Figure 12-4. *Current location in a Windows desktop family app*

■ **Note**   Ensure that Location Services is enabled in your Windows device to get the current location.

12.2 Respond to Geolocator Location Updates

Problem

You want to frequently check if there is any change to the location within the app.

Solution

Use the getGeopositionAsync method of the Geolocator class defined in the Windows.Devices. Geolocation namespace. Subscribe to the PositionChanged and the LocationChanged events to track the change in location and respond from the Windows Mobile or desktop family app.

How It Works

1.   Create a new Universal Windows project using the Universal Windows template, which can be found under **JavaScript ➤ Windows ➤ Universal** node of the New Project dialog in Microsoft Visual Studio 2015. This creates a single project in the Visual Studio Solution with the necessary files in it to start with.

2.   Enable the **Location** capability in the package.appxmanifest file in the project.

3. Open the **default.html** file from Visual Studio Solution Explorer, and then add
    the following code under the body tag of each file.

```html
<div>
    <button id="start">Start Tracking</button><br />
    <br />
    <button id="stop">Stop Tracking</button><br />
</div>
<br />
<div>
    <table>
        <tr>
            <td>
                Latitude
            </td>
            <td>
                <div id="latitude">
                </div>
            </td>
        </tr>
        <tr>
            <td>
                Longitude
            </td>
            <td>
                <div id="longitude">

                </div>
            </td>
        </tr>
        <tr>
            <td>
                Accuracy
            </td>
            <td>
                <div id="accuracy">
                </div>
            </td>
        </tr>
        <tr>
            <td>
                <div id="Status"></div>
            </td>
        </tr>
    </table>
</div>
```

The preceding HTML code is similar to the code in the Recipe 12.1, but includes an additional div tag to
display the status.

4. Open **default.js (/js/default.js)** in the project from Visual Studio Solution
    Explorer and replace the code in the file with the following:

```
(function () {
    "use strict";
    var app = WinJS.Application;
    var activation = Windows.ApplicationModel.Activation;

    app.onactivated = function (args) {
        if (args.detail.kind === activation.ActivationKind.launch) {
            if (args.detail.previousExecutionState !== activation.
            ApplicationExecutionState.terminated) {
            } else {
            }
            args.setPromise(WinJS.UI.processAll().
                    done(function () {

                        // Add an event handler to the button.
                        document.querySelector("#start").addEventListener("click",
                            Starttracking);

                        // Add an event handler to the button.
                        document.querySelector("#stop").addEventListener("click",
                            Stoptracking);

                }));
        }
    };
    var geolocation = null;
    // Start tracking
    function Starttracking() {
        if (geolocation == null)
        {
            geolocation = new Windows.Devices.Geolocation.Geolocator();
            geolocation.reportInterval = 100;
        }
        if (geolocation != null)
        {
            geolocation.addEventListener("positionchanged", onPositionChanged);
            geolocation.addEventListener("statuschanged", onStatusChanged);
        }
    }
    // On change of location position , update the UI
    function onPositionChanged(args) {
        document.getElementById('latitude').innerHTML = args.position.coordinate.
        point.position.latitude;
        document.getElementById('longitude').innerHTML = args.position.
        coordinate.point.position.longitude;
        document.getElementById('accuracy').innerHTML = args.position.coordinate.
        accuracy;
    }
```

```
        // Stop the tracking
        function Stoptracking()
        {
            if (geolocation != null) {
                geolocation.removeEventListener("positionchanged",
                onPositionChanged);
            }
        }
        // event handler for the Status Changed method.
        function onStatusChanged(args) {
            var Status = args.status;
            document.getElementById('Status').innerHTML =
                getStatus(Status);
        }
        // Gets the status
        function getStatus(Status) {
            switch (Status) {
                case Windows.Devices.Geolocation.PositionStatus.ready:
                    return "Ready";
                    break;
                case Windows.Devices.Geolocation.PositionStatus.initializing:
                    return "Initializing";
                    break;
                case Windows.Devices.Geolocation.PositionStatus.disabled:
                    return "Location is disabled . Check the Location settings in
                    your device or Appxmanifest file";
                    break;
                case Windows.Devices.Geolocation.PositionStatus.notInitialized:
                    return "Not Initialized";
                default:
                    return "Status us unknown";
            }
        }

        app.oncheckpoint = function (args) {

        };

        app.start();
    })();
```

The first step is to add the click event handler for the Start Tracking and the Stop Tracking buttons. The document.querySelector is used to add the event listener.

```
        document.querySelector("#start").addEventListener("click",Starttracking);
        document.querySelector("#stop").addEventListener("click",Stoptracking);
```

A new instance of the Geolocator class is created in the Starttracking method and the reportInterval is set. The reportInterval defines the minimum time interval between location updates, in milliseconds.

```
geolocation = new Windows.Devices.Geolocation.Geolocator();
geolocation.reportInterval = 100;
```

The positionchanged and the statuschanged event listeners are added to the geolocation instance:

```
geolocation.addEventListener("positionchanged", onPositionChanged);
geolocation.addEventListener("statuschanged", onStatusChanged);
```

The positionchanged event is raised when there is a change in location. The statuschanged event is raised when the ability of the Geolocator to provide updated location changes; for example, if the location is disabled or initialized, and so forth.

The getStatus method returns the message based on the Windows.Devices.Geolocation.PositionStatus.

When you don't need to track the location, just remove the positionchanged event listener, as follows:
`geolocation.removeEventListener("positionchanged", onPositionChanged);`

5. Now, build and run the project in the emulator.

6. In the app, click the **Start Tracking** button. The app subscribes for the location updates via the Geolocator's Onpositionchanged event and displays the location information (see Figure 12-5).

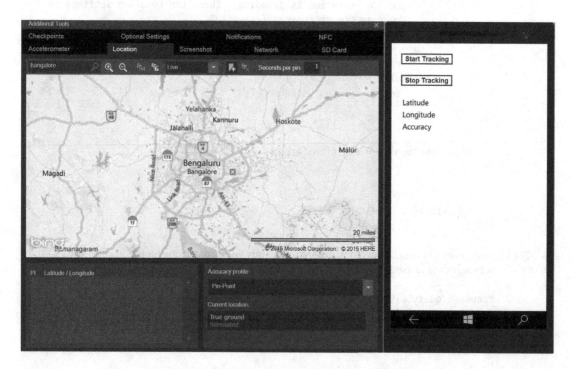

Figure 12-5. *Location updates using the Windows Mobile emulator's additional tools*

When the app is run on Windows desktop using the Local Machine option, you should see the screen shown in Figure 12-6.

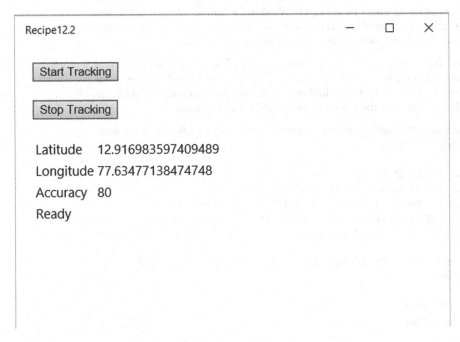

Figure 12-6. *Location updates in Windows desktop using Local Machine option*

■ **Note**   The Windows Mobile emulator provides additional tools that let the developer test location-based apps during development, as shown in Figure 12-5.

12.3 Detect the User's Location with HTML5

Problem

You don't know where you are. The Windows app needs to determine and display your current location.

Solution

Apart from the Windows Runtime API, the WinJS app can utilize the W3C Geolocation API to detect a user's current location by using HTML5 from the Windows app.

How It Works

1. Create a new Universal Windows project using the Universal Windows template, which can be found under **JavaScript ➤ Windows ➤ Universal** node of the New Project dialog in Microsoft Visual Studio 2015. This creates a single project in the Visual Studio Solution with the necessary files in it to start with.

2. The first step to integrate the location functionality in the app is to declare the Location capability in the package.appxmanifest file of the Windows app. From Visual Studio Solution Explorer, double-click the **package.appxmanifest** file. In the GUI designer, click the **Capabilities** tab and select **Location**.

3. Open the **default.html** file of the Windows app and add the following code under the body tag of the file.

```
<h1>Current Location using HTML5</h1>
<button id="btnLocation">Get Location</button> <br />
<label>Latitude</label> <div id="latitude"></div><br />
<label>Longitude</label> <div id="longitude"> </div><br />
<div id="status"> </div><br />
```

4. Open **default.js (/js/default.js)** in the project. Replace the code in the file with the following:

```
(function () {
    "use strict";

    var app = WinJS.Application;
    var activation = Windows.ApplicationModel.Activation;

    app.onactivated = function (args) {
        if (args.detail.kind === activation.ActivationKind.launch) {
            if (args.detail.previousExecutionState !== activation.
            ApplicationExecutionState.terminated) {
            } else {
            }
            args.setPromise(WinJS.UI.processAll().
                done(function () {

                    // Add an event handler to the button.
                    document.querySelector("#btnLocation").
                    addEventListener("click",
                        GetLocation);

            }));

        }
    };
```

```
    var nav = null;
    function GetLocation() {
        if (nav == null) {
            nav = window.navigator;
        }

        var geoloc = nav.geolocation;
        if (geoloc != null) {
            geoloc.getCurrentPosition(Onsuccess, Onerror);
        }
    }

    // after getting the location information
    function Onsuccess(position) {
        document.getElementById("latitude").innerHTML =
            position.coords.latitude;
        document.getElementById("longitude").innerHTML =
            position.coords.longitude;

    }
    // On error when trying to get the location
    function Onerror(error) {
        var errorMessage = "";
        switch (error.code) {
            case error.PERMISSION_DENIED:
                errorMessage = "Location is disabled";
                break;
            case error.POSITION_UNAVAILABLE:
                errorMessage = "Data unavailable";
                break;
            case error.TIMEOUT:
                errorMessage = "Timeout error";
                break;
            default:
                break;
        }

        document.getElementById("status").innerHTML = errorMessage;
    }

    app.oncheckpoint = function (args) {
    };

    app.start();
})();
```

5. Add the click event handler for the Get Location button. The document. querySelector is used to get the button control, and the addEventListener method is used to add the click event and map it to the GetLocation method.

```
document.querySelector("#btnLocation").addEventListener("click",
                            GetLocation);
```

The getCurrentPosition method of the window.navigator.geolocation class is used to get the user's current location.

```
if (nav == null) {
        nav = window.navigator;
    }

    var geoloc = nav.geolocation;
    if (geoloc != null) {
        geoloc.getCurrentPosition(Onsuccess, Onerror);
    }
```

Once the current position is successfully retrieved, the control is passed to the Onsuccess method to process the coordinates and display it. On an error, the Onerror method is invoked, which displays the error message in case of an issue getting the location information.

6. Build and run the project on the local machine.

7. Click the **Get Location** button in the app, as shown in Figure 12-7. The app immediately prompts the user to allow the app to use the location API. Once you click **Allow**, you should immediately see the latitude and the longitude of the current location.

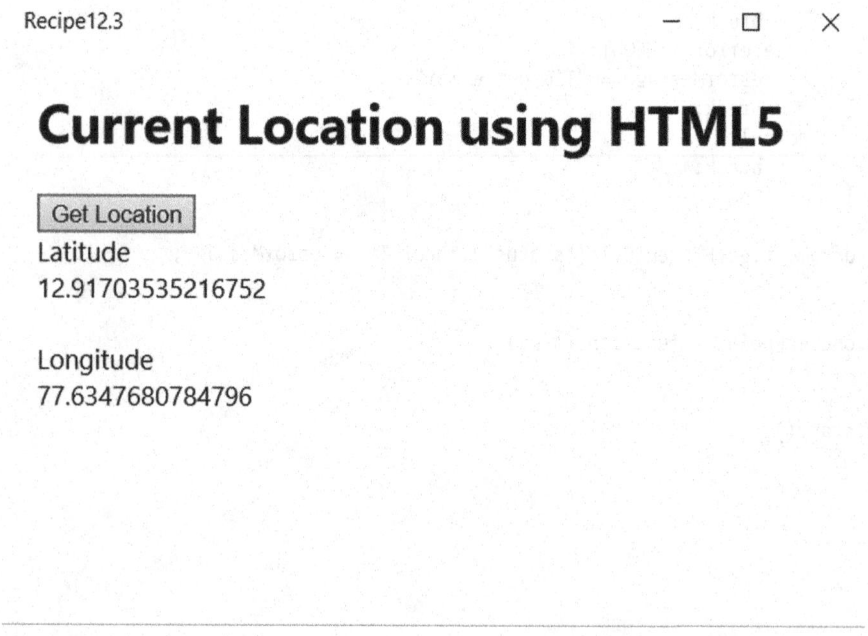

Recipe12.3   —   □   ✕

Current Location using HTML5

Get Location

Latitude
12.91703535216752

Longitude
77.6347680784796

Figure 12-7.   *Current location in Windows Store app using HTML5*

■ **Note** The W3C Geolocation API currently works only for the Windows desktop device family apps. When you run the same on the Windows Mobile emulator, the status displays as disabled.

12.4 Detect Location Updates with HTML5

Problem

You want to frequently check if there is any change in the location within the app.

Solution

You can use the W3C Geolocation API in HTML5 to detect location changes from your Windows app.

How It Works

1. Create a new Universal Windows project using the Universal Windows template, which can be found under **JavaScript ➤ Windows ➤ Universal** node of the New Project dialog in Microsoft Visual Studio 2015. This creates a single project in the Visual Studio Solution with the necessary files in it to start with.

2. The first step to integrate the location functionality in the app is to declare the Location capability in the package.appxmanifest file of the Windows app. From Visual Studio Solution Explorer, double-click the **package.appxmanifest** file. In the GUI designer, click the **Capabilities** tab and check **Location**.

3. Open the **default.html** file of the Windows app and add the following code under the body tag of the file:

```
<h1>Current Location using HTML5</h1>
<button id="btnstart">Start</button> <button id="btnstop">Stop</button> <br />
<label>Latitude</label> <div id="latitude"></div><br />
<label>Longitude</label> <div id="longitude"> </div><br />
<div id="status"> </div><br />
```

4. Open **default.js (/js/default.js)** in the Windows project and replace the code in the file with the following:

```
(function () {
    "use strict";

    var app = WinJS.Application;
    var activation = Windows.ApplicationModel.Activation;
```

```
        app.onactivated = function (args) {
            if (args.detail.kind === activation.ActivationKind.launch) {
                if (args.detail.previousExecutionState !== activation.
                ApplicationExecutionState.terminated) {
                } else {
                }
                args.setPromise(WinJS.UI.processAll().
                    done(function () {
                        document.querySelector("#btnstart").addEventListener("click",
                            starttracking);
                        document.querySelector("#btnstop").addEventListener("click",
                            stoptracking);

                    }));

            }
        };
        var geolocation = null;
        var positionInstance;
        // on click of the start tracking
        function starttracking() {
            if (geolocation == null) {
                geolocation = window.navigator.geolocation;
            }
            if (geolocation != null) {
                positionInstance = geolocation.watchPosition(onsuccess, onerror);
            }
        }
        // on click of the stop tracking button
        function stoptracking() {
            geolocation.clearWatch(positionInstance);
        }
        // on success of getting the location
        function onsuccess(pos) {
            document.getElementById('latitude').innerHTML = pos.coords.latitude;
            document.getElementById('longitude').innerHTML = pos.coords.longitude;
        }

        // On error when trying to get the location
        function Onerror(error) {
            var errorMessage = "";
            switch (error.code) {
                case error.PERMISSION_DENIED:
                    errorMessage = "Location is disabled";
                    break;
                case error.POSITION_UNAVAILABLE:
                    errorMessage = "Data unavailable";
                    break;
```

```
            case error.TIMEOUT:
                errorMessage = "Timeout error";
                break;
            default:
                break;
        }

        document.getElementById("status").innerHTML = errorMessage;
    }

    app.oncheckpoint = function (args) {

    };

    app.start();
})();
```

5. Add the click event handler for the Start Tracking and Stop Tracking buttons. The document.querySelector is used to get the button control and the addEventListener method is used to add the click event to the tracking buttons.

The tracking is handled by the watchPosition method of the window.navigator.geolocation class, as follows:

```
if (geolocation == null) {
        geolocation = window.navigator.geolocation;
}
if (geolocation != null) {
        positionInstance = geolocation.watchPosition(onsuccess, onerror);
}
```

When the coordinates are retrieved, the Onsuccess method is invoked, which is used to process the result and display it. When there is any issue getting the location, the Onerror method is invoked with the appropriate error code, which can be used by the developer to display a user-friendly message for each error code.

To stop the track, the clearWatch method of the geolocation needs to be called by providing the watchid parameter that was retrieved initially with the watchPosition function.

```
geolocation.clearWatch(positionInstance);
```

6. Build and run the project on the local machine.

7. In the app, click the **Start** button. The app immediately prompts the user to allow the app to use the location API. Once you click **Allow**, you should immediately see the latitude and the longitude of the current location, and the tracking of the location begins, as shown in Figure 12-8.

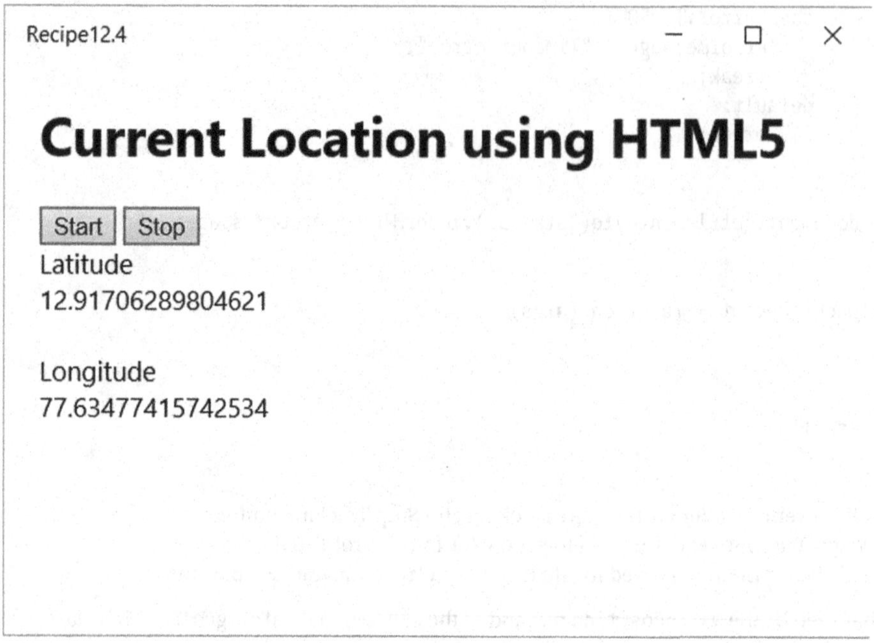

```
Recipe12.4                                        —   □   ✕

Current Location using HTML5

[ Start ] [ Stop ]
Latitude
12.91706289804621

Longitude
77.63477415742534
```

Figure 12-8. *Detect location updates in Windows Store app using HTML5*

■ **Note** The W3C Geolocation API currently works only for the Windows desktop device family. It is not supported on Windows 10 Mobile.

12.5 Display Maps in the Built-in Maps App

Problem

You want to display a map and plot the location in the built-in Maps app.

Solution

Use the `bingmaps:` URI scheme from your Universal Windows app to display the map in the built-in Maps app.

How It Works

1. Create a new Universal Windows project using the Universal Windows template, which can be found under **JavaScript ➤ Windows ➤ Universal** node of the New Project dialog in Microsoft Visual Studio 2015. This creates a single project in the Visual Studio Solution with the necessary files in it to start with.

2. Open the **default.html** file from the project, and add the following code under the body tag of the file:

```
<h1>Display Map</h1>
<button id="btnDisplayMap">Display Map</button> <br />
```

3. Open **default.js (/js/default.js)** in the project and replace the code in the file with the following:

```
(function () {
    "use strict";

    var app = WinJS.Application;
    var activation = Windows.ApplicationModel.Activation;

    app.onactivated = function (args) {
        if (args.detail.kind === activation.ActivationKind.launch) {
            if (args.detail.previousExecutionState !== activation.
            ApplicationExecutionState.terminated) {
            } else {
            }
            args.setPromise(WinJS.UI.processAll().
                done(function () {

                    // Add an event handler to the button.
                    document.querySelector("#btnDisplayMap").
                    addEventListener("click",
                        DisplayMap);

            }));
        }
    };
// Method to display the Built-in Map.
    function DisplayMap() {

        var latitude = "12.917264";
        var longitude = "77.634786";
        var uri = "bingmaps:?cp="+ latitude + "~" + longitude + "lvl=10";
        Windows.System.Launcher.launchUriAsync(new Windows.Foundation.Uri(uri));
    }
    app.oncheckpoint = function (args) {

    };

    app.start();
})();
```

The `bingmaps:` URI scheme can be used to launch the Maps app from your Windows app. The LaunchUriAsync method is generally used to launch another app from the Windows Store app using the URI scheme. In this case, the `bingmaps:` URI scheme is used to launch the Maps app.

■ **Note** When using the `LaunchUriAsync` method, the user is taken to another app on the device and the user has to manually return to your app after using the Maps app.

Developers can provide appropriate parameters to the URI scheme to display the location, or even to display the route on the map. For example, the following URI scheme opens the Bing Maps app and displays a map centered over the city of Bangalore in India:

```
Bingmaps:? Cp=12.917264~77.634786
```

Developers can use the some of the parameters shown in Table 12-1 along with the `bingmaps:` URI scheme.

Table 12-1. Examples of the Different Parameters Used with the bingmaps: URI

Parameter	Example
cp (Center Point)	cp=40.726966~-74.006076
bb (Bounding box)	bb=39.719_-74.52~41.71_-73.5
q (Query term or search term)	q=mexican%20restaurants
lvl (Zoom Level)	lvl=10.50
trfc (Specify to include traffic information in map)	trfc=1
rtp (route)	rtp=adr.One%20Microsoft%20Way,%20Redmond,%20WA~pos.45.23423_-122.1232

■ **Note** Bing Maps includes a lot of parameters; Table 12-1 shows only a few of them. More information about the parameters for Bing Maps can be found at `http://msdn.microsoft.com/en-us/library/windows/apps/xaml/jj635237.aspx`.

4. Now, build the project and run it. Click the **Display Map** button on the screen. If you are running the Windows app on the Windows Mobile emulator, you should see the built-in map with the location being plotted, as shown in Figure 12-9.

Figure 12-9. Built-in maps in the Windows Mobile app

If the app is run on Windows desktop using the Local Machine option, the Maps app shows the location (see Figure 12-10).

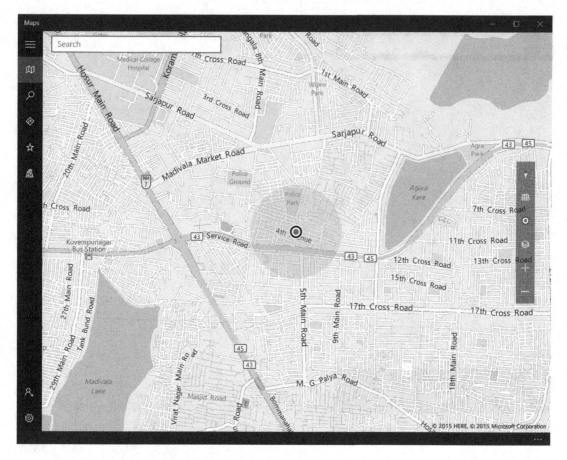

Figure 12-10. *Built-in maps in Windows desktop family*

■ **Note**   The `bingmaps:` URI scheme is a replacement for the MapsTask launcher that was available in Windows Phone 8.1 and earlier versions.

12.6 Display Directions in the Built-in Maps App

Problem

You want to display the directions or route from one location to another in the built-in Maps apps of the Windows device.

Solution

The `bingmaps:` URI scheme with the `rtp` parameter can be used from your Windows app to display the map in the built-in Maps app, as well as show the point-to-point driving directions from one location to another.

How It Works

1. Create a new Universal Windows project using the Universal Windows template, which can be found under **JavaScript ➤ Windows ➤ Universal** node of the New Project dialog in Microsoft Visual Studio 2015. This creates a single project in the Visual Studio Solution with the necessary files in it to start with.

2. Open the **default.html** file from the project using Visual Studio Solution Explorer, and add the following code under the body tag of each file:

```
<h1>Display Map</h1>
<button id="btnDisplayRoute">Display Route</button> <br />
```

3. Open **default.js (/js/default.js)** in the project and replace the code in the file with the following:

```
(function () {
    "use strict";

    var app = WinJS.Application;
    var activation = Windows.ApplicationModel.Activation;

    app.onactivated = function (args) {
        if (args.detail.kind === activation.ActivationKind.launch) {
            if (args.detail.previousExecutionState !== activation.
            ApplicationExecutionState.terminated) {
            } else {
            }
            args.setPromise(WinJS.UI.processAll().
                done(function () {
                    // Add an event handler to the button.
                    document.querySelector("#btnDisplayRoute").
                    addEventListener("click",
                        DisplayRoute);

                }));
        }
    };
    function DisplayRoute() {

        var fromAddress = "adr.HSR Layout 5th sector, Bangalore";
        var toAddress = "adr.Microsoft India,Signature Building,Bangalore";
        var uri = "bingmaps:?rtp=" + fromAddress + "~"+ toAddress;
        Windows.System.Launcher.launchUriAsync(new Windows.Foundation.Uri(uri));
        //Windows.Services.Maps.MapManager.showDownloadedMapsUI()
    }
    app.oncheckpoint = function (args) {
    };

    app.start();
})();
```

The `bingmaps:` URI scheme can be used to launch the Maps app from your Windows apps. The `LaunchUriASync` method is generally used to launch another app from the Windows app using the URI scheme. In this case, the `bingmaps:` URI scheme with the `rtp` parameter is used to launch the built-in map and then display the driving directions from the specified address to the specified location.

■ **Note** When the `LaunchUriASync` method is used, the user is taken to another app on the device; the user has to manually return to your app after using the Maps app.

Developers can include the `trfc=1` parameter along with the URI to display the traffic information.

```
"bingmaps:?rtp=adr.HSR Layout 5th sector, Bangalore~adr.Microsoft India,Signature
Building,Bangalore&trfc=1";
```

In the preceding URI scheme, the `adr.` defines the address. The `rtp` takes two waypoints to find the route. The `trfc` parameter is provided to display the traffic information as well.

4.   Build the project and run it. Click the **Display Map** button on the screen. If you are running the Windows app on a Windows Mobile emulator, you should see the built-in map with the location being plotted, as shown in Figure 12-11.

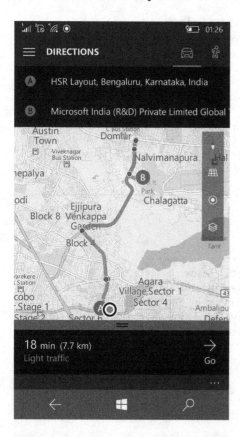

Figure 12-11. Directions in Windows Mobile

If the Windows app is run on the desktop family, the Maps app is used to show the location, as shown in Figure 12-12.

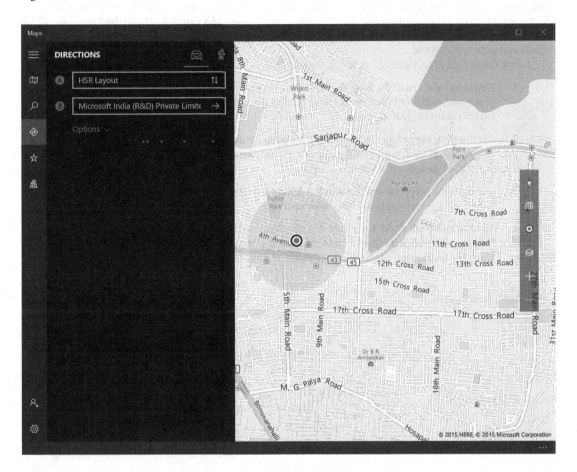

Figure 12-12. *Directions in Windows app*

■ **Note**　The `bingmaps:` URI scheme is a replacement for the MapsDirectionsTask launcher in Windows Phone 8.

12.7 Bing Maps Control in the Windows Store App

Problem

You want to use the maps in your Windows app instead of launching the built-in Maps app.

Solution

Use the Bing Maps AJAX Control 7.0 to add map functionality within the Universal Windows app developed using WinJS.

How It Works

Bing Maps is an online mapping service from Microsoft that allows users to use the map solution from Microsoft and utilize various features of the Bing maps. Bing Maps AJAX Control 7.0 and the Bing Maps REST Services provide unique opportunities for developers to easily include location and search features into their mobile and web applications.

To use Bing Maps AJAX Control 7.0, follow these steps:

1. Download and install the **Bing Maps SDK** for Windows Store apps (for Windows 8.1, which also works for Windows 10) from http://go.microsoft.com/fwlink/?LinkID=322092.

2. Get the **Bing Maps** key. Go to the **Bing Maps Account Center** at https://www.bingmapsportal.com and create a key for the application. You have to use this key in the Windows Store app.

3. Create a new project using the Windows Store app template in Microsoft Visual Studio 2013, which creates a Windows Store app.

4. Add the reference of the Bing Maps for JavaScript to the project. In Solution Explorer, right-click the project references and select **Add Reference** and **Bing Maps for JavaScript.** Click **OK**, as shown in Figure 12-13.

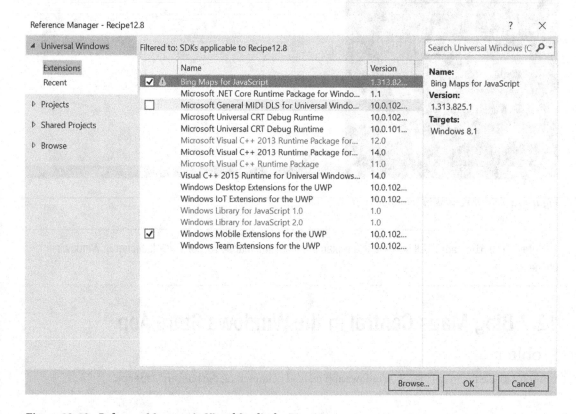

Figure 12-13. Reference Manager in Visual Studio for Bing Maps

5. Open the **default.html** file in the project and add the following code in the body
    tag of the file:

    ```
    <div id="myMap"></div>
    ```

6. In the `default.html` file, also add the reference to the Bing Maps JavaScript files:

    ```
    <!-- Bing Maps references -->
        <script type="text/javascript" src="ms-appx:///Bing.Maps.JavaScript//js/
    veapicore.js"></script>
        <script type="text/javascript" src="ms-appx:///Bing.Maps.JavaScript//js/
    veapimodules.js"></script>
    ```

7. Open **default.js (/js/default.js)** and replace the code in the file with the
    following:

    ```
    (function () {
        "use strict";

        var app = WinJS.Application;
        var activation = Windows.ApplicationModel.Activation;

        app.onactivated = function (args) {
            if (args.detail.kind === activation.ActivationKind.launch) {
                if (args.detail.previousExecutionState !== activation.
                ApplicationExecutionState.terminated) {
                } else {
                }
                args.setPromise(WinJS.UI.processAll().
                    done(function () {
                        Microsoft.Maps.loadModule('Microsoft.Maps.Map', { callback:
                        GetMap });

                    }));
            }
        };
        var map;
        function GetMap() {
            //   Microsoft.Maps.loadModule('Microsoft.Maps.Map', { callback: GetMap });
            var loc = new Microsoft.Maps.Location(13.0220, 77.4908);
            // Initialize the map
            map = new Microsoft.Maps.Map(document.getElementById("myMap"), {
                credentials: "Bing Map Key",
                zoom: 10
            });
            var pin = new Microsoft.Maps.Pushpin(loc);
            map.entities.push(pin);
    ```

```
            // Center the map on the location
            map.setView({ center: loc, zoom: 10 });
        }

        app.oncheckpoint = function (args) {

        };

        app.start();
    })();
```

The `loadModule` of the `Microsoft.Maps` function needs to be called first to load the map. `loadModule` has an optional culture parameter that can be used to identify the localized language and the region. The GetMap callback function is specified for `loadModule`.

```
Microsoft.Maps.loadModule('Microsoft.Maps.Map', { callback: GetMap });
```

An instance of the `Microsoft.Maps.Map` is created by specifying the container `div` element and the Bing Map API key.

```
// Initialize the map
map = new Microsoft.Maps.Map(document.getElementById("myMap"), {
    credentials: "Bing Map API Key",
});
```

The location on the map where the pushpin is to be added is identified using the `map.entities.push` method.

```
var loc = new Microsoft.Maps.Location(13.0220, 77.4908);
var pin = new Microsoft.Maps.Pushpin(loc);
map.entities.push(pin);
```

Finally, the map is displayed by setting the location at the center and with a zoom level value of 10.

8. Build the application and run it in the Windows emulator. You should be able to view the map and the pushpin added to the map, as shown in Figure 12-14.

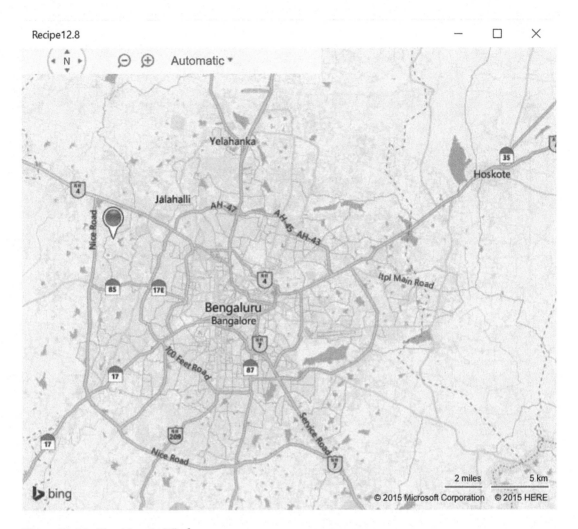

Figure 12-14. *Bing Maps in Windows app*

The Bing Maps AJAX Control provides additional APIs that let developers integrate additional Maps functionalities, such as displaying traffic information, directions, and so forth.

Currently, the WinJS library does not provide the Maps control out of the box in the SDK, and hence Bing Maps AJAX Control is a good alternate solution for the same.

■ ■ ■

CHAPTER 13

Building Apps That Connect to the Cloud

Microsoft Azure Mobile Services provides one of the easiest ways for developers to store data from a Windows app to the SQL Azure database in the cloud. By using Microsoft Azure Mobile Services, developers need not worry about creating and hosting their own web service. Most things are handled by Microsoft Azure Mobile Services.

This chapter covers some of the recipes on setting up and using Microsoft Azure Mobile Services from your Universal Windows app for data storage and retrieval.

13.1 Creating a New Mobile Service in Microsoft Azure

Problem

You need to create a new mobile service in Microsoft Azure Mobile Services that can be utilized by your Universal Windows app.

Solution

Log in to the Microsoft Azure Management portal and use the Mobile Services section to create a new mobile service.

How It Works

The Microsoft Azure Mobile Management portal provides the necessary options for developers to manage various resources, like virtual machines, mobile services, cloud services, and so forth.

Follow these steps to create a new mobile service in Microsoft Azure:

1. Log in to the Microsoft Azure Management portal by navigating to **http://manage.windowsazure.com** and providing your login credentials.

2. You can create a new mobile service by clicking the +**New** button in the bottom bar and then selecting **Compute ➤ Mobile Service ➤ Create**, as shown in Figure 13-1.

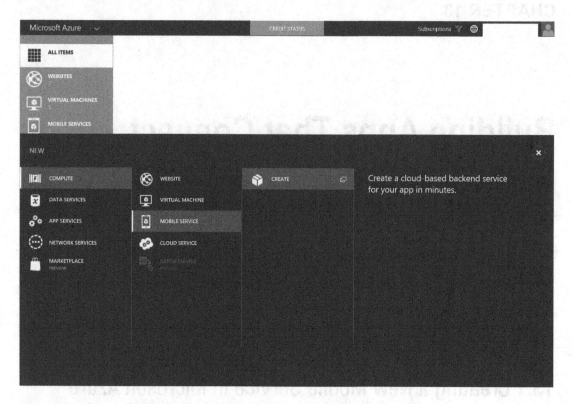

Figure 13-1. *Microsoft Azure dashboard for creating a new mobile service*

3. Provide the details of the mobile service. This includes the URL to access the mobile service, subscription, region, back end, and so forth. You can provide the Mobile Service name as **winjsrecipes**. Currently, Microsoft Azure supports JavaScript and .NET back ends. Select **JavaScript** in this recipe and click the **Next** button, as shown in Figure 13-2.

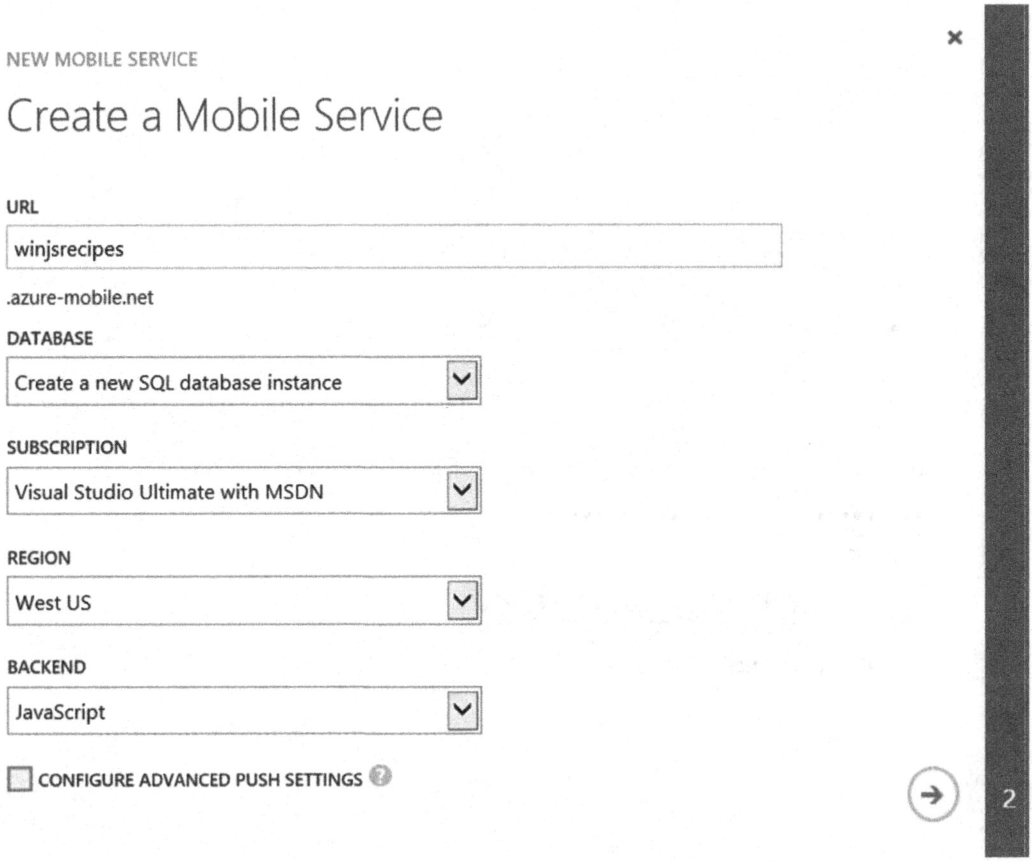

NEW MOBILE SERVICE

Create a Mobile Service

URL

winjsrecipes

.azure-mobile.net

DATABASE

Create a new SQL database instance

SUBSCRIPTION

Visual Studio Ultimate with MSDN

REGION

West US

BACKEND

JavaScript

☐ CONFIGURE ADVANCED PUSH SETTINGS ❓

Figure 13-2. *New Mobile Service dialog*

4. If you selected **Create a new SQL database instance**, you have to provide the existing database settings information, as shown in Figure 13-3. Complete the mobile service creation.

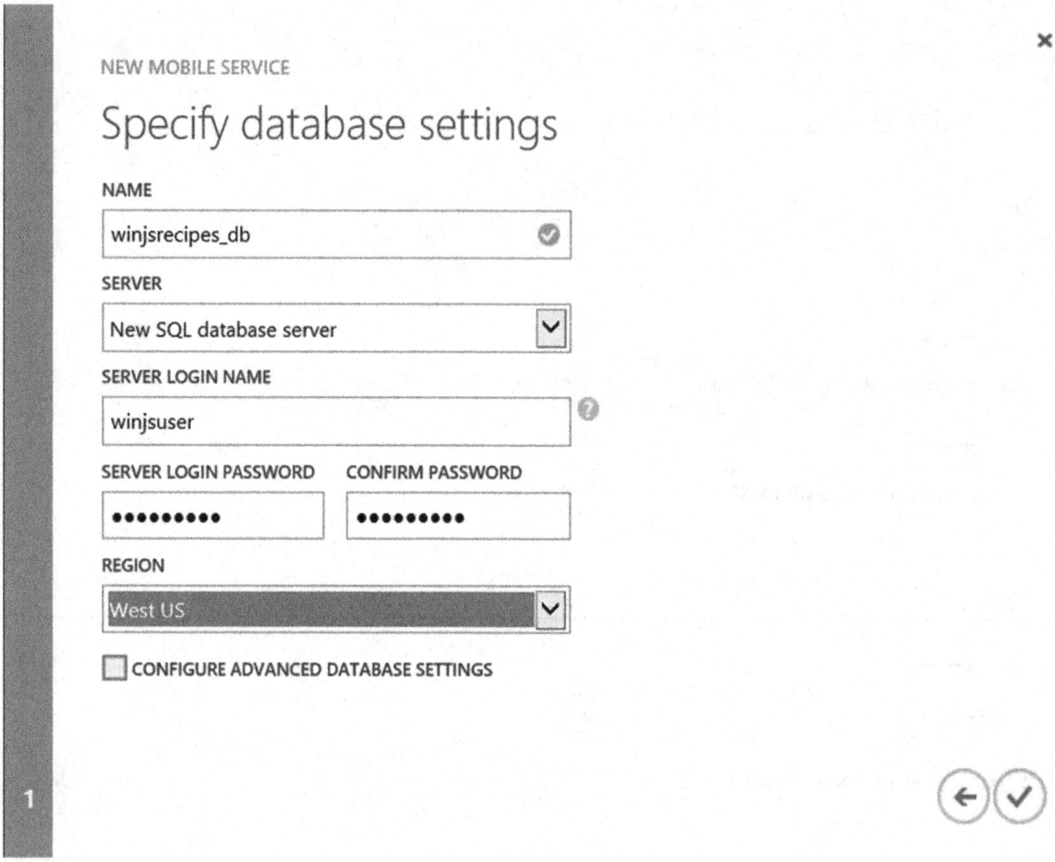

NEW MOBILE SERVICE

Specify database settings

NAME

winjsrecipes_db

SERVER

New SQL database server

SERVER LOGIN NAME

winjsuser

SERVER LOGIN PASSWORD   CONFIRM PASSWORD

•••••••••   •••••••••

REGION

West US

☐ CONFIGURE ADVANCED DATABASE SETTINGS

Figure 13-3. *New Mobile Service database settings dialog*

5.   Within a few minutes, the mobile service is ready and displayed in the Mobile
Service overview screen.

You can also use Visual Studio 2015 to create the mobile service in Microsoft Azure. To create a mobile
service from Visual Studio 2015, follow these steps:

1.   Launch Visual Studio 2015 and open the **Server Explorer** window.

2.   In the Server Explorer window, right-click **Azure** and select Conn**ect to
Microsoft Azure...** in the context menu, as seen in Figure 13-4. Provide your
Microsoft Azure login credentials. This imports the Azure subscription to Visual
Studio.

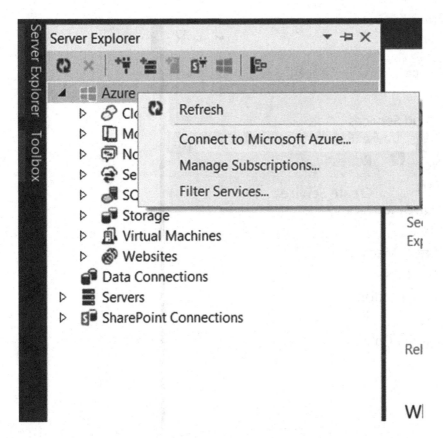

Figure 13-4. Connect to Azure from the Visual Studio Server Explorer window

3. The next step is to create the mobile service from Server Explorer. Right-click **Mobile Services** and select **Create Service**, as demonstrated in Figure 13-5.

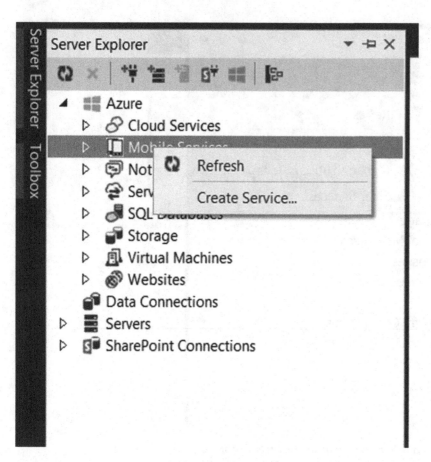

Figure 13-5. Create a Service from Visual Studio 2015

4. In the Create Mobile Service dialog, provide the necessary information for the mobile service to be created, which includes the URL, region, database information, and so forth. Name the recipe **winjs**, as shown in Figure 13-6.

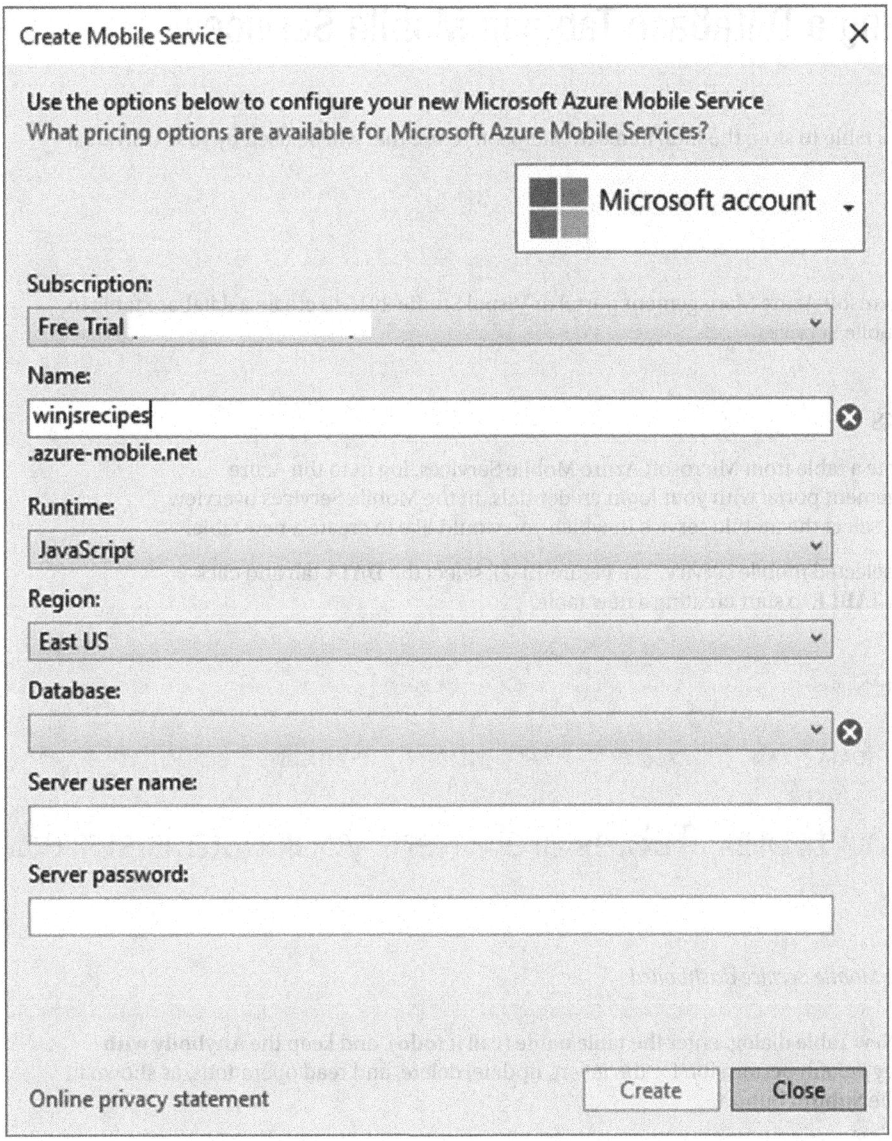

Create Mobile Service ✕

Use the options below to configure your new Microsoft Azure Mobile Service
What pricing options are available for Microsoft Azure Mobile Services?

■■ Microsoft account ▾
■■

Subscription:
Free Trial ▾

Name:
winjsrecipes ❌
.azure-mobile.net

Runtime:
JavaScript ▾

Region:
East US ▾

Database:
▾ ❌

Server user name:

Server password:

Online privacy statement   Create   Close

Figure 13-6. New Mobile Service dialog in Visual Studio 2015

■ **Note**   You need to have a Microsoft Azure subscription. If you haven't yet subscribed to it, then you need to visit `http://azure.microsoft.com/en-us/`. You can get a free trial account if you want to try Microsoft Azure.

13.2 Creating a Database Table in Mobile Services

Problem

You need to create a table to store the todo items in Microsoft Azure that will be used by your Universal Windows app.

Solution

You can use the Microsoft Azure Management portal or Visual Studio 2015 to create a database table in Microsoft Azure Mobile Services.

How It Works

1. To create a table from Microsoft Azure Mobile Services, log in to the Azure Management portal with your login credentials. In the Mobile Services overview screen, select the mobile service in which you would like to create a new table.

2. In the selected mobile service (see Figure 13-7), select the **DATA** tab and click **ADD A TABLE** to start creating a new table.

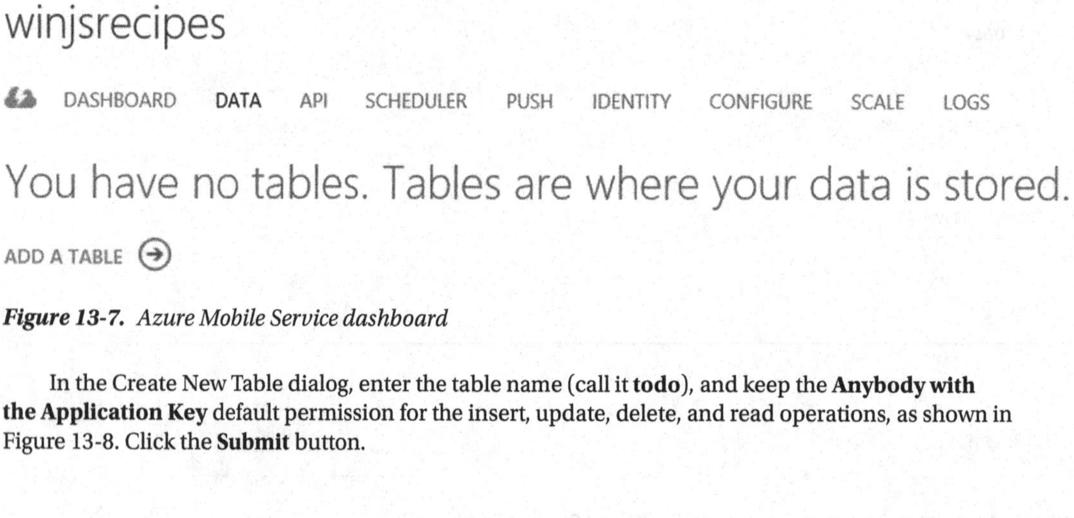

winjsrecipes

DASHBOARD   **DATA**   API   SCHEDULER   PUSH   IDENTITY   CONFIGURE   SCALE   LOGS

You have no tables. Tables are where your data is stored.

ADD A TABLE ➔

Figure 13-7. Azure Mobile Service dashboard

In the Create New Table dialog, enter the table name (call it **todo**), and keep the **Anybody with the Application Key** default permission for the insert, update, delete, and read operations, as shown in Figure 13-8. Click the **Submit** button.

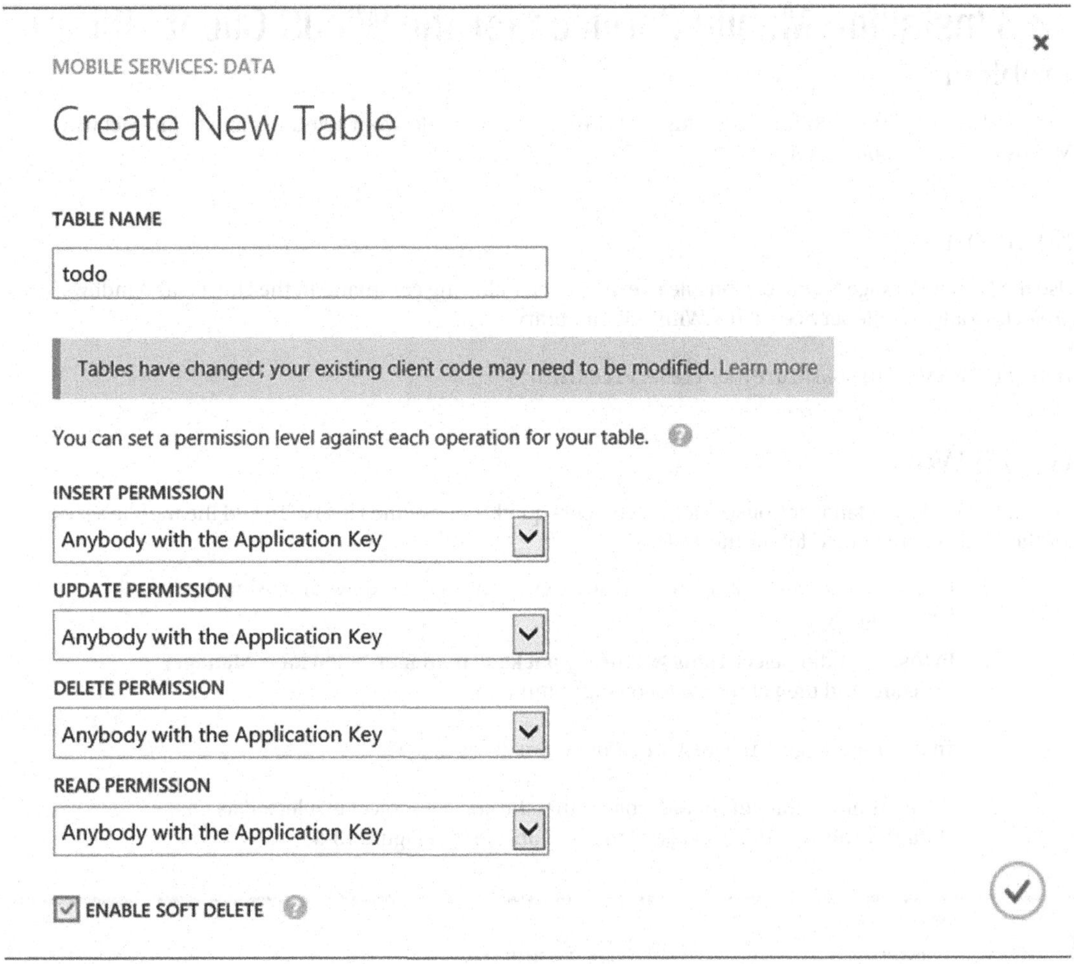

MOBILE SERVICES: DATA

Create New Table

TABLE NAME

todo

Tables have changed; your existing client code may need to be modified. Learn more

You can set a permission level against each operation for your table. ②

INSERT PERMISSION

Anybody with the Application Key

UPDATE PERMISSION

Anybody with the Application Key

DELETE PERMISSION

Anybody with the Application Key

READ PERMISSION

Anybody with the Application Key

☑ ENABLE SOFT DELETE ②

Figure 13-8. *Table creation within the Mobile Services in Microsoft Azure*

Note that you did not specify the columns for the todo table. One option is to go ahead and add the columns to the table from the dashboard, which is a preferred option. The other option is to use the Dynamic schema, where the columns are created dynamically based on the data that you insert (which makes it easier to develop a new mobile service). Use the second option in this recipe. Developers can disable the Dynamic schema from the dashboard.

13.3 Installing Mobile Services for the WinJS Client Library

Problem

You need to install the mobile services for the WinJS client library for your Windows app to interact with Microsoft Azure Mobile Services.

Solution

Use the NuGet Package Manager Console to execute the following command in the Universal Windows projects to add mobile services to the WinJS client library:

```
Install-Package WindowsAzure.MobileServices.Winjs
```

How It Works

The NuGet Package Manager Console lets developers quickly install the library. To add the mobile services for the WinJS client library, follow these steps.

1. Launch Visual Studio 2015 and create a new Universal Windows app using the JavaScript template.

2. In Visual Studio, select **Tools ➤ Library package manager ➤ Package Manager Console**, and then enter the following command:

    ```
    install-package WindowsAzure.MobileServices.WinJS
    ```

3. Before running this command, ensure that the correct project is selected as **Default project** in the Package Manager Console (see Figure 13-9).

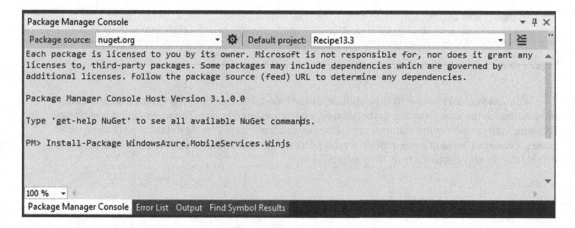

Figure 13-9. Project selection in the Package Manager Console

Once the installation is successful, you will see the new JavaScript files in the JS folder of the project in the Solution Explorer, as shown in Figure 13-10.

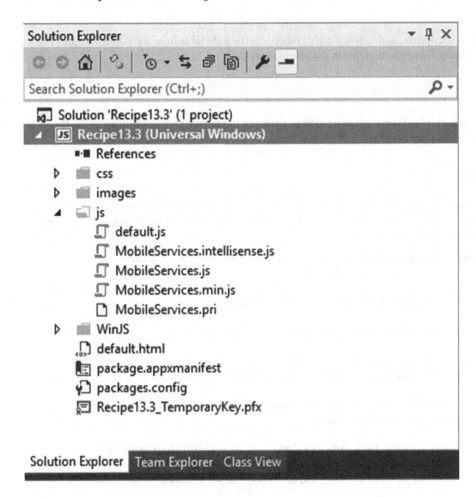

Figure 13-10. *Universal project in Solution Explorer after installation of library*

4. To use the WinJS library for mobile services, you must add a reference to the MobileServices.min.js script in the HTML page.

    ```
    <script src="js/MobileServices.min.js"></script>
    ```

    You can now access the Mobile Services client library from your Windows Store project.

13.4 Performing the CRUD Operation

Problem

You need to create, read, update, and delete (CRUD) records in the todo table from the Windows app. (The creation of the todo table was demonstrated in the previous recipe.)

Solution

You can perform the basic CRUD operations for tables created in the mobile service by using the methods exposed via the mobile service library.

How It Works

In the previous recipe, you created a mobile service with the name winjsrecipes and a table called todo. In this recipe, you will explore how to interact with the todo database table from the Windows apps.Microsoft Azure Mobile Services:CRUD operations:

1. Open the **default.html** page in the Windows app and add the following reference to the mobile service library head section:

    ```
    <script src="js/MobileServices.min.js"></script>
    ```

2. In the same file, add the following code to the body tag.

    ```
    <div style="margin:38px 18px 18px 18px">
            <h4 style="margin-bottom:18px">winjsrecipes</h4>

            <div>Enter some text below and click Save to insert a new TodoItem item
            into your database</div>

            <input type="text" id="textInput" style="width:240px;vertical-
            align:middle;margin-right:10px;" />
            <button id="buttonSave" style="vertical-align:middle">Save</button>

            <div>Click refresh below to load the unfinished TodoItems from your
            database. Use the checkbox to complete and update your TodoItems</div>

            <button id="buttonRefresh" style="width:100%">Refresh</button>

            <div id="TemplateItem" data-win-control="WinJS.Binding.Template">
                <input type="checkbox" style="margin-right:5px" data-win-
                bind="checked: complete; dataContext: this; innerText: text" />
            </div>

            <div id="listItems"
                data-win-control="WinJS.UI.ListView"
                data-win-options="{ itemTemplate: TemplateItem, layout: {type:
                WinJS.UI.ListLayout} }">
            </div>
        </div>
    ```

3. Open the **default.js** file from the JS folder and replace it with the following code:

```
// For an introduction to the Blank template, see the following documentation:
// http://go.microsoft.com/fwlink/?LinkID=392286
(function () {
    "use strict";

    var app = WinJS.Application;
    var activation = Windows.ApplicationModel.Activation;

    app.onactivated = function (args) {
        if (args.detail.kind === activation.ActivationKind.launch) {
            if (args.detail.previousExecutionState !== activation.
            ApplicationExecutionState.terminated) {
            } else {
            }
            args.setPromise(WinJS.UI.processAll());

            var client = new WindowsAzure.MobileServiceClient(
                            "https://winjsrecipes.azure-mobile.net/",
                            "<Application Key2>"
                        );

            var todoTable = client.getTable('todo');

            var todoItems = new WinJS.Binding.List();

            var insertTodoItem = function (todoItem) {

                todoTable.insert(todoItem).done(function (item) {
                    todoItems.push(item);
                });
            };

            var refreshTodoItems = function () {

                todoTable.where({ complete: false })
                    .read()
                    .done(function (results) {
                        todoItems = new WinJS.Binding.List(results);
                        listItems.winControl.itemDataSource = todoItems.
                        dataSource;
                    });
            };

            var updateCheckedTodoItem = function (todoItem) {

                todoTable.update(todoItem).done(function (item) {
                    todoItems.splice(todoItems.indexOf(item), 1);
                });
            };
```

```
buttonSave.addEventListener("click", function () {
    insertTodoItem({
        text: textInput.value,
        complete: false
    });
});

buttonRefresh.addEventListener("click", function () {
    refreshTodoItems();
});

listItems.addEventListener("change", function (eventArgs) {
    var todoItem = eventArgs.target.dataContext.backingData;
    todoItem.complete = eventArgs.target.checked;
    updateCheckedTodoItem(todoItem);

});

refreshTodoItems();

        }
    };

    app.oncheckpoint = function (args) {

    };

    app.start();
})();
```

4. Run the application on the Windows desktop using the Local Machine option.
    You should see screens like the ones shown in Figure 13-11. You should be able
    to add, delete, or update the data from your app to the mobile service.

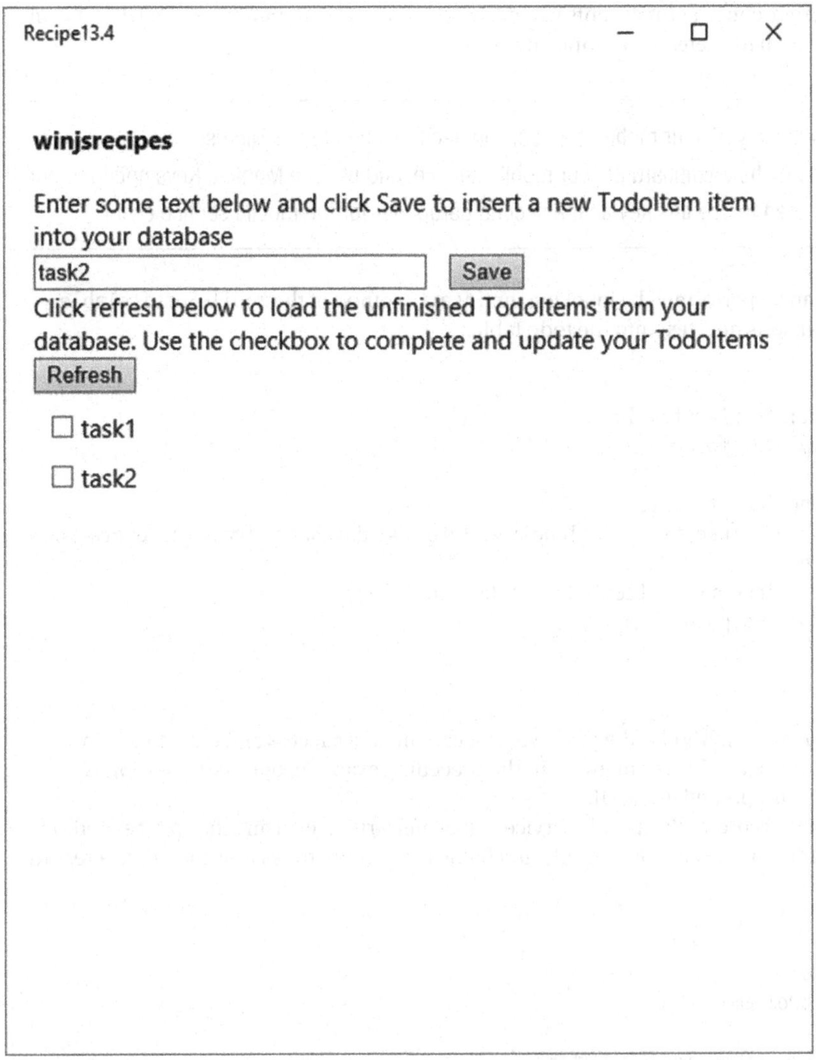

Figure 13-11. Windows app with insert and refresh options

Before performing any operation on the Microsoft Azure Mobile Services from a Windows app, you must first connect to the service and get the access to the remote service. Access to the remote service client is available by using the `MobileServiceClient` object. Similarly, access to the remote table is available by using the `MobileServiceTable` object.

Here's how to get the `MobileServiceClient` and the table reference:

```
var client = new WindowsAzure.MobileServiceClient(
                    "https://winjsrecipes.azure-mobile.net/",
                    "<Enter the Application Key>"
            );

var todoTable = client.getTable('todo');
```

The MobileServiceClient constructor accepts two parameters. The first parameter is the URL of your mobile service and the second parameter is the application key.

___

■ **Note**   To get the application key of your mobile service, you need to log in to the Microsoft Azure Management portal, navigate to the dashboard of your mobile service, and use the Manage Keys option to get the application key. You will need to use this key as the second parameter for the mobile service client.

___

The insert operation can be performed by invoking the insert method of the MobileServiceTable object. The following code inserts new text into the todo table:

```
insertTodoItem({
                text: textInput.value,
                complete: false
            });
var insertTodoItem = function (todoItem) {
            // This code inserts a new TodoItem into the database. When the operation
            completes
            todoTable.insert(todoItem).done(function (item) {
                todoItems.push(item);
            });
        };
```

The return type of the insert method is the promise. You can include success and error functions to handle the operation results of the insert method. In the preceding example, once the insertion is successful, the todoItems list is updated in the UI.

The update of an existing record in the mobile service can be performed by using the update method defined in the MobileServiceTable class. For example, the following demonstrates how to update a record in the todo table:

```
var todoItem = { id:1 };
todoItem.complete = true;
updateCheckedTodoItem(todoItem);

var updateCheckedTodoItem = function (todoItem) {
            // This code takes a freshly completed TodoItem and updates the database.
When the MobileService
            // responds, the item is removed from the list
            todoTable.update(todoItem).done(function (item) {
                todoItems.splice(todoItems.indexOf(item), 1);
            });
        };
```

When updating the record, it is necessary to include the primary key in the record to be updated. In this example, the id field is the primary key. The id column is automatically created and made the primary key when a new Azure Mobile Services is created. This field is an autoincrement column.

The deletion of a record can be performed by calling the del() method of the MobileServiceTable class. For example, the following example demonstrates how to delete a record from the todo table:

```
var deleteItem = { id:1};
todoTable.del(deleteItem);
```

Similar to the update method, the del method also requires the primary key of the object to be passed.

13.5 Data Retrieval with Paging

Problem

You need to control the amount of data returned to your Universal Windows app from Microsoft Azure Mobile Services.

Solution

Use the take and skip query methods on the client to get the specific number of records from the mobile service.

How It Works

Let's use the previous recipe as the starting point for this one.

1. Add six more todo items from the app by changing the text and clicking the **Save** button.

2. Open the **default.js** file and replace the refreshTodoItems method with the following code.

```
var refreshTodoItems = function () {
    // Define a filtered query that returns the top 2 items.
    todoTable.where({ complete: false })
        .take(2)
        .read()
        .done(function (results) {
            todoItems = new WinJS.Binding.List(results);
            listItems.winControl.itemDataSource = todoItems.dataSource;
        });
};
```

This example returns the top two items on the todo table, which are not marked as complete.

3. Run the application in the Windows desktop using the Local Machine option. You should see the first three todo items from the service, as shown in Figure 13-12.

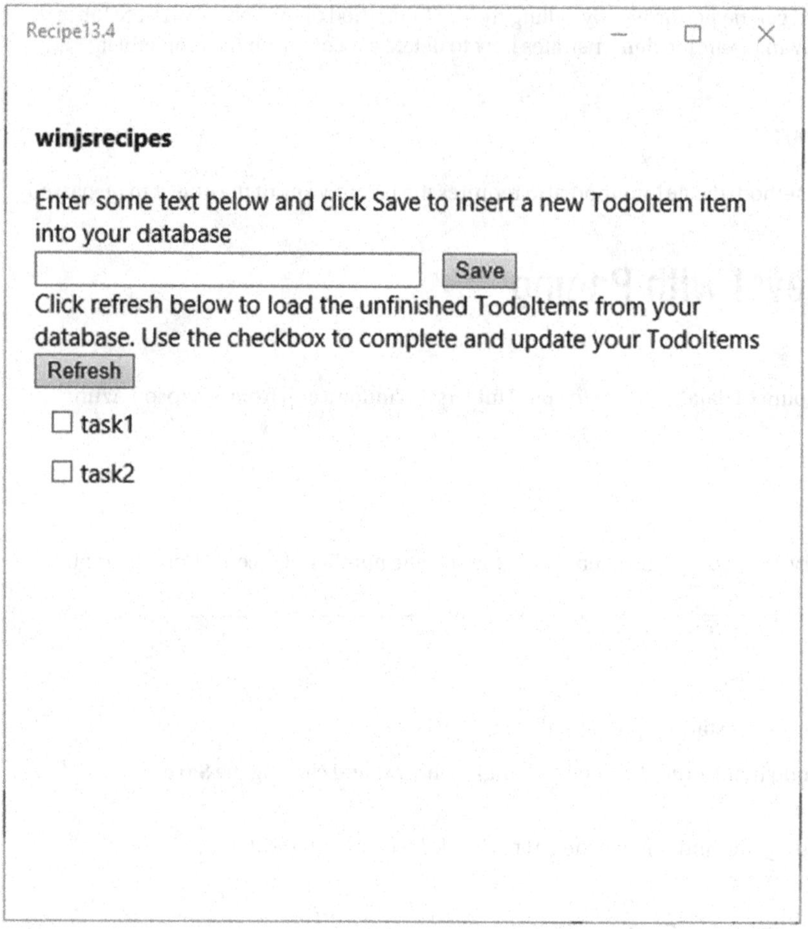

Figure 13-12. Windows app displaying only two records with paging

What if you want to skip a certain number of items on the table and then return records after that? You can use the skip method to achieve this.

The following is a code snippet that skips the first four records and returns the four records after that. This is similar to the page 2, which can show four more records.

```
var refreshTodoItems = function () {

            todoTable.where({ complete: false })
                .skip(4)
                .take(4)
                .read()
                .done(function (results) {
                    todoItems = new WinJS.Binding.List(results);
                    listItems.winControl.itemDataSource = todoItems.dataSource;
                });
        };
```

■ **Note**   Mobile Services has an automatic page limit of up to 50 items in a response. The `skip`/`take` methods can help in retrieving more records (if needed) in a single response.

13.6 Sorting Returned Data from the Mobile Service
Problem
You need to sort the data that is returned by the mobile service from your Universal Windows app.

Solution
You can use the `orderBy` or `orderByDescending` function in the query.

How It Works
Let's use the previous recipe as the starting point for this one. You will be updating the `refreshTodoItems` method to sort the records.

1. Open the **default.js file** and replace the `refreshTodoItems` method with the following code to sort by text in descending order.

```
var refreshTodoItems = function () {

            todoTable.where({ complete: false }).orderByDescending("text")
                .read()
                .done(function (results) {
                    todoItems = new WinJS.Binding.List(results);
                    listItems.winControl.itemDataSource = todoItems.
                    dataSource;
                });
        };
```

When you run the application in the Windows desktop using the Local Machine option, you will notice that the list is now sorted in descending order, as shown in Figure 13-13.

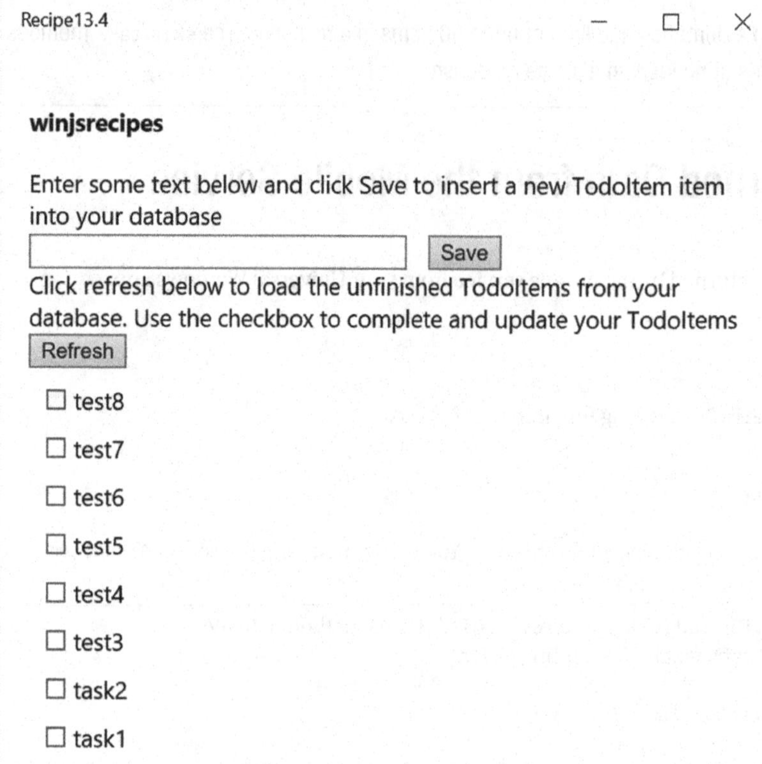

Recipe13.4 — ☐ ✕

winjsrecipes

Enter some text below and click Save to insert a new TodoItem item into your database

☐ [_____] Save

Click refresh below to load the unfinished TodoItems from your database. Use the checkbox to complete and update your TodoItems

Refresh

☐ test8

☐ test7

☐ test6

☐ test5

☐ test4

☐ test3

☐ task2

☐ task1

Figure 13-13. *Windows app displaying sorted data from a mobile service*

To sort the data in ascending order, the orderBy method can be used to specify the column on which to sort the records. The following example demonstrates how to sort the todo table by the "text" column in ascending order.

```
todoTable.where({ complete: false }).orderBy("text")
                .read()
```

13.7 Performing Validation in a Server Script
Problem

You want to perform validation in the server-side JavaScript in Microsoft Azure Mobile Services.

Solution

You can define the validations in the server scripts (insert, update, delete, etc.). This can be modified either from Visual Studio 2015 or from the Mobile Services dashboard.

How It Works

Let's use the previous recipe sample to demonstrate how validation can be performed in Azure Mobile Services and then display a message within the Windows app.

Assume that you want to validate the length of the data that is submitted when inserting a new record. You have to register a script that validates data that is less than six characters. If the text length is less than or equal to six characters, you need to display an error message.

1. Open the **Server Explorer** window in Visual Studio and expand the mobile service table.

2. Double-click the **insert.js** file to start modifying it within Visual Studio. You can also right-click and select the **Edit Script** option to edit the file, as shown in Figure 13-14. Note that when you modify and save the file, the file is automatically updated in Microsoft Azure.

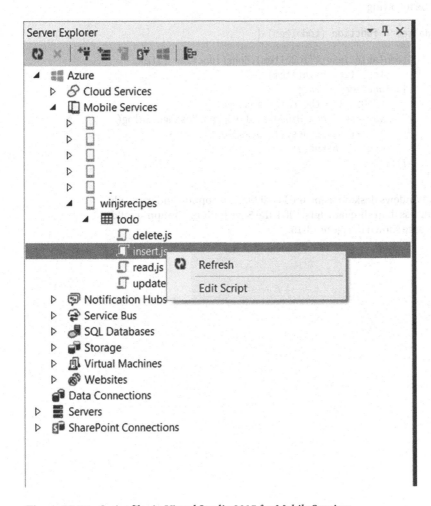

Figure 13-14. Script files in Visual Studio 2015 for Mobile Services

3. Replace the **insert.js** file with the following code snippet.

```
function insert(item, user, request) {

    if (item.text.length <= 6) {
        request.respond(statusCodes.BAD_REQUEST, 'Text length must be greater
than 6 characters');
    } else {
        request.execute();
    }

}
```

4. Open the **default.js** file from the project and replace the insertTodoItem function with the following:

```
var insertTodoItem = function (todoItem) {

                todoTable.insert(todoItem).done(function (item) {
                    todoItems.push(item);
                }, function (error) {
                    // Display the error message
                    var msg = new Windows.UI.Popups.MessageDialog(
                        error.request.responseText);
                    msg.showAsync();
                });
            };
```

5. Run the app in Windows desktop using the Local Machine option and try to add a todo item with less than six characters. Click the **Save** button. The app should display the message shown in Figure 13-15.

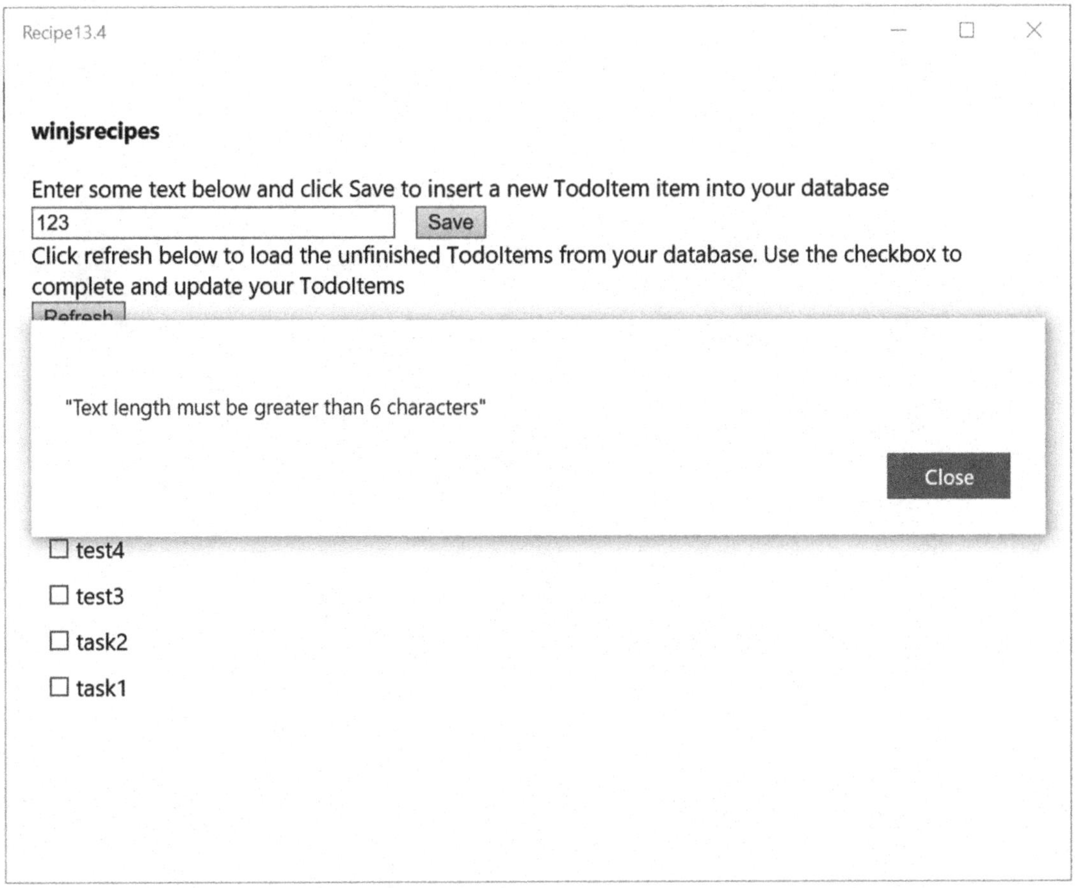

Figure 13-15. *Windows app displaying a validation message from a mobile service*

Alternatively, you can modify the scripts from the SCRIPT tab, which can be found by selecting the table in the DATA tab in the Azure Management portal.

■ ■ ■

CHAPTER 14

Tiles and Notifications

As we all know, in Windows 8, Microsoft introduced a new way to launch applications using tiles, which are an iconic part of the user experience. With Windows 10, there are additional features that are exciting and different. This chapter provides an overview of the tiles and notifications available in Windows 10. You will explore how to create tiles and notifications of different types.

14.1 Create a Default Tile

Problem

You need to add a default tile in your application.

Solution

Use the `package.appxmanifest` to provide information for the UWP app tiles and display.

How It Works

Create a new Universal Windows app project in Visual Studio 2015. Open the `package.appxmanifest` for your project. This opens the manifest editor window, as shown in Figure 14-1.

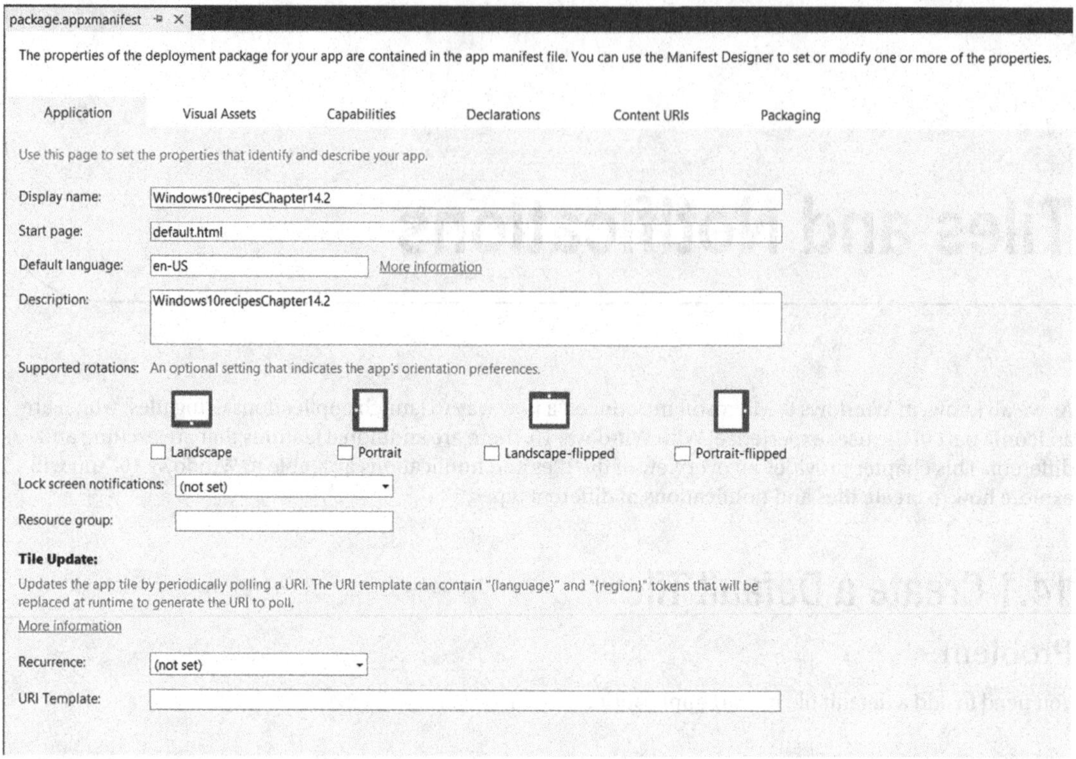

Figure 14-1. Application package.appmanifest

Select the **Applications** tab, if it is not selected. Change the value of **Display name** if required. The display name is the app name that is listed installed/available in the apps list and displayed in your app's title.

In the app manifest, click the **Visual Assets** tab. Under the **Tiles and Logos** section, change the image provided for logos and select **logos** in the Windows manifest. Change or enter a new ShortName for the app, which should be 13 characters; otherwise, it will be truncated. Select the appropriate tile size on which the short mime is displayed. You can enter your preferred background color in W3DC format (for example, #FFFFFF) or use the default background color.

Compile the project and run the app to test the tile title and images logo created with the app.

14.2 Create Adaptive Tiles

Adaptive tiles are a new addition in Windows 10. For adaptive tiles, there are new lightweight XML templates that allow developers to design tile notification content—based on their own requirements—to support different devices and displays.

Problem

You want to create adaptive tiles for your UWP app.

Solution

Just like standard tiles, use the adaptive tiles template to provide the content of the tile. For creating adaptive tiles, there are adaptive tiles templates, which can be used to create different types of tiles.

The Notifications Visualizer (`https://www.microsoft.com/store/apps/9nblggh5xsl1`) helps developers design the adaptive tiles. It provides instant visual previews. This helps you quickly design the adaptive tiles and test. It provides an easy way configure tile properties like text, font, display colors, show name, background images, badge value, and so forth, as well.

Adaptive templates work across different types of notifications and different form factors. The adaptive tile appearance depends on the device where the app is installed and the type of notification—tile or toast.

The adaptive tile XML Schema syntax is as follows:

```
<tile>
  <visual>
      <binding template="TileMedium">
      ...
      </binding>
      <binding template="TileWide">
      ...
      </binding>
      <binding template="TileLarge">
...
      </binding>
      </visual>
</tile>
```

In the binding element is key, where the content of each tile size is specified. In one XML payload, you can specify multiple binding. The following are different types of tile size that can be specified in the `template` parameter of the `binding`:

- `TileSmall`
- `TileMedium`
- `TileWide`
- `TileLarge` (desktop only)

How It Works

Adaptive tiles templates are based on XML. Let's use the Notification Visualizer to generate the XML for the adaptive tile.

Create a new Universal Windows app project in Visual Studio 2015. This creates a new Windows app project. Open the **default.html** page from the project in the Visual Studio Solution Explorer. Add the following HTML markup within the body tag of `default.html`.

```
<input type="button" value="Update Adaptive Tile" id="btnUpdateAdaptiveTile" />
```

This HTML adds a simple HTML button on the `default.html` page with the text, "Update Adaptive Tile".

277

Now, right-click the project in the Solution Explorer and select **Add ➤ New JavaScript file**. Provide a name for the file: **LoadTileandNotifications.js**. Add the following code:

```
function GetControl() {
        WinJS.UI.processAll().done(function () {
                var adaptiveTilebutton = document.getElementById("btnUpdateAdaptiveTile");
                adaptiveTilebutton.addEventListener("click", AddAdaptiveTiles, false);
        }
document.addEventListener("DOMContentLoaded", GetControl);
```

In the preceding code, you added an event handler, AddAdaptiveTiles(), for the btnUpdateAdaptiveTile HTML button. You then added the getControl method when default.html was loaded.

Reopen default.html and add a reference to the LoadTileandNotifications.js file.

```
<script src="/js/LoadTileandNotifications.js"></script>
```

Now, let's add an AddAdaptiveTiles()event handler method using the following code snippet in the LoadTileandNotifications.js file.

```
    function AddAdaptiveTiles() {
        var adaptivetileXml = "<tile><visual displayName=\"UWP recipes\" branding=\"name\">"
+ "<binding template=\"TileSmall\"><group><subgroup><text hint-style=\"subtitle\"> Windows
10 Apps receipes </text><text hint-style=\"subtitle\">Adaptive Tiles</text></subgroup></
group></binding>"
+ "<binding template=\"TileMedium\"><group><subgroup><text hint-style=\"subtitle\"> Windows
10 Apps receipes </text><text hint-style=\"subtitle\">Adaptive Tiles</text></subgroup></
group></binding>"
+ "<binding template=\"TileLarge\"><group><subgroup><text hint-style=\"subtitle\"> Windows
10 Apps receipes </text><text hint-style=\"subtitle\">Adaptive Tiles</text></subgroup></
group></binding>"
+ "<binding template=\"TileWide\"><group><subgroup><text hint-style=\"subtitle\"> Windows 10
Apps recipes </text><text hint-style=\"subtitle\">Adaptive Tiles</text></subgroup></group></
binding>"
+ "</visual></tile>";
        var adaptivetileDom = Windows.Data.Xml.Dom.XmlDocument();
        adaptivetileDom.loadXml(adaptivetileXml);
        var notifications = Windows.UI.Notifications;
        var tileNotification = new notifications.TileNotification(adaptivetileDom);
        notifications.TileUpdateManager.createTileUpdaterForApplication().
        update(tileNotification);
    }
```

In this event listener function, you created an XmlDocument object, adaptivetileDom, which is used to load adaptivetileXml. adaptiveXml contains the XML payload for adaptiveTile, which contains the following adaptive tile bindings:

- TileSmall

- TileMedium

- TileLarge

- TileWide

In the preceding code, the `Windows.UI.Notifications` namespace is used.

In `adaptivetileXml`, all tiles have the following display name: UWP recipes. The next parameter is branding, which is set to `Name`. This displays the name value at the bottom of the tile.

The `<group>` and `<subgroup>` elements are used to semantically group the content displayed on the tile. In this case, "Windows 10 Apps recipes" is displayed first and then "Recipes on Tiles" is displayed on the next line. Both text elements are grouped together.

In the `TileLarge` binding, we are also displaying the image in the tile along with text content. This image is displayed in line with text, but you can also set it to be the background of the tile.

The `hint-width` attribute is used to specify the width of column when there are multiple columns presented in the tile.

Once XMLDocument is created, create a `tileNotification` object of type `Windows.UI.Notifications.TileNotification()` and pass the `adaptivetileXml` XmlDocument object as a parameter to the `TileNotification` class. The `TileNotification` object is used to define the tile and visual elements related to the tile.

After this, send the notification to the app's tile using the `TileUpdateManager` class, which changes the content of the specified tiles that the updater is bound to by using the `createTileUpdaterForApplication().update()` method.

When you run the application on a Windows 10 device, click the **Update Adaptive Tile** button to update the tile dynamically, as shown in Figure 14-2.

Figure 14-2. *Windows 10 adaptive tile update using Windows.UI.Notifications.TileNotification()*

14.3 Create a Toast Notification with Visual Content

Problem

You want to create an interactive toast notification, to be displayed with an image, to override the application logo and inline image thumbnail in a toast.

Solution

Windows 10 UWP provides toast notifications, which are developed using an XML template similar to adaptive tiles. Toast notification XML contains mainly three key elements: visual, action, and audio. The `ToastNotificationManager` is used to send toast notifications. Use the `ToastNotificationManager` to send new notifications to the app.

How It Works

In the previous section, you created an adaptive tile with an XML Schema. In a similar manner, you will create an interactive toast notification that notifies the user on a new book added in the Apress catalog.

Use the same project. Add the following HTML markup within the `<body>` tag of `default.html`.

```
<input type="button" value="Display Toast" id="btnDisplayToast" />
    <br />
```

This creates a simple Display Toast HTML button on the `default.html` page.

Open **LoadTileandNotifications.js** and add the following code in the existing `GetControl()` method:

```
var toastNotificationbutton = document.getElementById("btnDisplayToast");
        toastNotificationbutton.addEventListener("click", DisplayToastNotification, false);
```

In the preceding code, you basically get a reference to the `btnDisplayToast` button and associate the click event handler with the `AddToastNotification()` method.

Add a new `AddToastNotification` event method with the following code snippet:

```
function AddToastNotification()
  {
        var toastXML = "<toast><visual>"
+ "<binding template=\"ToastGeneric\"><text>Apress Catalog</text><text>Apress is working on
new Windows 10 Receipes guide</text>"
+ "<image placement=\"appLogoOverride\" src=\"/images/Alarm.png\" /><image
placement=\"inline\" src=\"/images/Pattern-Blue-Dots-background.jpg\" /></binding>"
+ " </visual>"
    + "</toast>";
        var toastNotificationDom = Windows.Data.Xml.Dom.XmlDocument();
        toastNotificationDom.loadXml(toastXML);
        var notifications = Windows.UI.Notifications;

        // Get the toast notification manager for the current app.
        var notificationManager = notifications.ToastNotificationManager;
        // Create a toast notification from the XML, then create a ToastNotifier object
        // to send the toast.
        var toast = new notifications.ToastNotification(toastNotificationDom);
        notificationManager.createToastNotifier().show(toast);

}
```

In the preceding event listener method, the `adaptivetileXml` variable contains the XML payload for the toast notification, which is similar to "Adaptive Tiles", but in the `<binding>` element, the template value is set to `ToastGeneric`.

Then create a new `toast` object of type `ToastNotification` and specify the `toastNotificationDom` XmlDocument. After this, send the notification to the app's tile using the `ToastNotificationManager` class, which sends the content of the specified toast.

Run the application in the emulator in the default page. Click the **Display Toast** button to test the output, as shown in Figure 14-3.

Figure 14-3. *Toast notification from UWP app*

You can create toast notifications associated with your app and notify users dynamically while the app is running. In the next recipe, you will learn how to add actions to toast notifications.

14.4 Create a Toast Notification with Actions

Problem

You want to create an interactive toast notification to be displayed with possible actions for the user.

Solution

Add the <Actions> element to the toast notification XML.

How It Works

In previous recipe, you created an adaptive toast notification with XML Schema. In a similar manner, you will create an interactive toast notification with actions that will notify users on a new book added in the Apress catalog and allow the users to take actions.

Let's use same project as in the previous recipe. Open the **LoadTileandNotifications.js** file. Add a new method, AddInteractiveToastNotification().

```
function AddInteractiveToastNotification()
{
    var toastXML = "<toast><visual>"
+ "<binding template=\"ToastGeneric\"><text>Apress Catalog</text><text>Apress is working on
new Windows 10 Receipes guide</text>"
+ "<image placement=\"appLogoOverride\" src=\"/images/Alarm.png\" /><image
placement=\"inline\" src=\"/images/Pattern-Blue-Dots-background.jpg\" /></binding>"
+ " </visual>"
+ "<actions><action content=\"check\" arguments=\"check\" imageUri=\"/images/storelogo.png\"
/><action content=\"cancel\" arguments=\"cancel\" /></actions>"
```

```
+ " <audio src=\"ms-winsoundevent:Notification.Reminder\"/>"
+ "</toast>";
        var toastNotificationDom = Windows.Data.Xml.Dom.XmlDocument();
        toastNotificationDom.loadXml(toastXML);
        var notifications = Windows.UI.Notifications;

        // Get the toast notification manager for the current app.
        var notificationManager = notifications.ToastNotificationManager;
        // Create a toast notification from the XML, then create a ToastNotifier object
        // to send the toast.
        var toast = new notifications.ToastNotification(toastNotificationDom);
        notificationManager.createToastNotifier().show(toast);
    }
```

In the AddInteractiveToastNotification() event handler method, the only difference is in XML payload, where you added additional elements to allow users to take actions. It also plays a notification sound when the toast notification is sent to the app. Actions are specified under the <actions><action> element.

In default.html, add the following line for a new button to display an interactive notification event:

```
<p>
        <input type="button" value="Display interactive Toast"
id="btnDisplayinteractiveToast" />
        <br />
</p>
```

This code adds a new button, **Display Interactive Toast**. To associate the AddInteractiveToastNotification() method with the btnDisplayinteractiveToast button, let's add the following lines of code in the existing GetControl() method.

```
  var toastinteractiveNotificationbutton = document.getElementById("btnDisplayinteractiveTo
ast");
            toastinteractiveNotificationbutton.addEventListener("click",
AddInteractiveToastNotification, false);
```

The preceding code is the same as previous recipe, where you associated a button click event handler with a method. In this case, you associate the button with the btnDisplayinteractiveToast id to the AddInteractiveToastNotification() method.

Compile the project and run it in the emulator. When the default.html page is loaded, press the **Display Interactive Toast** button. On button click notifications are displayed to users with two different possible actions. A notification sound is also played, as shown in Figure 14-4.

Figure 14-4. *Interactive toast notification from app*

In this recipe, you learned how to interact with users via toast notifications. You also learned how to get users to take actions based on toast notifications.

14.5 Create a Scheduled Tile and Toast Notification

Problem

You want to create an interactive toast notification to be displayed with a reminder to the user.

Solution

Add an `<Actions>` element in the tile and toast notification XML.

How It Works

In the previous recipe, you created an adaptive toast notification with XML Schema. In a similar manner, let's create an interactive toast notification with actions that notify users on a new book added in the Apress catalog and allow users to take actions.

Let's use same project as in the previous recipe. Open the **LoadTileandNotifications.js** file and add the following `AddScheduledTileNotification()` method.

```
function AddScheduledTileNotification() {

        var adaptivetileXml = "<tile><visual displayName=\"Future recipes\"
        branding=\"name\">"
+ "<binding template=\"TileSmall\"><group><subgroup><text hint-style=\"subtitle\"> Updated
Tiles </text><text hint-style=\"subtitle\">Adaptive Tiles</text></subgroup></group></
binding>"
```

```
+ "<binding template=\"TileMedium\"><group><subgroup><text hint-style=\"subtitle\"> Updated
Tiles </text><text hint-style=\"subtitle\">Adaptive Tiles</text></subgroup></group></
binding>"
+ "<binding template=\"TileLarge\"><group><subgroup><text hint-style=\"subtitle\"> Updated
Tiles </text><text hint-style=\"subtitle\">Adaptive Tiles</text></subgroup></group></
binding>"
+ "<binding template=\"TileWide\"><group><subgroup><text hint-style=\"subtitle\"> Updated
Tiles </text><text hint-style=\"subtitle\">Adaptive Tiles</text></subgroup></group></
binding>"
+ "</visual></tile>";
        var adaptivetileDom = Windows.Data.Xml.Dom.XmlDocument();
        adaptivetileDom.loadXml(adaptivetileXml);
        var currentTime = new Date();
        //notification should appear in 3 seconds
        var startTime = new Date(currentTime.getTime() + 3 * 1000);
        var scheduledTile = new Windows.UI.Notifications.ScheduledTileNotification(adaptive
        tileDom, startTime);
        //Give the scheduled tile notification an ID
        scheduledTile.id = "Future_Tile";
        var tileUpdater = Windows.UI.Notifications.TileUpdateManager.
        createTileUpdaterForApplication();
        tileUpdater.addToSchedule(scheduledTile);

}
```

In this method, we set up new XML for the tile in a local variable, adaptivetileXml. We then created a local object, adaptivetileDom, of type XMLDocument, in which we loaded adaptiveXml text.

To send a scheduled update to tile, we first need to set the scheduled time, for which we create a startTime local variable and set the value to the current time and 3 seconds. For sending a scheduled update of the tile, create a tileUpdater object of type Windows.UI.Notifications.TileUpdateManager. createTileUpdaterForApplication() and then call addToSchedule method to send the update at a configured time.

To execute the preceding method, add an HTML button and bind an event handler to execute the preceding method. Open **default.html** and add the following HTML snippet to add an HTML button with text, Scheduled Adaptive Tile.

```
<p>
        <input type="button" value="Scheduled  Adaptive Tile" id="btnScheduledAdaptiveTile" />
        <br />
</p>
```

Next, open **LoadTileandNotifications.js** and update the existing LoadTileandNotifications() method with the following lines of code:

```
    var ScheduledAdaptiveTilebutton = document.getElementById("btnScheduledAdaptiveTile");
            ScheduledAdaptiveTilebutton.addEventListener("click",
AddScheduledTileNotification, false);
```

This adds a new onclick event handler to the btnScheduledAdaptiveTile button and associates the AddScheduledTileNotification method to be executed when the **Scheduled Adaptive Tile** button is clicked.

To test this, compile and run the app. When the default.html page is loaded, click **Scheduled Adaptive Tile** button. This sends a notification to the tile in 3 seconds. You can validate by checking the tile title and text, which change on scheduled time.

In this recipe, you sent an update to the UWP app tile at a scheduled time. Scheduled updates are useful when sending dynamic updated based on changes in content, such as with weather apps, email apps, travel schedule apps, and so forth.

14.6 Create or Update a Badge on a Tile

Problem

You want to add a badge to a tile.

Solution

Use the <badge> element in the tile XML payload to display a badge. Use BadgeNotificationto create a badge.

How It Works

In the existing project, we will add an additional method, UpdateTileBadge, to show how to create a badge update on a tile. Open **LoadTileandNotifications.js** and add the following method:

```
function UpdateTileBadge()

{
    AddAdaptiveTiles();
    var badgeXml = "<badge value=\"alarm\"/>";
    var badgeDom = Windows.Data.Xml.Dom.XmlDocument();
    badgeDom.loadXml(badgeXml);
    var notifications = Windows.UI.Notifications;
    var badgeNotification = new notifications.BadgeNotification(badgeDom);
    notifications.BadgeUpdateManager.createBadgeUpdaterForApplication().
    update(badgeNotification);
}
```

In this method, we call the AdaptiveTiles() method to display adaptive tiles.

Then we add badgeXML, which contains the XML payload for the badge to display an alarm on the tile. In badgeXml, we set the value for the badge to "Alarm".

Then we create a badgeNotifications object of type Windows.UI.Notifications.BadgeNotification and pass the XML for badge notification.

Following this, call the createBadgeUpdaterForApplication.update() method to update the tile with a badge notification.

Now open **default.html** and add a new button to test the UpdateTileBadge() method for updating the tile with a badge.

```
<p> <input type="button" value="Update Badge" id="btnUpdateBadge" />
    <br />
    </p>
```

Next, open the **LoadTileandNotifications.js** and update the GetControl()method with the following lines of code:

```
var badgeUpdatebutton = document.getElementById("btnUpdateBadge");
        badgeUpdatebutton.addEventListener("click", UpdateTileBadge, false);
```

This will add a new onclick event handler the btnUpdateBadge button and associate UpdateTileBadge method to be executed when the **Update Badge** button is clicked.

When you compile and run this app, click the **Update Badge** button on the default.html page. This will update the tile and the app tile will display the badge with a Windows alarm glyph displayed in the right-hand corner, as shown in Figure 14-5.

Figure 14-5. Badge notification on a Windows UWP adaptive tile

There are different types of Windows glyphs that can be specified in the badge XML, such as alarm, alert, available, error, paused, new message, and so forth.

■ **Note**   In UWP apps, badges are displayed in the lower-right corner.

In this chapter, you learned about UWP app tiles and various ways to update tiles, and how to add notifications via tiles, and how to dynamically update the content of adaptive tiles.

CHAPTER 15

■ ■ ■

Device Capabilities

This chapter provides an overview of the device capabilities in a Windows 10 app. You will also learn about how to develop Bluetooth, text to speech, speech to text, and sensor capabilities in your UWP apps. The chapter also provides an overview of Cortana integration in apps.

15.1 How to Specify Device Capabilities in an App Package Manifest

Problem

You need to specify different devices' capabilities required by your Windows 10 app.

Solution

Use the app package manifest file to specify the DeviceCapability element and associated child elements.

How It Works

Open the project that you are working on for your Windows 10 app in Visual Studio 2015.

From Solution Explorer, locate the Package.appmanifest file. Double-click the file to open it. Click the **Capabilities** tab. Select the device capabilities that your app will use. This adds the capabilities list in the application (see Figure 15-1).

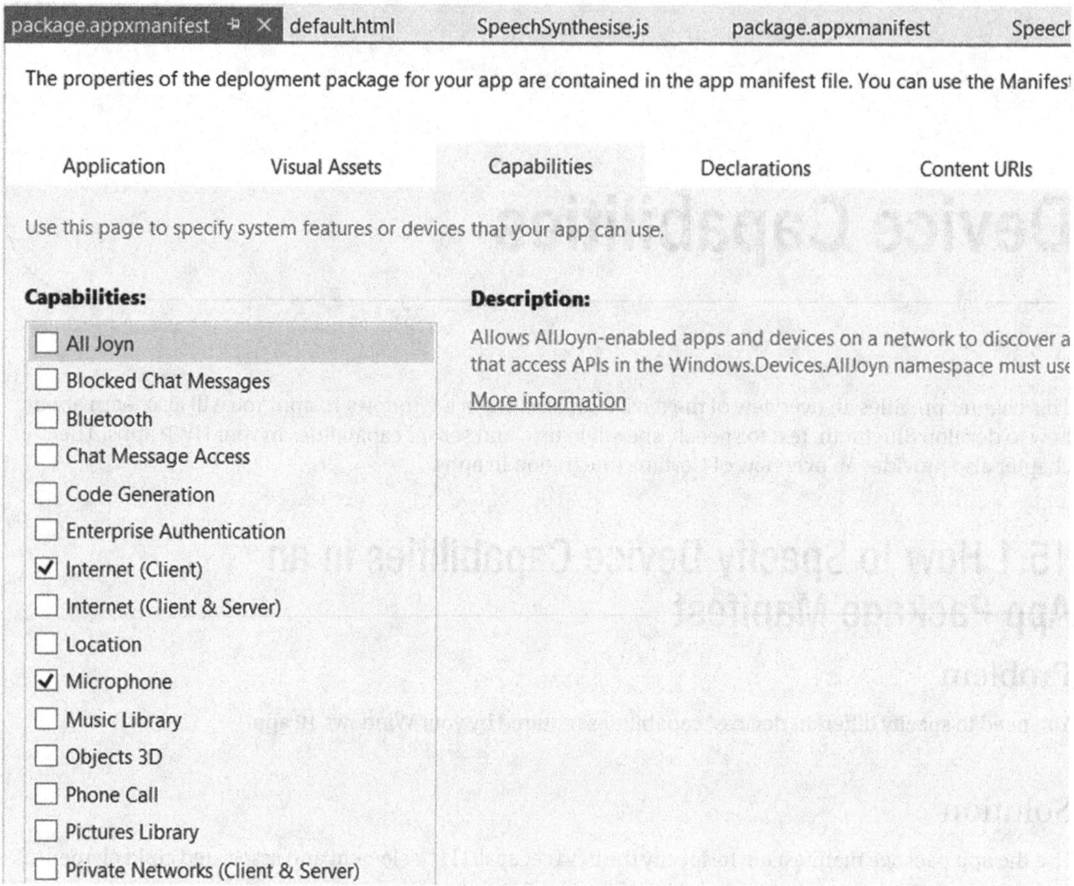

| package.appxmanifest ⊹ ✕ | default.html | SpeechSynthesise.js | package.appxmanifest | Speech |

The properties of the deployment package for your app are contained in the app manifest file. You can use the Manifes

| Application | Visual Assets | Capabilities | Declarations | Content URIs |

Use this page to specify system features or devices that your app can use.

Capabilities:

- ☐ All Joyn
- ☐ Blocked Chat Messages
- ☐ Bluetooth
- ☐ Chat Message Access
- ☐ Code Generation
- ☐ Enterprise Authentication
- ☑ Internet (Client)
- ☐ Internet (Client & Server)
- ☐ Location
- ☑ Microphone
- ☐ Music Library
- ☐ Objects 3D
- ☐ Phone Call
- ☐ Pictures Library
- ☐ Private Networks (Client & Server)

Description:

Allows AllJoyn-enabled apps and devices on a network to discover a that access APIs in the Windows.Devices.AllJoyn namespace must use

More information

Figure 15-1. *Capabilities tab in app package.appmanifest file*

You can also open the app `package.appmanifest` file in an XML editor and add the device capabilities using the `<Capability>` element under the `<Capabilities>` element; for example:

```
<Capabilities>
    <Capability Name="internetClient" />
    <Capability Name="allJoyn" />
    <Capability Name="codeGeneration" />
    <Capability Name="internetClientServer" />
    <uap:Capability Name="blockedChatMessages" />
    <uap:Capability Name="chat" />
    <uap:Capability Name="videosLibrary" />
    <uap:Capability Name="phoneCall" />
    <uap:Capability Name="removableStorage" />
    <DeviceCapability Name="microphone" />
    <DeviceCapability Name="webcam" />
</Capabilities>
```

In this example, the following capabilities were enabled for the app to use: chat, video library, phone call, and removable data storage such as USB drives, microphones, and webcams. Please note that there are a few capabilities, like the webcam, that cannot be specified using the package.manifest visual interface. You have to do this using a code file.

15.2 How to Specify Device Capabilities for Bluetooth for Windows Apps

Problem

You need to access the Bluetooth device in your Windows 10 app.

Solution

Use the DeviceCapability element of package.manifest to define the device capabilities for accessing a Bluetooth device. This is for both Bluetooth Rfcomm and Gatt APIs.

How It Works

1. Open your Windows Universal Windows app project in Visual Studio 2015.

2. From Solution Explorer, locate the Package.appmanifest file. Right-click and open the Package.appmanifest file in the XML editor.

3. Locate the <Capabilities> section. Add the following elements under <Capabilities>:

```
<DeviceCapability Name="bluetooth.rfcomm">
  <Device Id="any">
    <Function Type="name:obexObjectPush"/>
    <Function Type="name:serialPort"/>
    <Function Type="name:genericFileTransfer"/>
  </ Device>
</DeviceCapability>
```

In the preceding code, the <DeviceCapability> element has the Name attribute, which is specified as "bluetooth.rfcomm" for accessing a Bluetooth RFCOMM device. The <Device> element is set to "any" to allow access to any device that matches the function types specified in the <function> elements.

The <DeviceCapability> can also be used to specify device capabilities for a Bluetooth GATT device, as shown in the following code snippet:

```
<DeviceCapability Name="bluetooth.genericAttributeProfile">
  <Device Id="any">
    <Function Type="name:battery"/>
    <Function Type="name:bloodPressure"/>
    <Function Type="serviceId:aaaaaaa"/>
  </ Device>
</DeviceCapability>
```

In the preceding code, DeviceCapabilities for a Bluetooth GATT "any" device support mentioned functions with specified service names and service ids.

15.3 How to Find Devices Available for a UWP App

Problem

You want to get a list of devices that are connected to a system—externally connected or available for a UWP app.

Solution

Use the Windows.Devices.Enumeration.DevicePicker class to enumerate through devices that are discoverable by the app.

How It Works

Create a new project using the **Windows Universal (Blank App)** template in Microsoft Visual Studio 2015.

Open the **default.html** page from the project in Visual Studio Solution explorer. Add the following HTML markup to display a button and label:

```
<body class="win-type-body">
    <div>
        <h2 id="sampleHeader" class="win-type-subheader">Description:</h2>
        <div id="scenarioDescription">
            Recipe to demo DevicePicker to allows users of your app to pick a device
        </div>
    </div>
    <div id="scenarioContent">
        <button id="showDevicePickerButton" >Show Device Picker</button>
    </div>
</body>
```

Right-click the js folder from Solution Explorer. Add a DevicePicker.js JavaScript file. Add a reference to this js file in default.html.

```
<script src="/js/DevicePicker.js"></script>
```

Open the devicePicker.js in Visual Studio and add the following script:

```
(function () {
    "use strict";

    var DevEnum = Windows.Devices.Enumeration;
    var devicePicker = null;

    var page = WinJS.UI.Pages.define("../default.html", {
        ready: function (element, options) {
```

```
// Hook up button event handlers
                       document.getElementById("showDevicePickerButton").
                       addEventListener("click", showDevicePicker, false);
}
    });
```

In the preceding code, we have declared a variable of type `Windows.Devices.Enumeration`. This object will be later used to create the `DevicePicker` object.

The page variable is used to bind the rest of the `js` script to the default page when its DOM is loaded.

In the `ready()` function, we bind an event handler, `showDevicePicker`, to the `showDevicePickerButton` button.

Add the following `showDevicePicker()` method, which will get the devices available:

```
function showDevicePicker() {
    var buttonRect;
    devicePicker = new DevEnum.DevicePicker();
    buttonRect = document.getElementById("showDevicePickerButton").
    getBoundingClientRect();
    var rect = { x: buttonRect.left, y: buttonRect.top, width: buttonRect.width, height:
    buttonRect.height };

        // Show the picker
        devicePicker.show(rect);

}

})();
```

In the `showDevicePicker()`event handler, which is called on click of `showDevicePickerButton` button, we create a `Windows.Devices.Enumeration.DevicePicker` object and create a rectangle object to show the picker UI output.

Compile this project and run it using the Mobile emulator to get a list of all the devices, as shown in Figure 15-2.

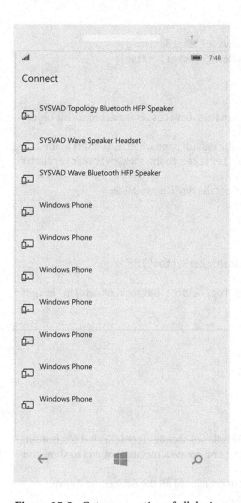

Figure 15-2. *Get enumeration of all devices available to app on system*

15.4 How to Create an Audio Stream and Output Speech Based on Plain Text

Problem

You need to add a voice facility in your app to allow it to read text.

Solution

Use `Windows.Media.SpeechSynthesis.SpeechSynthesizer()` to develop audio/voice output based on text in your UWP app.

How It Works

Microsoft has provided predefined voices that can be used to synthesize speech in a single language.

Create a new project using the **Windows Universal (Blank App)** template in Microsoft Visual Studio 2015. In the project package.appmanifest file, click the **Capabilities** tab and select the **Microphone** and **Internet** check boxes. This allows the app to use the audio feed.

Open the default.html page from the project in Visual Studio Solution Explorer. Add the following HTML markup within the <body> tag of default.html.

```
<body class="win-type-body">
    <div id="scenarioView">
        <div>
            <h2 id="sampleHeader" class="win-type-subheader">>Convert text to speech.</h2>
        </div>
    <div id="scenarioContent">
        <button id="btnSpeak" class="win-button">Speak</button>
        <select id="voicesSelect" class="win-dropdown"></select>
        <textarea id="textToSynthesize" style="width: 100%" name="textToSynthesize"
        class="win-textarea"> Hello World! This is an example of Windows 10 Universal
        Windows App Recipes</textarea>
        <p id="errorTextArea"></p>
    </div>
    </div>
    <div id="contentWrapper">
        <div id="contentHost"></div>
        <div id="statusBox">
            Status:
            <div id="statusMessage"></div>
        </div>
    </div>
</body>
```

When the app is started in the Mobile emulator in debug mode, what's shown in Figure 15-3 is displayed.

Figure 15-3. *Text to speech GUI with drop-down list to select the language*

As you can see, four main controls were added:

- A Speak button

- A drop-down list to allow users to select available languages

- A text box that contains predefined text. This text is converted to audio by the app

- A Status label that displays a message when voice is played and stopped

Right-click the project in Solution Explorer and select **Add ➤ New JavaScript file**. Provide a name for the file. In this example, let's name the file **SpeechSynthesise.js**. Add the following code in the file:

```
var page = WinJS.UI.Pages.define("../default.html", {
        ready: function (element, options) {
            try {
                synthesizer = new Windows.Media.SpeechSynthesis.SpeechSynthesizer();
                audio = new Audio();
                var btnSpeak = document.getElementById("btnSpeak");
```

```
            var voicesSelect = document.getElementById("voicesSelect");
            btnSpeak.addEventListener("click", speakFn, false);
            voicesSelect.addEventListener("click", setVoiceFunction, false);

            var rcns = Windows.ApplicationModel.Resources.Core;
            context = new rcns.ResourceContext();
            context.languages = new Array(synthesizer.voice.language);
            listbox_GetVoices();
            audio_SetUp();
        } catch (exception) {
            if (exception.number == -2147467263) {// E_NOTIMPL

                // If media player components aren't installed (for example, when using
                an N SKU of windows)
                // this error may occur when instantiating the Audio object.
                statusMessage.innerText = "Media Player components are not available.";
                statusBox.style.backgroundColor = "red";
                btnSpeak.disabled = true;
                textToSynthesize.disabled = true;
            }
        }
    },

    unload: function (element, options) {
        if (audio != null) {
            audio.onpause = null;
            audio.pause();
        }
    }
});
```

Declare the following variables:

```
var synthesizer;
    var audio;

    // localization resources
    var context;
    var resourceMap;
```

The ready() function is executed when DOM is loaded for the default.html page on the device where the app is loaded. In this function, create a local synthesizer object of type Windows.Media.SpeechSynthesis.SpeechSynthesizer(), which provides access to the functionality of an installed speech synthesis engine on a Microsoft device and controls the speech synthesis engine (voice).

The second object is audio, which is for playing audio. Then we associate event listeners for the Speak button and voicesSelect drop-down HTML controls.

We also create a local rcns object of type Windows.ApplicationModel.Resources.Core. This object is used to enumerate all available resources in the device. It is later used to get installed voices and display them using drop-down controls.

In the preceding code, we also declare local variables that are used in other methods called on-click of the Speak button and the voicesSelect drop-down list. Notice that we are also catching an exception in case the media player components are missing in the device and audio cannot be played. If an exception occurs, we capture it and display the StatusMessage error message in the HTML div object.

Add the following method:

```
function audio_SetUp() {
        audio.onplay = function () { // executes when the voice begins playing
            statusMessage.innerText = "Playing";
        };

        audio.onpause = function () { // executes when the user presses the stop button
            statusMessage.innerText = " Audio Completed";
            btnSpeak.innerText = "Speak";
        };

        audio.onended = function () { // executes when the voice finishes playing
            statusMessage.innerText = "Completed";
            btnSpeak.innerText = "Speak";
            voicesSelect.disabled = false;
        };
    }
```

audio_SetUp() method Sets up the voice element's events so the app UI updates based on the current state of voice playback.

Next, add the following method:

```
 function speakFn() {
        var btnSpeak = document.getElementById("btnSpeak");
        if (btnSpeak.innerText == "Stop") {
            voicesSelect.disabled = false;
            audio.pause();
            return;
        }

        // Changes the button label. You could also just disable the button if you don't
        want any user control.
        voicesSelect.disabled = true;
        btnSpeak.innerText = "Stop";
        statusBox.style.backgroundColor = "green";

        // Creates a stream from the text. This will be played using an audio element.
        synthesizer.synthesizeTextToStreamAsync(textToSynthesize.value).done(
            function (markersStream) {
                // Set the source and start playing the synthesized audio stream.
                var blob = MSApp.createBlobFromRandomAccessStream(markersStream.ContentType,
                markersStream);
                audio.src = URL.createObjectURL(blob, { oneTimeOnly: true });
                markersStream.seek(0);
                audio.play();
            },
```

```
    function (error) {
        errorMessage(error.message);
    });
}
```

speakFn() is the main method that is invoked when the user clicks on the Speak/Stop button on the app. The synthesizer.synthesizeTextToStreamAsync() method is used for converting the text in the text box into a Blob stream. It then plays the stream through audio.

Next, add the following method to allow users to select different audio voice options from resources.

```
function setVoiceFunction() {
    /// <summary>
    /// This is called when the user selects a voice from the drop down.
    /// </summary>
    if (voicesSelect.selectedIndex !== -1) {
        var allVoices = Windows.Media.SpeechSynthesis.SpeechSynthesizer.allVoices;

        // Use the selected index to find the voice.
        var selectedVoice = allVoices[voicesSelect.selectedIndex];

        synthesizer.voice = selectedVoice;

        // change the language of the sample text.
        context.languages = new Array(synthesizer.voice.language);
    }
}
```

In this method, we used Windows.Media.SpeechSynthesis.SpeechSynthesizer.allVoices() to get all installed speech synthesis engines (voices) in the allVoices object.

Next, add the following method to create items out of the device installed voices. The voices are then displayed in a voicesSelect drop-down control.

```
function listbox_GetVoices() {
    /// <summary>
    /// This creates items out of the system installed voices. The voices are then
    displayed in a listbox.
    /// This allows the user to change the voice of the synthesizer in your app based on
    their preference.
    /// </summary>

    // Get the list of all of the voices installed on this machine.
    var allVoices = Windows.Media.SpeechSynthesis.SpeechSynthesizer.allVoices;

    // Get the currently selected voice.
    var defaultVoice = Windows.Media.SpeechSynthesis.SpeechSynthesizer.defaultVoice;
    var voicesSelect = document.getElementById("voicesSelect");
    for (var voiceIndex = 0; voiceIndex < allVoices.size; voiceIndex++) {
        var currVoice = allVoices[voiceIndex];
        var option = document.createElement("option");
        option.text = currVoice.displayName + " (" + currVoice.language + ")";
        voicesSelect.add(option, null);
```

```
        // Check to see if we're looking at the current voice and set it as selected in
        the listbox.
        if (currVoice.id === defaultVoice.id) {
            voicesSelect.selectedIndex = voiceIndex;
        }
    }
}
```

Lastly, in case of any error message, there is a generic errorMessage() method to display an error on the errorTextArea object.

```
function errorMessage(text) {
    /// <summary>
    /// Sets the specified text area with the error message details.
    /// </summary>
    var errorTextArea = document.getElementById("errorTextArea");

    errorTextArea.innerText = text;
}
```

Once you are done creating the SpeechSynthesise.js file, make sure that you add a reference in the default.html file.

```
<script src="/js/SpeechSynthesise.js"></script>
```

When you run the application in the Windows 10 Mobile emulator, the app opens the default.html file. Press the Speak button to play the sound in the current default voice. Update the value in the Status div, as shown in Figure 15-4.

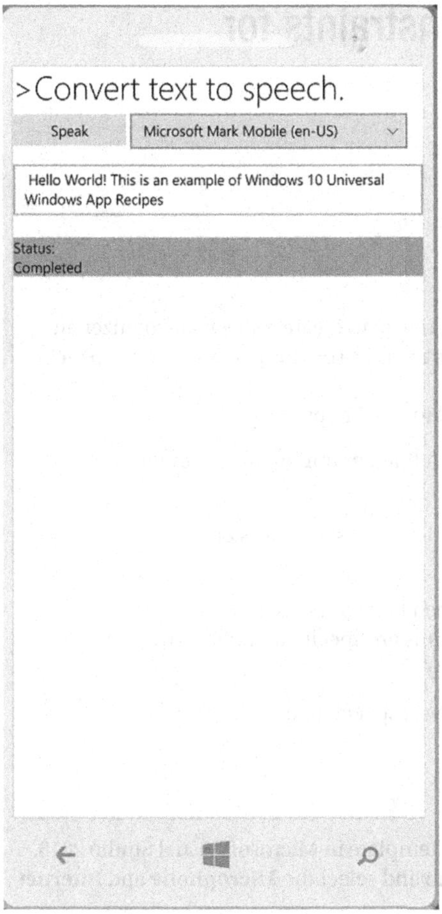

>Convert text to speech.

| Speak | Microsoft Mark Mobile (en-US) ∨ |

Hello World! This is an example of Windows 10 Universal Windows App Recipes

Status:
Completed

Figure 15-4. *Text to speech app*

In this recipe, you learned how to convert text to audio using the `Windows SpeechSynthesizer()` class. Note that you can also specify text in the SSML language and pass it to an object of `Windows.Media.SpeechSynthesis.SpeechSynthesizer()` to convert specified text into audio.

15.5 How to Specify Recognition Constraints for Speech Recognition

Problem

You need to create an app that allows speech recognition.

Solution

Use the `Windows.Media.SpeechRecognition.SpeechRecognizer` object to create a speech recognizer and use `Windows.Media.SpeechRecognition.SpeechRecognitionListConstraint` to specify different speech recognition constraints.

There are three possible speech constraints that can be used in UWP apps.

- `SpeechRecognitionTopicConstraint`: Based on predefined grammar and relies on an Internet connection.

- `SpeechRecognitionListConstraint`: Based on a predefined list of words and phrases.

- `SpeechRecognitionGrammarFileConstraint`: A Speech Recognition Grammar Specification (SRGS) file is added and all the constraints are specified in this XML file.

This recipe uses `SpeechRecognitionListConstraint` to convert speech to text.

How It Works

Create a new project using the **Windows Universal (Blank App)** template in Microsoft Visual Studio 2015. In the project `package.appmanifest` file, click the **Capabilities** tab and select the **Microphone** and **Internet** check boxes. This allows the app to use the audio feed.

Open the `default.html` file and copy the following code:

```
<body class="win-type-body">
    <div id="scenarioView">
        <div>
            <h2 id="sampleHeader" class="win-type-subheader">Speech to Text</h2>
            <div id="scenarioDescription">
                <p>Speech recognition using a custom list-based grammar.</p>
            </div>
        </div>
        <div id="scenarioContent">
            <div>
                <button id="btnSpeak" class="win-button">Speak</button>
            </div>
            <p id="errorTextArea"></p>
        </div>
    </div>
</body>
```

Right-click the project in Solution Explorer and select **Add ➤ New JavaScript file**. Provide a name for the file. In this example, let's name it **Speechrecognisation.js**.

Add the following code to the Speechrecognisation.js file:

```
(function () {
    "use strict";

    function GetControl() {
        WinJS.UI.processAll().done(function () {
            var btnSpeak = document.getElementById("btnSpeak");
            btnSpeak.addEventListener("click", buttonSpeechRecognizerListConstraintClick,
false);

            var resultTextArea = document.getElementById(resultTextArea);

        });

    }

    document.addEventListener("DOMContentLoaded", GetControl);
```

The preceding code adds an event receiver to the btnSpeak button. Now add a buttonSpeechRecognizerListConstraintClick function, which is triggered when the user clicks the Speak button on the user preference form control.

```
function buttonSpeechRecognizerListConstraintClick() {
    // Create an instance of SpeechRecognizer.
    var speechRecognizer =
      new Windows.Media.SpeechRecognition.SpeechRecognizer();

    // You could create this array dynamically.
    var responses = ["Yes", "No", "Hello", "Hello World"];

    // Add a web search grammar to the recognizer.
    var listConstraint =
        new Windows.Media.SpeechRecognition.SpeechRecognitionListConstraint(
        responses,
        "YesOrNo");

    speechRecognizer.uiOptions.audiblePrompt = "Say what you want to search for…";
    speechRecognizer.uiOptions.exampleText = "Ex. 'Yes', 'No', 'Hello'";
    speechRecognizer.constraints.append(listConstraint);
    var resultTextArea = document.getElementById(resultTextArea);
    // Compile the default dictation grammar.
    speechRecognizer.compileConstraintsAsync().done(
      // Success function.
      function (result) {
          // Start recognition.
          speechRecognizer.recognizeWithUIAsync().done(
            // Success function.
            function (speechRecognitionResult) {
                // Do something with the recognition result.
                speechRecognizer.close();
```

```
            },
            // Error function.
            function (err) {
                if (typeof errorTextArea !== "undefined") {
                    errorTextArea.innerText = "Speech recognition failed.";
                }
                speechRecognizer.close();
            });
    },
    // Error function.
    function (err) {
        if (typeof errorTextArea !== "undefined") {
            errorTextArea.innerText = err;
        }
        speechRecognizer.close();
    });

}
})();
```

The preceding code declares a variable named speechRecognizer. It is assigned to the Windows.Media.SpeechRecognition.SpeechRecognizer() class, which denotes a container for the speech recognizer object. The next line has the responses static array variable to store the recognized speech constraint values.

It is then referenced in an object instance of type Windows.Media.SpeechRecognition.SpeechRecognitionListConstraint(), which loads all the values specified in the responses array.

Following are the UI settings for the speech recognizer. Pass the SpeechRecognitionListConstraint listcontraint to the speechRecognizer object.

Then we call speechRecognizer.compileConstraintsAsync() method to asynchronously compile all constraints specified by the constraints property. This method execution provides output of type SpeechRecognitionCompilationResult, which is captured using the speechRecognitionResult success function. We also capture errors and display them using the errorTextArea element.

Once you done with the Speechrecognisation.js file, make sure you add a reference in default.html.

```
<script src="js/Speechrecognisation.js"></script>
```

That's it. The speech recognition is based on predefined constraints and is available in the app. It can be used to capture user inputs.

When you run the application in the Windows Mobile emulator, it looks like what's shown in Figure 15-5. Click **Go** and say specific words, such as "Yes," "No," or "Hello." The speech recognizer will validate it.

Figure 15-5. *Speech recognition based on a custom list of words*

15.6 How to Launch Your App with Cortana Voice Command in Foreground

Problem

You want to provide users the ability to use Cortana voice commands to launch your app in the foreground.

Solution

Use the Voice Command Definition (VCD) file to define the voice commands, which contain commands to activate the app. When the app is installed and executed, the VCD file is installed in Cortana.

Users can speak commands specified in the VCD file to launch the app. User voice commands are recognized by Cortana with the help of the Windows Speech platform and the cloud-hosted Microsoft Speech Recognition Service. Both services try to identify the speech and Cortana receives the text and launches the application and voice commands in the application with the onactivated event.

303

How It Works

Create a new project using the Windows Universal (Blank App) template in Microsoft Visual Studio 2015.

Add a new video command definition file, CortanaVoiceCommands.xml, in the project. Add the following XML code to the file:

```xml
<?xml version="1.0" encoding="utf-8" ?>
<VoiceCommands xmlns="http://schemas.microsoft.com/voicecommands/1.2">
  <CommandSet xml:lang="en-gb" Name="CortanaVoiceCommandSet">
    <AppName>Win10Recipes</AppName>
    <Example> Show Win10 Recipes </Example>

    <Command Name="showDevicesAvailableRecipes">
      <Example>Show</Example>
      <ListenFor RequireAppName="BeforeOrAfterPhrase">{command}</ListenFor>
      <ListenFor RequireAppName="ExplicitlySpecified">Listening to command </ListenFor>
      <Feedback> Recipes available in App </Feedback>
      <Navigate/>
    </Command>

    <PhraseList Label="command">
      <Item>Devices</Item>
      <Item>Text to Speech</Item>
    </PhraseList>
  </CommandSet>

</VoiceCommands>
```

In this Video Command Definition file, there are a few main elements. The <CommandSet> element defines the commands used to activate your app and execute a command. The <CommandSet> element also has the xml:Lang attribute to specify the command language. In this example, we are using GB English.

The <CommandPrefix> is unique name to our application. It's used as a prefix or suffix in the voice command to activate the app. The <Commmand> element is for commanding what the user can speak. The <ListenFor> element specifies the text that should be recognized by Cortana. The <Feedback> element specifies the text that is spoken by Cortana when launching the app. The <Navigate> element indicates that the voice command is to launch the app in the foreground.

If you want to launch the app by voice command in the background, use <VoiceCommandService>.

Once the VCD file is created, install the commands specified by a VCD file. To do this, use the installCommandDefinitionsFromStorageFileAsync method.

Open default.js from Solution Explorer. In this, call the onactivated method and add the following code:

```
//load vcd
        var storageFile = Windows.Storage.StorageFile;
        var wap = Windows.ApplicationModel.Package;
        var voiceCommandManager = Windows.ApplicationModel.VoiceCommands.
        VoiceCommandDefinitionManager;
        wap.current.installedLocation.getFileAsync("CortanaVoiceCommands.xml")
    .then(function (file) {
        voiceCommandManager.installCommandDefinitionsFromStorageFileAsync(file);
    });
        var activationKind = args.detail.kind;
        var activatedEventArgs = args.detail.detail;
```

In the preceding code, we used the `Windows.ApplicationModel.Package.current.`
`installedLocation.getFileAsync` method to get reference to the VCD file. The
`installCommandDefinitionsFromStorageFileAsync` method was called to install the commands specified
in the file. Now we have to specify how the app responds to the voice commands matching the VCD file. For
this, first check whether `IActivatedEventArgs.Kind` is VoiceCommand. Replace the following code after the
standard code in `default.js` to check activation argument types:

```
if (args.detail.kind === activation.ActivationKind.launch) {
    if (args.detail.previousExecutionState !== activation.
        ApplicationExecutionState.terminated) {
        // TODO: This application has been newly launched. Initialize your
        application here.
    } else {
        // TODO: This application was suspended and then terminated.
        // To create a smooth user experience, restore application state here so
        that it looks like the app never stopped running.
    }
    args.setPromise(WinJS.UI.processAll());
}

else if (activationKind == Windows.ApplicationModel.Activation.ActivationKind.
voiceCommand)
{
    var speechRecognitionResult = activatedEventArgs[0].Result;
    // Get the name of the voice command and the text spoken
    var voiceCommandName = speechRecognitionResult.RulePath[0];
    switch(voiceCommandName)
    {
    case "showDevicesAvailableRecipes":
        var textSpoken = speechRecognitionResult.semanticInterpretation.
        properties[0];
        var url = "Devices.html";
        nav.history.backStack.push({ location: "/Devices.html" })
        break;
        default:
            break;

    }
}


};

app.oncheckpoint = function (args) {
        // TODO: This application is about to be suspended. Save any state that
        needs to persist across suspensions here.
        // You might use the WinJS.Application.sessionState object, which is
        automatically saved and restored across suspension.
```

```
                // If you need to complete an asynchronous operation before your application
                is suspended, call args.setPromise().
        };

        app.start();
```

The preceding code checked for the Windows.ApplicationModel.Activation.ActivationKind value, which specifies the kind of activation. Check if ActivationKind is voiceCommand or by any other means. If the app is launched using a voice command, then you need to get the text spoken by the user in the speechRecognitionResult variable; to get the string, use activatedEventArgs.

The activatedEventArgs has a property called Result that provides the SpeechRecognitionResult.

To get text spoken by the user, use speechRecognitionResult.RulePath[0] and store it in the voiceCommandName local variable.

Using this text (voiceCommandName), you can decide which app page has to be displayed. For this, switch case and match the voicecommandName value with the command name specified in the VCD file. In CortanaVoiceCommands.xml, you specify command name showDevicesAvailableRecipes. If this is matched, show the application page to the user in devices.html. This way, the application is integrated with Cortana. When the user launches the app using voice commands, you can further enhance to launch application pages.

■ **Note**   You can't test this recipe using a Visual Studio Mobile emulator because Cortana needs a Microsoft account registration and sign in process, which does not work on a Mobile emulator. Instead, you need to install the app on a device and then run Cortana to test the app launching in the foreground.

CHAPTER 16

■ ■ ■

Additional Tools

The Windows SDK and Microsoft Visual Studio 2015 provide additional tools and features that let developers easily debug and test their Windows apps. This chapter covers some of these tools, such as the JavaScript Console window, DOM Explorer, Diagnostic Tools, the Windows 10 Mobile emulator Additional Tools. These tools make a developer's life much easier when it comes to testing an app in various scenarios.

16.1 JavaScript Console Window

Problem

You want to view the JavaScript errors or write debug messages when debugging your Universal Windows Platform app.

Solution

Use the JavaScript Console window in Visual Studio 2015 to view the JavaScript errors or write debug messages when debugging your Universal Windows Platform app.

How It Works

Microsoft Visual Studio 2015 provides a tool called the JavaScript Console window that allows developers to do the following:

- Display and modify the value of variables.

- Run JavaScript code that can execute within the current context.

- View JavaScript errors, exceptions, and messages.

- Display the messages from the app to the console window.

The JavaScript Console window is displayed when your app runs. Alternatively, you can open the JavaScript Console window from Visual Studio Menu Debug ➤ Windows ➤ JavaScript Console, as shown in Figure 16-1.

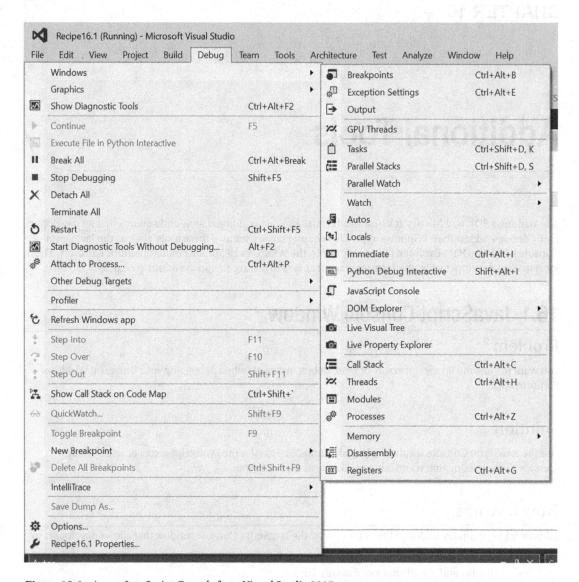

Figure 16-1. *Access JavaScript Console from Visual Studio 2015*

To test this functionality, create a new Universal Windows Platform app from Visual Studio 2015 using the JavaScript template.

Build the solution and run it using the **Local Machine** option. You should see the app running on the desktop. Switch to Visual Studio with your app still running. Notice the JavaScript console lists all possible JavaScript errors in the page, as shown in Figure 16-2.

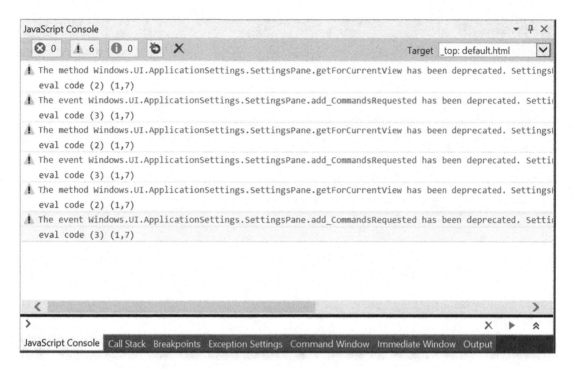

Figure 16-2. JavaScript Console window displaying list of warnings and errors

The JavaScript console provides the following options:

- View error messages
- View warning messages
- View messages
- Options to clear the console

Developers can also write debug messages that can be displayed when the app runs in debug mode from Visual Studio 2015. This is achieved by using the console.log method.

Let's open the **default.js** file from the project's js folder and add the following code to the first line of the file, just below the use strict option.

```
console.log("This is a custom log message");
```

When you run the app and view the JavaScript Console window, you see the message in it, as shown in Figure 16-3.

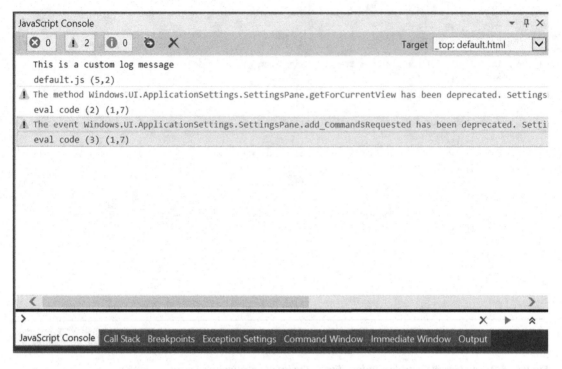

Figure 16-3. *JavaScript Console window displaying the log message*

Table 16-1 lists some of the common commands to manipulate messages in the console window.

Table 16-1. *JavaScript Console Window Commands*

Command Name	Description
assert(expression, message)	Sends a message if expression evaluates to false.
clear()	Clears the messages from the console window.
debug(message)	Sends a message to the console window; it is identical to the console.log
error(message)	Sends an error message to the console window. The message text is red and includes an error symbol.
info(message)	Sends a message to the console window; the message is prefaced with an information symbol.
log(message)	Sends a message to the console window.

16.2 DOM Explorer
Problem

You need to inspect the properties of the app's HTML element, as well as debug and modify the HTML and CSS-style element properties.

Solution

Use DOM Explorer in Visual Studio 2015 to inspect and modify the values of the HTML and CSS elements for debugging purposes.

How It Works

Web developers and Internet Explorer users should be aware of DOM Explorer, which is a popular debugging tool. The F12 Developer tools in Microsoft Edge and Internet Explorer provide this option.

Since the UWP app supports development with web technologies, DOM Explorer is supported by UWP apps and apps created using Visual Studio tools for Apache Cordova.

Developers can access DOM Explorer in Windows using the Visual Studio Menu Debug ➤ Windows ➤ DOM Explorer, as shown in Figure 16-4.

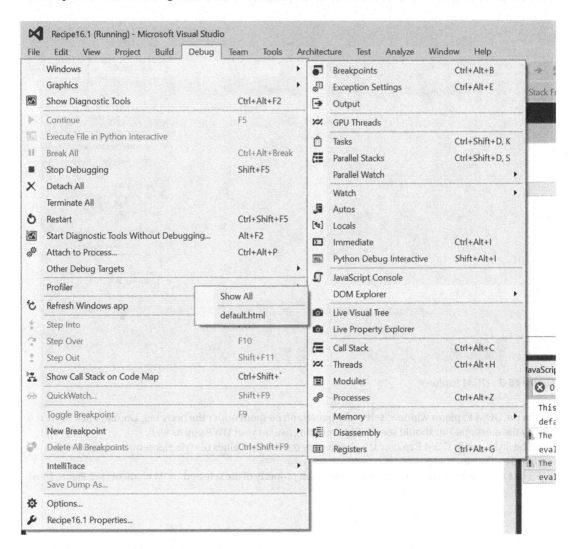

Figure 16-4. Access DOM Explorer from Visual Studio 2015

You can do the following using DOM Explorer in Visual Studio:

- Inspect the live DOM

- Select the elements

- Debug CSS styles

- Debug the layout

- View DOM event listeners

- Debug a WebView control

Open an existing UWP app developed with JavaScript and run it in the **Local Machine** option.

Switch to Visual Studio and select the DOM Explorer tab. You can use the F12 shortcut key when the app is running to display DOM Explorer in F12 developer tools, as shown in Figure 16-5.

Figure 16-5. *DOM Explorer*

In the DOM Explorer window, select the paragraph element under the body tag. Double-click the text to modify the message. You should see the text updating live on your UWP app as well.

The Styles tab in DOM Explorer lets developers modify the values of style elements and see how it is rendered on the app page.

The Computed tab shows the final value for each property of the selected DOM element (see Figure 16-6) .

Figure 16-6. *Computed tab in DOM Explorer*

The Layout tab displays the element's box model and shows what your app's layout looks like, considering the offset and margin (see Figure 16-7).

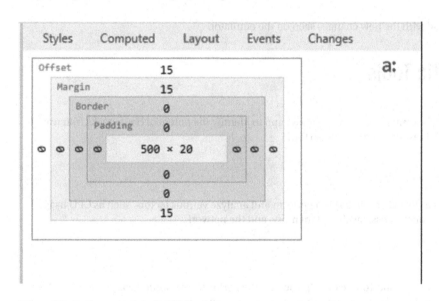

Figure 16-7. *Layout tab in DOM Explorer*

You can also refresh your app while debugging. To do this, follow these steps.

1. When the app is running in an emulator, open the **default.html** file in Visual Studio and modify the source code.

2. Click the **Refresh Windows app** button in the Debug toolbar or hit the F4 shortcut key (see Figure 16-8).

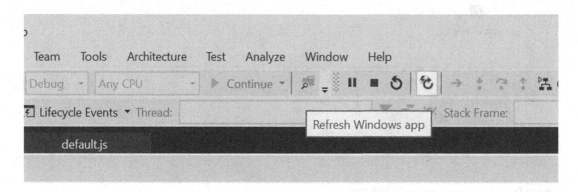

Figure 16-8. *Refresh Windows app button in Visual Studio*

The app pages reload with the new changes seen on the emulator.

16.3 Diagnostic Tools

Problem

You want to analyze the performance of your Windows app to identify the potential bottlenecks. You want to analyze the CPU usage, UI responsiveness, and so forth.

Solution

Use the Diagnostic Tools in Visual Studio 2015 to perform and analyze various factors, such as CPU usage, GPU usage, HTML UI responsiveness, JavaScript memory, and the network.

How It Works

Visual Studio profilers or Diagnostic Tools can help you find the performance bottlenecks in your Windows app. They show you where the code in your app spends most of the time.

You can launch Visual Studio 2015 Diagnostic Tools by navigating to the **Debug** menu and selecting **Start Diagnostic Tools Without Debugging**, as shown in Figure 16-9.

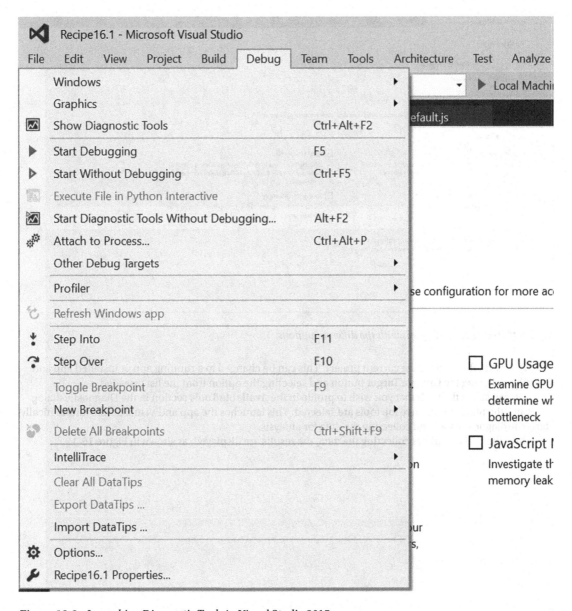

Figure 16-9. *Launching Diagnostic Tools in Visual Studio 2015*

The Visual Studio Diagnostic Tools (see Figure 16-10) provide the following options for developers to test on their apps:

- CPU usage
- GPU Usage
- HTML UI responsiveness
- JavaScript memory
- Network

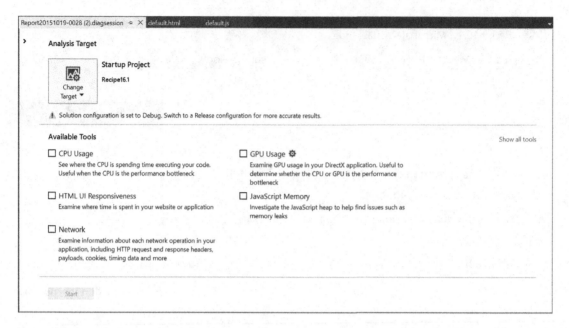

Figure 16-10. Diagnostic Tools with the different options

By default, the target is the current project. This can be changed to a running app or installed app and so forth by clicking the **Change Target** button and selecting the option from the list provided.

You can select the tools that you wish to profile in the **Available Tools** section in the Diagnostic dialog.

Click the Start button once the tools are selected. This launches the app and Visual Studio automatically starts the diagnostic tool and collecting the data for analysis.

Once the tool completes collecting the data, the results are displayed, as shown in Figure 16-11.

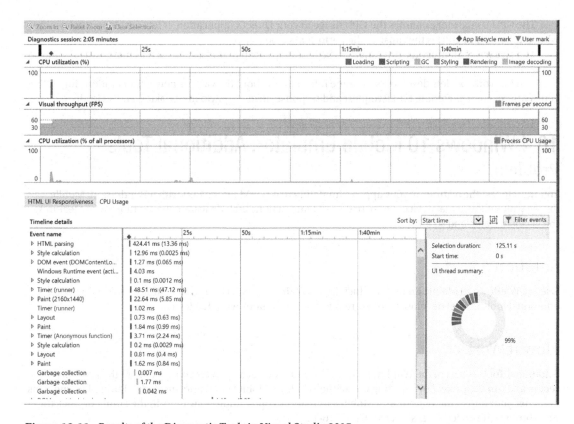

Figure 16-11. *Results of the Diagnostic Tools in Visual Studio 2015*

Understanding how the app uses the CPU is a good starting point for analyzing and identifying the performance issues in your app. The CPU usage tool displays information on where the CPU is spending time executing your JavaScript code.

When analyzing the CPU Usage report, developers can check the CPU utilization timeline graph and select the timeline segments to view details. The CPU utilization timeline graph shows the CPU activity of the app from all the processor cores of the device.

The UI Responsiveness tool can help developers identify the following issues:

- UI responsiveness. The app could be slow to respond if the UI thread is getting blocked. The possible reasons for this include excessive synchronous JavaScript code, synchronous XHR requests, or even processor-intensive JavaScript code.

- Slow loading time caused by resources.

The GPU Usage tool examines the GPU usage in your DirectX application. It lets developers determine whether the CPU or GPU is the cause of the performance bottleneck.

The JavaScript Memory tool investigates the JavaScript heap to find issues such as memory leaks and so forth.

The Network tool lets developers examine information about the various network operations impacting your Windows app, including HTTP request and response headers, payloads, cookies, and so forth.

16.4 Windows 10 Mobile Emulator: Additional Tools

Problem

You want to test the features of your app by simulating real-world interaction with a Windows 10 Mobile device without the actual device. These real-world interactions include testing the location-aware features, the accelerometer, and so forth.

Solution

Use the Windows 10 Mobile emulator, which is part of the Universal Windows Platform tools. It includes additional tools that let developers to test real-world interactions with the device.

How It Works

Additional Tools is part of the Windows 10 Mobile emulator. Let's open the app created in the previous recipe and run the project by selecting one of the Windows Mobile emulators instead of Local Machine. This launches your app in the Windows 10 Mobile emulator. To open Additional Tools in the emulator, click the tools button (the >> icon), as shown in Figure 16-12.

Figure 16-12. Windows 10 Mobile emulator with Additional Tools feature

This opens the Additional Tools window, where developers can access tools like Location, Networking, and Accelerometer to test on the emulator (see Figure 16-13).

Figure 16-13. Additional Tools window in emulator

Simulate Mouse Input

You can click the **mouse input** button on the emulator toolbar to enable the mouse input. This ensures that any mouse clicks within the emulator will be sent as mouse events to the emulator's operating system. This is a very useful feature if your app is paired to a mouse that can be used as input.

Near Field Communications (NFC)

If your app uses Near Field Communication (NFC), the NFC tab (see Figure 16-14) might be a useful tool to test your app in scenarios such as proximity, or tap to share, card emulation, and so forth.

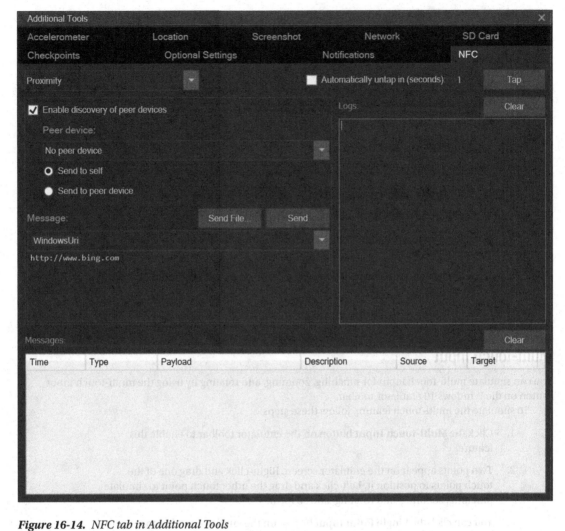

Figure 16-14. *NFC tab in Additional Tools*

You can test your app by simulating a pair of phones tapping together by using a pair of emulators. The NFC tool supports the following modes:

- Proximity mode
- HCE (host card emulation) mode
- Smart card reader mode

The NFC tab displays the following when you test this functionality:

- Mode selected
- Logs related to the tap and untapped event
- A transcript of all messages sent and received over the current connection

Note that you will receive a Windows Firewall prompt when you click the **Tap** button for the first time in the NFC tab.

You need to launch two emulators of different resolutions from Visual Studio to simulate a pair of phones tapping together.

Select **the Enable discovery of peer devices** check box. The peer device drop-down box displays the Microsoft emulators and the Windows machines running the simulator driver.

When both the emulators are running, follow these steps:

1. Select the target emulator.

2. Select the **Send to peer device** option.

3. Click the **Tap** button, which simulates the two devices tapping together.

4. Click the **Untap** button to disconnect the devices.

To simulate reading messages from a device, follow these steps:

1. Select the **Send to self** radio option to test scenarios that require only one NFC-enabled device.

2. Click the **Tap** button to simulate tapping a device to a tag. You should hear the notification sound.

3. Click the **Untap** button to disconnect.

Multi-touch Input

You can simulate multi-touch input for pinching, zooming, and rotating by using the multi-touch input button on the Windows 10 emulator toolbar.

To simulate the multi-touch feature, follow these steps:

1. Click the **Multi-touch Input** button on the emulator toolbar to enable this feature.

2. Two points appear on the emulator screen. Right-click and drag one of the touch points to position it. Left-click and drag the other touch point to simulate pinching, zooming, and rotating, and so forth.

3. You can click the **Single Point Input** button on the emulator toolbar to restore the normal input.

Accelerometer

The Accelerometer tool lets developers test Windows apps that track the movement of the phone (see Figure 16-15). It simulates the behavior in the emulator.

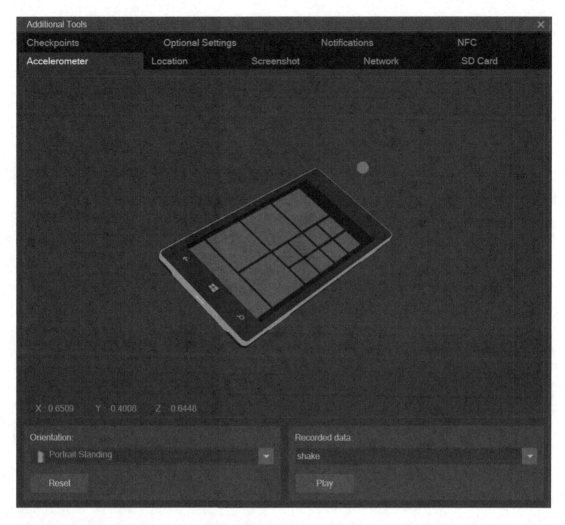

Figure 16-15. Accelerometer tool in Additional Tools

The accelerometer sensor can be tested with live input or prerecorded input. It can simulate the shaking of a phone with the recorded data.

1. Select the desired orientation from the orientation drop-down list.

2. In the middle of the accelerometer, you see a colored dot. Drag it to simulate the movement of the device in a 3D plane.

Location

You can test apps that use navigation and geo-fencing by using the Location tab.

You can simulate the movement from one location to another at different speeds and accuracy levels. The Location tool (see Figure 16-16) currently supports three modes:

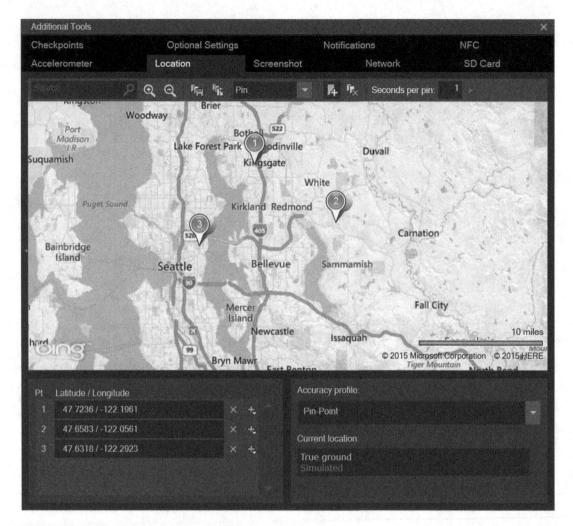

Figure 16-16. Location tab in Additional Tools

- *Pin mode*: Place pushpins on the map. You can then click the Play all points, the simulator sends the location of each pin to the emulator in a sequence at the interval specified.

- *Live mode*: When you place a pushpin on a map, the simulator sends the location of the pin to the emulator as you place them.

- *Route mode*: Place pushpins on a map to indicate the waypoints. The simulator calculates the route.

Users can also do the following in the Location tab:

- Search for a location using the search box.

- Zoom in and zoom out of a map.

- Save the current set of pushpin points to an XML file to reload it later.

- Clear all the points.

- Save the route and load it the next time you are in the Pin and Route modes.

Network

The Network tab lets developers test the app at different network speeds and signal strengths.

You can test your app on various network speeds, such as 2G, 3G, and 4G, and at different signal strengths, such as good, average, and poor.

This feature is especially useful when your app makes calls to web services or transfers data.

CHAPTER 17

■ ■ ■

Sideloading and Windows App Certification Kit

After you develop an app, it is important that you deploy the app and test it on various machines before you upload it to the Store. This chapter covers some of the recipes on how to generate an app package from command prompts and sideload your app on the machine, and later use the Windows App Certification Kit to test that the app is good enough to be published to the Windows Store. Chapter 18 includes a recipe to generate the app package interactively from Visual Studio, hence, that is not covered in this chapter.

17.1 Sideload Your App

Problem

You need to sideload your app on a Windows device without submitting it to the Windows Store so that testers can install and test it using the app package file that you have created.

Solution

Use PowerShell to run the Add-AppDevPackage file (which was created when generating the package file) to sideload your app on a Windows device.

How It Works

Your app's users cannot simply install a Universal Windows app the same way that they do with traditional desktop apps.

Universal Windows apps can only be downloaded from the Store and then installed on the device. If you have an app that you want to install without going to the Store, you can sideload the app on the device so that users can install and test it.

You can sideload the app package to a Windows 10 device by following these steps.

1. Enable your device for sideloading.

2. Install your app using PowerShell.

The first step to sideload the app is to ensure that the sideloading is enabled on your device. You can enable it on your Windows machine by launching the Settings app and visiting **Update & Security**. Select the **For developers** button, which displays various options for using the developer features. Select **Developer mode** to enable the sideloading for the device (see Figure 17-1).

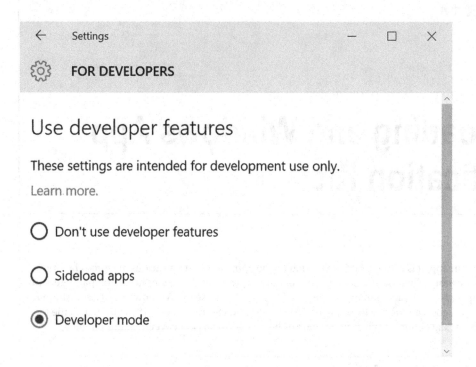

Figure 17-1. Enable Sideload apps and Developer mode in Windows 10

Once you select Developer mode, a confirmation dialog is displayed (see Figure 17-2) to confirm that you would like to turn on app sideloading. The **Sideload apps** option lets you install an .appx file and the certificate that is needed to run the app with the PowerShell script that was created along with the package. This option is more secure than Developer mode because you cannot install apps that are not trusted. But for this recipe, let's select **Developer mode** and proceed.

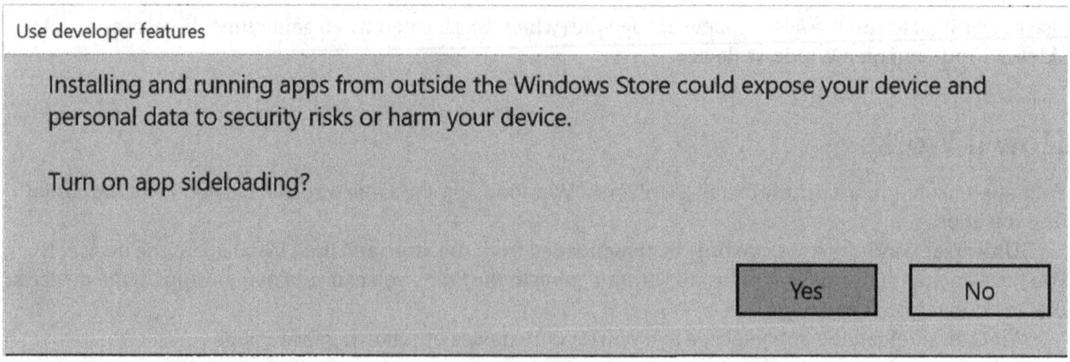

Figure 17-2. Confirmation dialog for enabling sideloading

The next step is to install the app on the machine. To do it, follow these steps.

1. Generate the package file for installation. This is covered in Chapter 18.

2. Copy the complete folder of the package file that you want to install onto the target machine. For example, if you have created the app bundle, the folder name will contain the version number and _test. If the version number is 1.0.0.0 and the project name is Recipe17.1, targeting AnyCPU, the folder would be **Recipe17.1_1.0.0.0_AnyCPU_Debug_Test**.

3. On the target machine that you want to sideload the app, open the folder. Right-click the **Add-AppDevPackage.ps1** file and click the **Run with PowerShell** button on the context menu, as shown in Figure 17-3.

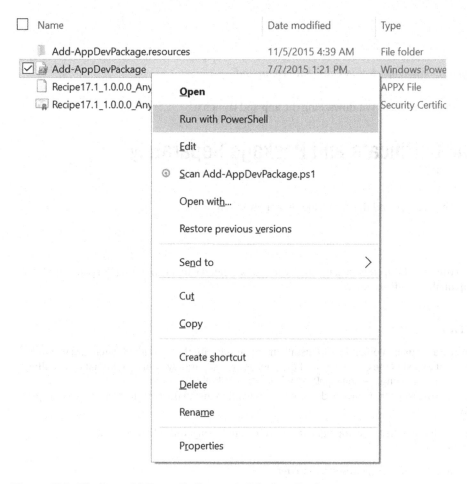

Figure 17-3. *The Run with PowerShell menu in Windows Explorer*

4. Follow the information shown in the PowerShell command. When the package is successfully installed, you will notice the **Your app was successfully installed** message in the command prompt, as shown in Figure 17-4.

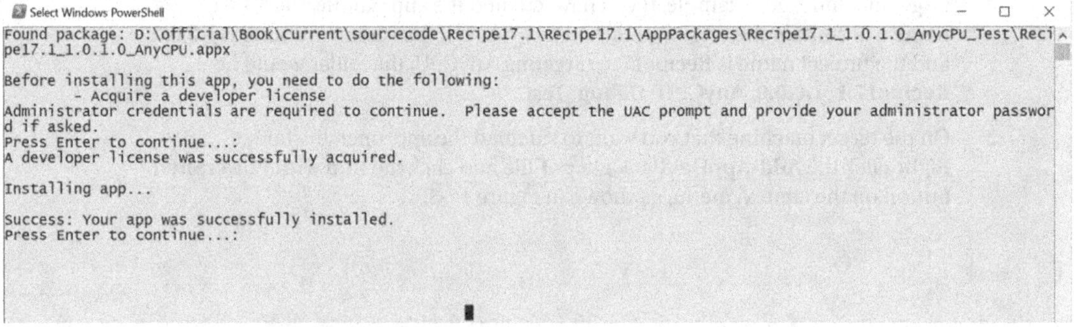

Figure 17-4. *App installation message in PowerShell command*

Now, click the **Start** button in Windows. Find the app and launch it.

17.2 Install Certificate and Package Separately

Problem

You need to install the package and the certificate separately in Windows.

Solution

Use PowerShell to run the Add-AppDevPackage file (which was created when generating the package file) to sideload your app on the Windows device.

How It Works

Recipe 17.1 demonstrated using PowerShell to install an app along with the certificate. There are instances where you might want to install the certificate and the package file separately. You can do that by installing the certificate first and then using the Add-AppDevPackage PowerShell command.

The following are the steps that you need to take if you want to install the certificate and the package file separately on a Windows desktop.

1. Open the folder where the app package was created. Ideally, this folder contains the following:

   - Add-AppDevPackage.resources folder

   - Add-AppDevPackage.resources PowerShell script file

   - ProjectName_Version_Platform.appx file

   - ProjectName_Version_Platform.cer security or certificate file

2. Double-click the certificate file (.cer) and then click the **Install Certificate** button on the Certificate screen (see Figure 17-5).

Figure 17-5. Install Certificate screen

3.   On the Certificate Import Wizard screen, select the **Local Machine** option under the Store Location group, as shown in Figure 17-6. Click **Next**.

Figure 17-6. Select store location from the Certificate Import Wizard

4. In the UAC dialog, click the **OK** button to continue.

5. In the next certificate import screen, select the **Place all certificates in the following store** radio button and click the **Browse** button (see Figure 17-7).

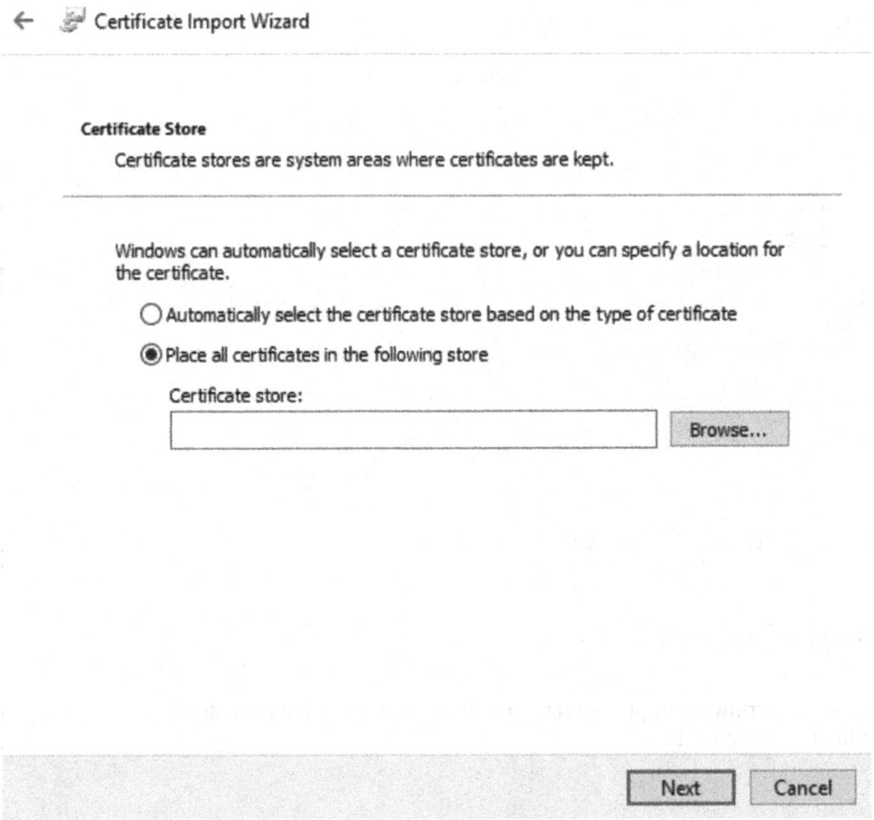

← ⚙ Certificate Import Wizard

Certificate Store

Certificate stores are system areas where certificates are kept.

Windows can automatically select a certificate store, or you can specify a location for the certificate.

○ Automatically select the certificate store based on the type of certificate

◉ Place all certificates in the following store

Certificate store:

| | Browse... |

| Next | Cancel |

Figure 17-7. Select the certificate store to place the certificate

6. In the Select Certificate Store pop-up screen, select **Trusted people** and click the **OK** button (see Figure 17-8).

Figure 17-8. *Select Certificate Store screen*

7. Click **Next** in the Certificate Import Wizard and then complete the certificate by clicking **Finish** (see Figure 17-9).

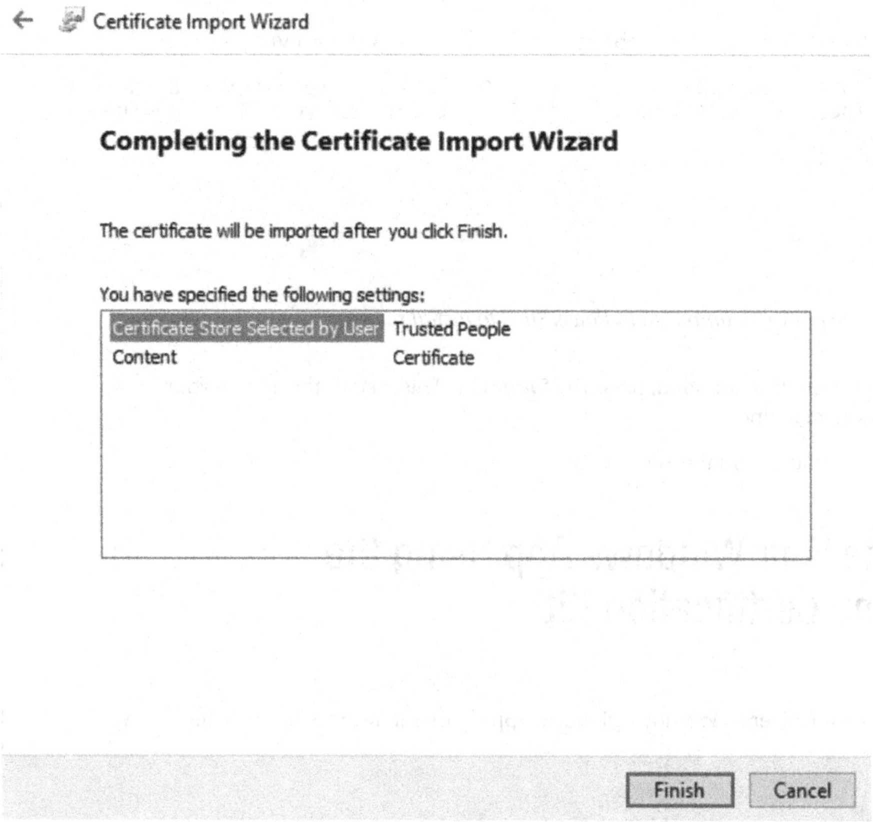

← 🎫 Certificate Import Wizard

Completing the Certificate Import Wizard

The certificate will be imported after you click Finish.

You have specified the following settings:

Certificate Store Selected by User	Trusted People
Content	Certificate

Finish   Cancel

Figure 17-9. *Completion of the certificate import process*

8. This installs the certificate to the Windows certificate store on the local machine. The next step is to install the app alone using the add-appxpackage cmdlet for PowerShell, as explained in the following steps.

9. Navigate to the **AppPackages** folder and identify the complete path of the package file (.appx) file that you want to install.

10. As shown in Figure 17-10, open Windows PowerShell from the Start menu and run the Add-appxpackage command by specifying the following parameters.

    ```
    Add-appxpackage –Path <Path to appx file>
    ```

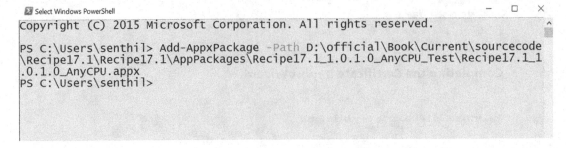

Figure 17-10. Add-appxpackage command in PowerShell to install the app

11. Once you enter the command, press the **Enter** key. This installs the app on your Windows 10 machine.

You can now start the app from the Start menu.

17.3 Validate Your Windows App Using the Windows App Certification Kit

Problem

You want to validate your Universal Windows Platform app by interactively using the Windows App Certification Kit.

Solution

Launch the Windows App Certification Kit from the Windows Start menu and specify the app that you want to validate and test.

How It Works

It is always better to validate and test your app locally before you submit it to the Store for certification. This provides more information to the developers in case the package has any issues.

The Windows App Certification Kit is a great tool that helps the developers validate and test your app locally. The Windows App Certification Kit is included in the Windows Software Development Kit (SDK) for Windows 10.

The following steps validate and test a Windows app using the Windows App Certification Kit.

1. From the Windows Start menu, search for **Windows app cert kit** and then click the **Windows App Cert Kit** desktop app (see Figure 17-11).

Figure 17-11. Windows App Certification Kit in the Start menu

2. In the Windows App Certification Kit, select the validation category that you want to perform. For example, if you are validating a Windows app, select **Validate Store App** (see Figure 17-12).

 Windows App Certification Kit 10.0   —   ☐   ✕

Select the validation to perform

Validate Store App
Test a Store app for submission to the Store

Validate Desktop App
Test a desktop app to qualify for Windows Desktop App Certification

Validate Desktop Device App
Test a desktop device app for compliance with value-added software requirements

Figure 17-12. *Selection of the type of app to perform validation*

3. Once you select the Store App option, you are provided with options to either select an app that is already installed on the machine or choose the package file that you want to validate. You can enable the **Browse for app you want to validate** radio button and click the **Browse** button to select the package file (see Figure 17-13).

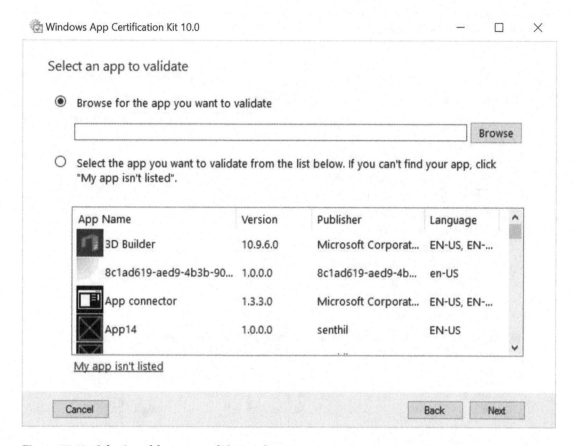

Figure 17-13. *Selection of the app to validate and test*

4. Once you have selected the app or the package file, click **Next** to continue. The
    subsequent screens display the tests workflows that are applicable for the app
    that you are testing (see Figure 17-14). If a test is not applicable to your app type,
    it is grayed out.

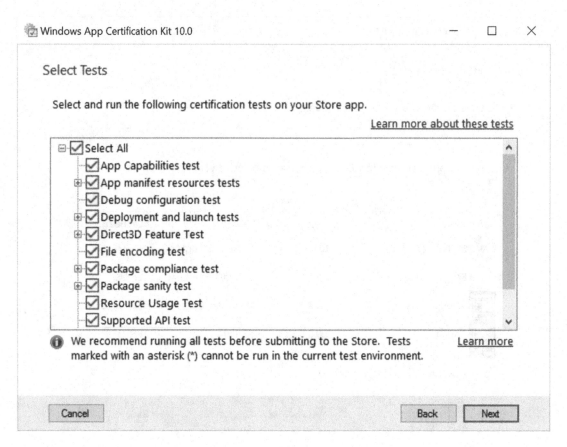

Figure 17-14. Types of tests applicable for the app

5. Click **Next**. The Windows App Certification Kit begins validating the app, as shown in Figure 17-15.

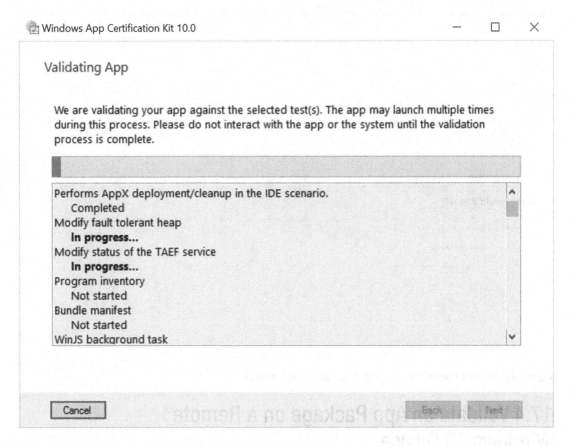

Figure 17-15. *Windows App Certification Kit validating the app*

6. Once the validation is complete, you are prompted to save the report in the XML file format, which displays the results, as shown in Figure 17-16. The Windows App Certification Kit creates an HTML file along with an XML report and saves them in a specified folder.

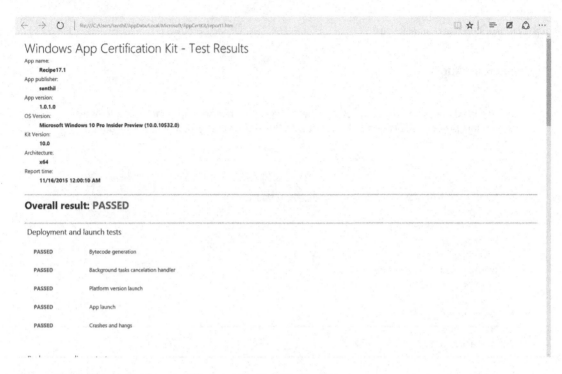

Figure 17-16. *Test results from the Windows App Certification Kit*

17.4 Validate an App Package on a Remote Windows 10 Device

Problem

You need to validate your app package in a remote Windows 10 machine and test it.

Solution

Install the remote tools for Visual Studio and the Windows App Certification Kit on a remote machine and use the **Remote Machine** option to validate the package on the remote machine.

How It Works

When generating the package file from Visual Studio, you also have the option of validating it on a remote machine.

To validate the package on a remote machine, follow these steps.

1. Enable your Windows 10 remote device for development by enabling **Developer mode** in the **Use developer features** in the Settings app, as shown in Figure 17-17. Note that the validation on the remote ARM device for Windows 10 is currently not supported.

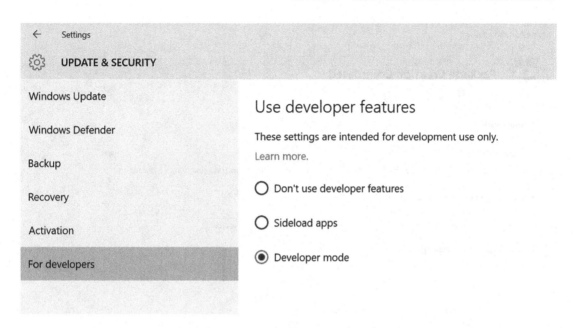

Figure 17-17. *Enabling Developer mode in the Settings app*

2. Download and install the remote tools for Visual Studio on the remote machine. Go to `http://www.microsoft.com/en-us/download/details.aspx?id=48155&N avToggle=True`. The remote tools for Visual Studio are used to run the Windows App Certification Kit.

3. Download the Windows App Certification Kit from `https://dev.windows.com/ en-us/develop/app-certification-kit` and install it on your remote machine.

4. Now, start creating a package from your Windows app. In the **Package Creation Completed** wizard, select the **Remote machine** option and click the ellipsis button (see Figure 17-18).

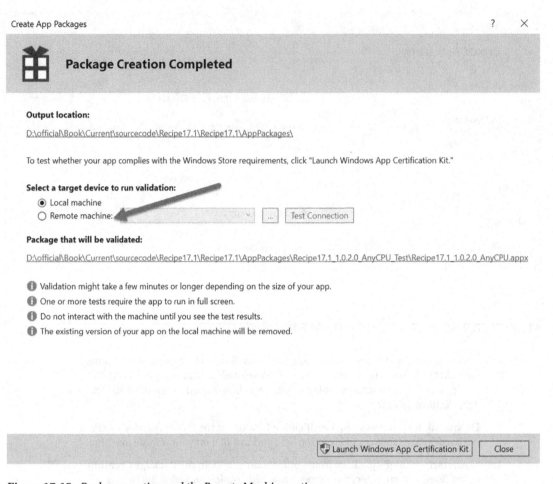

Figure 17-18. *Package creation and the Remote Machine option*

5. Enter your subnet/Domain Name Server (DNS)/IP address. Select the appropriate mode in Authentication Mode menu of Windows credentials (see Figure 17-19).

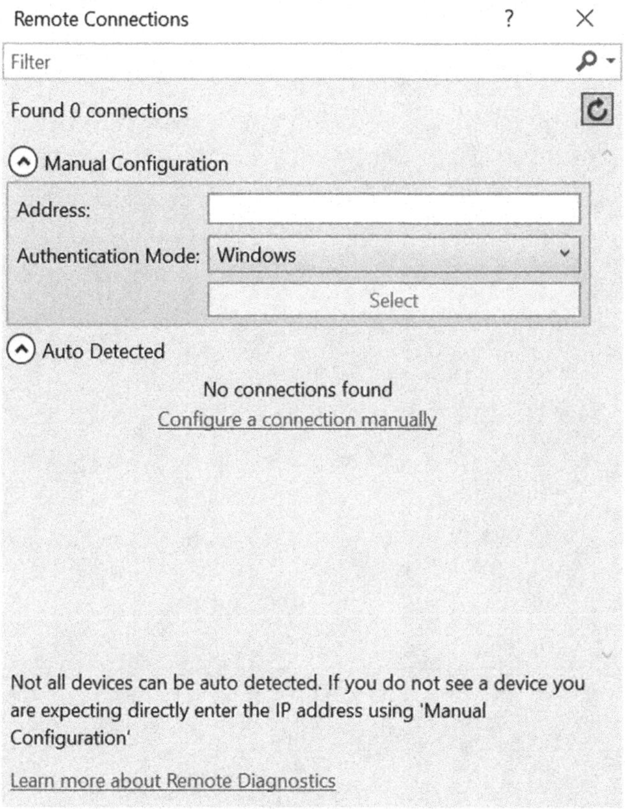

Figure 17-19. *Remote Connection screen*

6. Click the **Select** button and then the **Launch Windows App Certification Kit** button. If the remote tools are running on the remote machine, you are connected and the validation tests should begin.

CHAPTER 18

■ ■ ■

Store and Monetization

By now, you should have finished developing your Universal Windows platform application targeting the Windows 10 OS. You need to build your application and upload it to the Windows Store, where users search for and download apps. In this chapter, you will learn the things required to get your app in the Windows Store, and how to make money by making use of in-app advertising.

18.1 Create a Windows App Developer Account

Problem

You need to build and upload your application to the Windows Store. But to do this, you need to first log in to the Windows Dev Center using your developer account. You need to know how to create a developer account before you can start the upload phase.

Solution

Create a developer account online. There are two ways to start this process.

- Go directly to **http://dev.windows.com**.

- Access account registration through Visual Studio.

Access Account Registration Through the Windows Dev Center

The Windows Dev Center is a one-stop portal for Windows app development. This portal provides the tools that you need to get started with Windows 10 application development. There are code samples, tutorials on how to develop Windows 10 apps, and of course, the provision to submit your apps. The Windows Dev Center can be accessed at http://dev.windows.com. When you navigate to this page, you see a **Get a dev account** link. Click it and follow the onscreen instructions to finish creating your own dev account. A developer account allows you to submit your apps (for all Windows devices) to the Windows Store. It also allows you to manage your apps and get analytics on how your app is doing in the Store.

You can sign up under one of the following categories:

- *Individual*: This account type lets you develop and sell apps as an individual, a student, or an unincorporated group. The fee for this type of account is $19.

- *Company*: This account type is for companies that have a registered business name to develop and sell apps. The fee for this type of account is $99.

You need to provide the following to get an account:

- Your contact information
- The publisher name that you want displayed
- A payment method (VISA/MasterCard/PayPal)

Access Account Registration Through Visual Studio

You can also register as a developer via Visual Studio.

In Visual Studio, from the **Project** menu, select **Store ➤ Open Developer Account** (see Figure 18-1).

This action opens a new browser window and takes you directly to the account registration page. You have to follow the onscreen instructions to finish account registration.

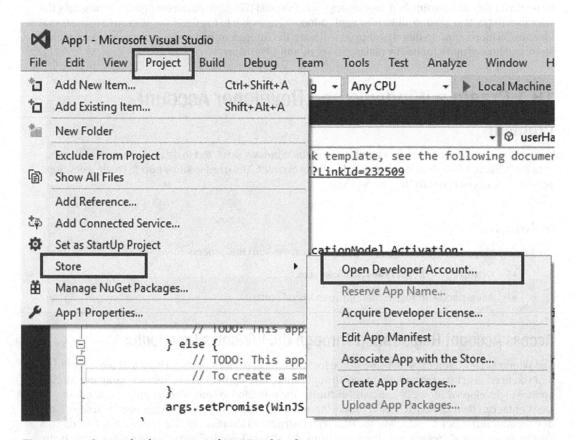

Figure 18-1. *Open a developer account from Visual Studio*

18.2 Package a Universal Windows Platform Application for Windows 10

Problem

You have completed the development of your app. You have finished account registration in the Windows Dev Center. Now you want to package your app so that you can submit it to the Store.

Solution

To sell or distribute Windows apps, you need to create what is known as an *application package* or an *appxupload package*, as it is technically termed. With the Universal Windows Platform (UWP), you generate one package (.appxupload). This package is uploaded to the Windows Store. Once the app is in the Store, it can then be installed and run on any Windows 10 device, including phones, tablets, PCs, and so forth.

How It Works

Packaging a Windows 10 app needs to be done as a two-step process. First, configure the package with certain properties and settings. Then, generate the package to upload to the Store.

Configuring an App Package

To create an app package, you need to first set certain properties and settings that describe your app. The app properties and settings are stored in a file called the *app manifest* file, which is in the root of your project under the name package.appxmanifest. Some of the properties/settings you set in the manifest are the images used for the application tile or the orientation that the app supports.

The application manifest file is an XML file. Visual Studio provides a GUI-based manifest designer/editor to edit this file. With the GUI designer/editor, it is easy to make changes to your application manifest.

The following steps provide instructions on how to configure the package:

1. In **Solution Explorer**, expand your application's project node.

2. Double-click the **package.appxmanifest** file. Visual Studio will launch the manifest designer/editor (see Figure 18-2).

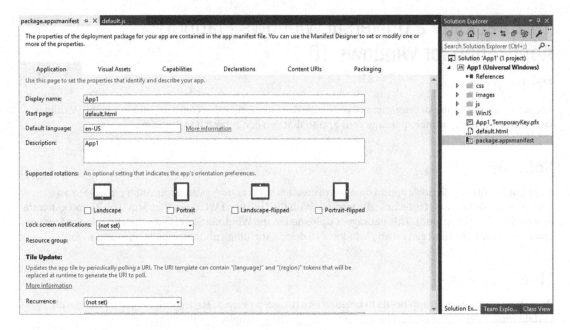

Figure 18-2. *Application package manifest editing*

The manifest file has several tabs to configure different aspects of your app.

- **Application**: Configures your app's display name, start page, the default language, description, supported orientations, lock screen notification mode, and tile update information.

- **Visual Assets**: Configures your app's visual assets, such as tile images and logos, the badge logo, and the splash screen (see Figure 18-3).

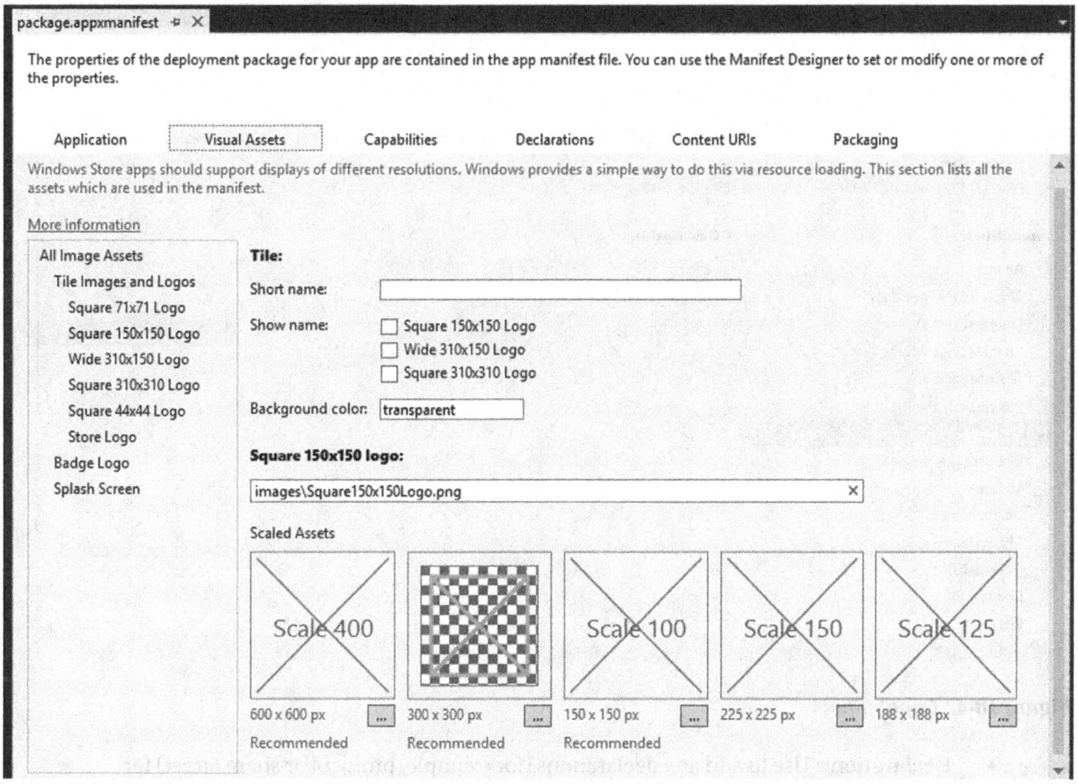

Figure 18-3. *Visual Assets*

- **Capabilities**: Any capabilities that your app needs has to be declared in this area of the manifest file (see Figure 18-4).

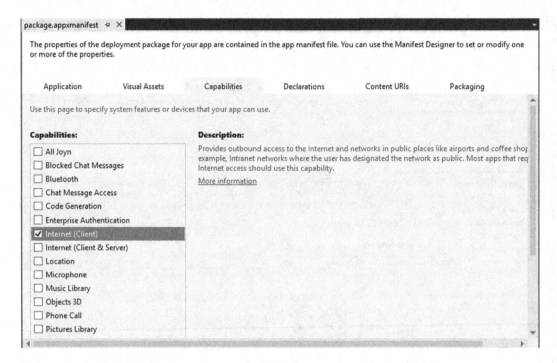

Figure 18-4. Capabilities

- **Declarations**: Use to add any declarations (for example, protocol or share target) for your app and sets their properties (see Figure 18-5).

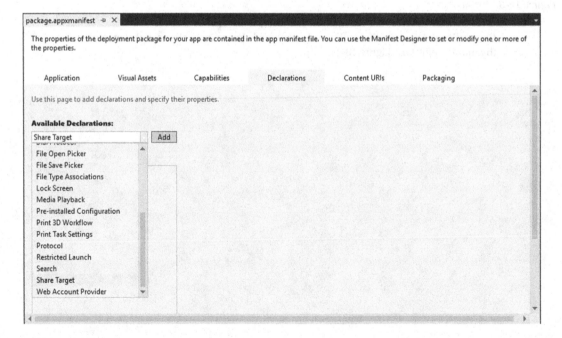

Figure 18-5. Declarations

- **Content URIs**: Specifies which pages in the app can be navigated to by a frame, and URIs that can be navigated to when loaded in a web view (see Figure 18-6).

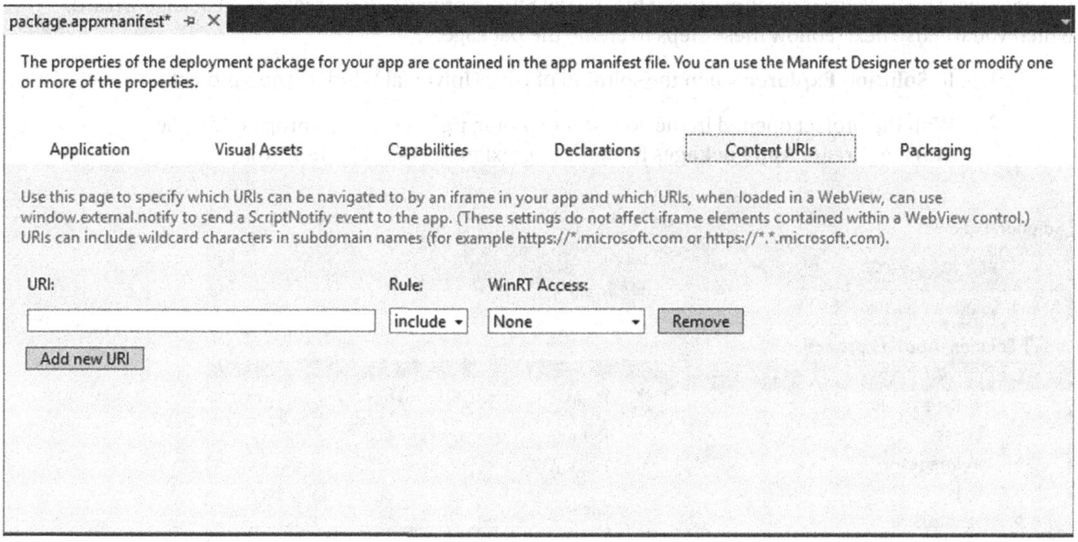

The properties of the deployment package for your app are contained in the app manifest file. You can use the Manifest Designer to set or modify one or more of the properties.

| Application | Visual Assets | Capabilities | Declarations | Content URIs | Packaging |

Use this page to specify which URIs can be navigated to by an iframe in your app and which URIs, when loaded in a WebView, can use window.external.notify to send a ScriptNotify event to the app. (These settings do not affect iframe elements contained within a WebView control.) URIs can include wildcard characters in subdomain names (for example https://*.microsoft.com or https://*.*.microsoft.com).

URI:

Rule: include ▾   WinRT Access: None ▾   Remove

Add new URI

Figure 18-6. Content URIs

- **Packaging**: Sets the package details, such as package name (note: this is not the application name, rather just the package name), package display name, version details, publisher, publisher display name, and package family name (see Figure 18-7).

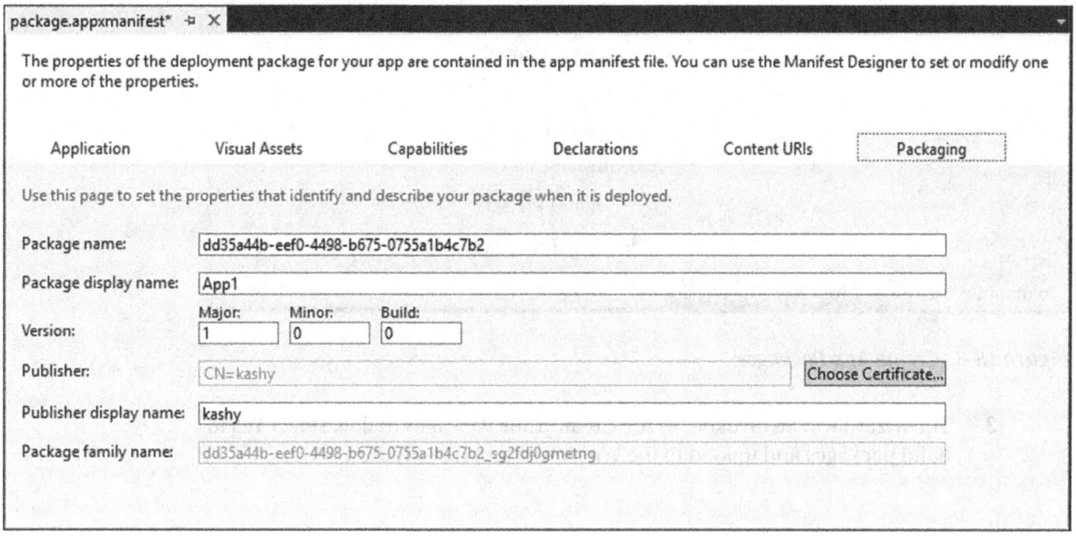

The properties of the deployment package for your app are contained in the app manifest file. You can use the Manifest Designer to set or modify one or more of the properties.

| Application | Visual Assets | Capabilities | Declarations | Content URIs | Packaging |

Use this page to set the properties that identify and describe your package when it is deployed.

Package name: dd35a44b-eef0-4498-b675-0755a1b4c7b2

Package display name: App1

Version: Major: 1 Minor: 0 Build: 0

Publisher: CN=kashy   Choose Certificate...

Publisher display name: kashy

Package family name: dd35a44b-eef0-4498-b675-0755a1b4c7b2_sg2fdj0gmetng

Figure 18-7. Packaging

353

Creating an App Package

After configuring the application package using the manifest file, the next thing to do is generate or create the package. The package is an appxupload file. Visual Studio provides the Create App Package wizard, which you will use next. Follow these steps to create the package:

1. In **Solution Explorer**, open the solution of your Universal Windows app project.

2. With the project opened in the Solution Explorer, right-click your project. Choose **Store ➤ Create App Packages** from the context menu (see Figure 18-8).

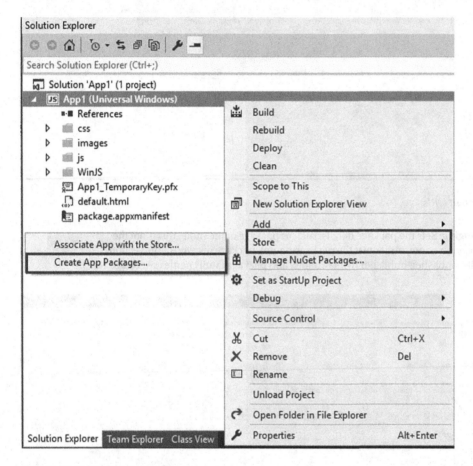

Figure 18-8. *Create App Packages*

3. The wizard will be invoked. In the Create Your Packages dialog, select **Yes** to build packages and upload to the Windows Store (see Figure 18-9).

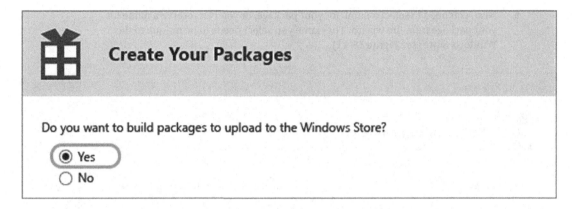

Figure 18-9. *Create App Package wizard*

If you chose No, Visual Studio would not create the required .appxupload file required for Store submission. This option should be used when you only want to sideload your app to run it on an internal device.

4. Next, you need to sign in to your Windows Dev Center account (see Figure 18-10).

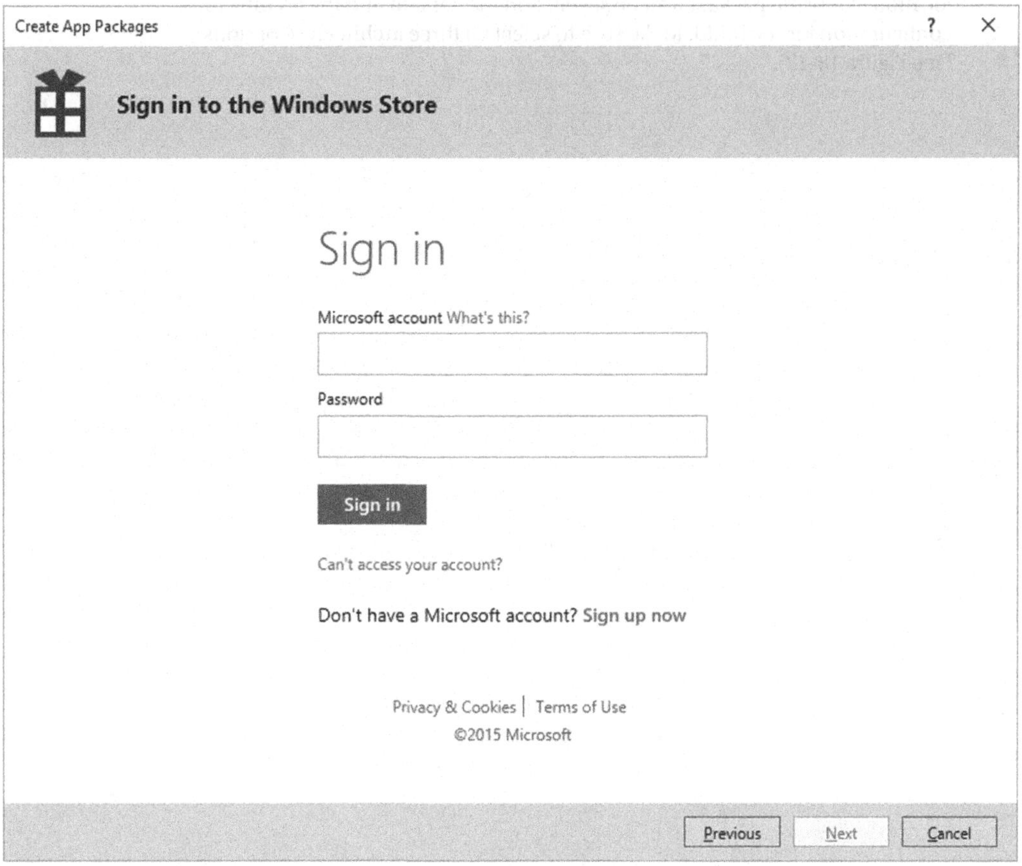

Create App Packages	? ✕

Sign in to the Windows Store

Sign in

Microsoft account What's this?

Password

Sign in

Can't access your account?

Don't have a Microsoft account? Sign up now

Privacy & Cookies | Terms of Use
©2015 Microsoft

Previous   Next   Cancel

Figure 18-10. *Create App Package Dev Center Sign in*

355

5.   Next, you need to select a name for your package, or you can reserve a name for your package from the wizard. The name you select needs to be unique to the Windows Store (see Figure 18-11).

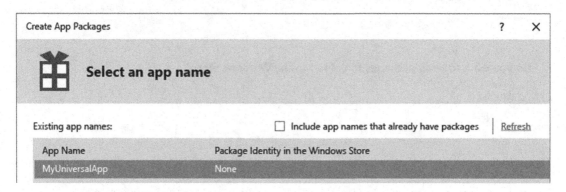

Figure 18-11. Selecting app name

6.   Next, you need to select and configure the package information: the output location where the package will be saved, and the version and the architecture configuration for the build. Make sure to select all three architecture options (see Figure 18-12).

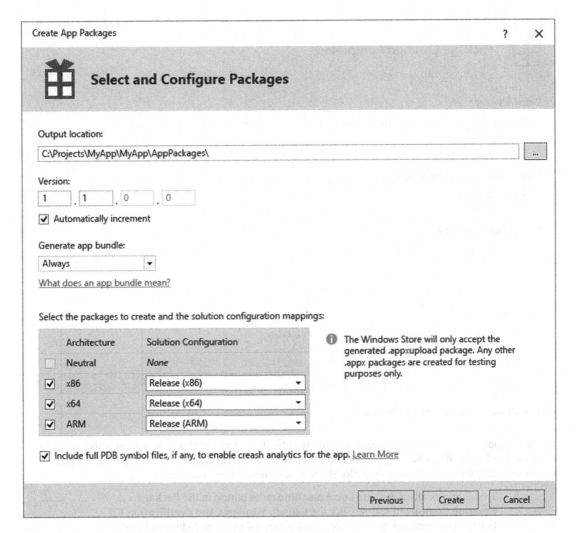

Figure 18-12. *Configuring package details*

7. Click **Create** to generate the appxupload package, which is generated at the selected output location. You can then submit the appxupload package to the Store.

Next, you see Package Creation Completed dialog (see Figure 18-13).

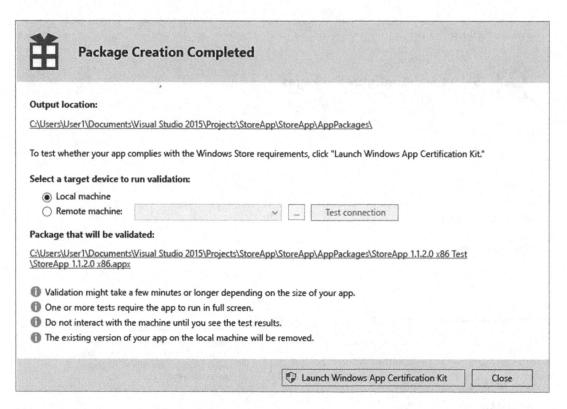

Figure 18-13. Creation Completion dialog

It is important that you validate your app before submitting it to store for certification. Validation can be done by using the Windows App Certification Kit (WACK) that is installed as part of the SDK on your machine. Validation can be done on your local machine or on a remote machine.

8.   To validate locally, select the **Local machine** radio button in the **Package Creation Completed** dialog. Click the **Launch Windows App Certification Kit** button. The Windows App Certification Kit performs tests and shows you the results.

9.   If your app has passed the tests, you are ready to submit your app to the Store.

18.3 Submit an App to the Windows Store

Problem

You have finished creating the package. An appxupload package has been generated for your app. You now need to submit the app to the Store for certification.

Solution

Once an appxupload package has been created for your app, the next step is to submit it to the store for certification. Once certified, your app is listed on the Windows Store so that users can search for it and download it for installation. You submit your app package to the Windows Store using the Windows Dev Center dashboard. The following outlines the process of submission.

1. Log in to the Windows Dev Center using your dev center account credentials. Head over to **http://dev.windows.com** and sign in.

2. Click the **Dashboard** link.

3. On the dashboard page, you see the My Apps section on the left-hand side of the page. Under this section, the app name you reserved during package creation is listed with an **In progress** status. Click the app name (see Figure 18-14).

My apps

MyUniversalApp1
In progress

MNOPEDIA
In progress

Socius
In progress

TechNet Newz
In the Store

City Context
In the Store

Curah
In the Store

Create a new app

Figure 18-14. Apps listing in Windows Dev Center dashboard

4. Next, you are presented with the App Overview page. Here you need to click the **Start your submission** button in the **Submissions** section.

5. Next, you are presented with the submission screen. Here you need to provide information related to pricing, the application properties, the application package, which countries you want your app to be available in, and any other instructions for certification team.

    a. **Pricing and availability**: Here you provide the pricing for your app or decide to list it as free. You also have option to choose the countries in which you want to list your app.

    b. **App Properties**: Here you provide information such as the category and subcategories to which your app belongs in, as well as the age rating, any hardware preferences, and app declarations.

    c. **Packages**: Here you submit the appxupload package that was generated by Visual Studio.

6. Once you have followed all the steps in the submission process, you can click the **Submit to the Store** button. Your package will then undergo a workflow. Your app is signed with a certificate, and then the certification team performs certification tests. Once certified by the certification team, your app is published to the Windows Store.

18.4 Use Windows Ad Mediation in Your UWP Apps

Problem

You have developed your Windows 10 app and you are thinking of monetizing it by running advertisements. You want to sign up with multiple ad providers to show their ads in your app. You need an ad mediator control for your app.

Solution

In-app advertisements are one of the ways in which you can earn money from your app. You can subscribe to advertisement providers and run their ads within your app. You get paid for impressions of the ads shown in your app. Different providers have different economics tied with the ad impressions. But to show ads, you need to first install Windows Ad Mediator, a control that helps you to show ads from multiple providers. Let's learn how to install an Ad Mediator control from Visual Studio.

1. Open your project in **Solution Explorer**. Expand your project if it is not expanded already.

2. From the menu bar, select **Tools ➤ Extensions and Updates** (see Figure 18-15).

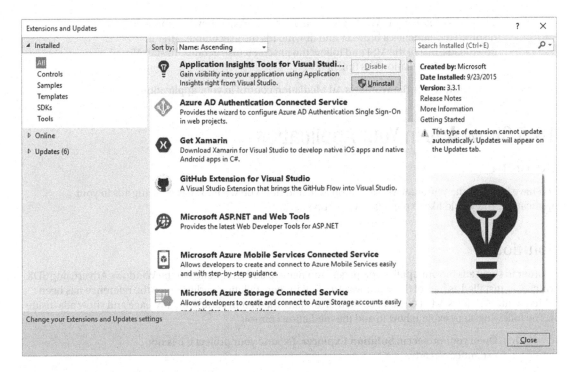

Figure 18-15. *Extension and Updates dialog*

3. Select **Online** from the left tree. Type **Windows Ad Mediation** in the dialog search bar (see Figure 18-16).

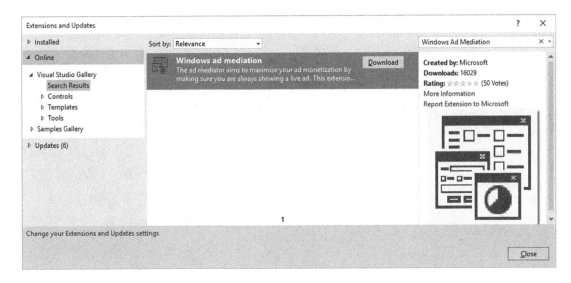

Figure 18-16. *Windows ad mediation*

4. Click **Download** on the Windows ad mediation package shown in the search results. This launches a browser and downloads the executable. After it downloads, install the MSI and follow the onscreen instructions. Restart Visual Studio once installation has finished.

You are now ready to use the Windows Ad Mediation control in your application.

18.5 Show Ads in Your Application

Problem

You have installed the Windows Ad Mediation SDK and now you want to start showing ads in your application. You would like to put ads in your app pages.

Solution

In order to show ads in your application pages, you need to add a reference to the Windows Advertising SDK, which was installed as part of the Windows Ad Mediation installation earlier. Once the reference has been added to the Windows Ad SDK, you can then instantiate mediation control on any page and show ads inside it. The following steps explain how to add the mediation control.

1. Open your project in **Solution Explorer**. Expand your project if it is not expanded already.

2. Right-click the **References** node and select **Add Reference** from the context menu.

3. In the **Reference Manager** dialog, select **Microsoft Advertising SDK for JavaScript** and click **OK** (see Figure 18-17).

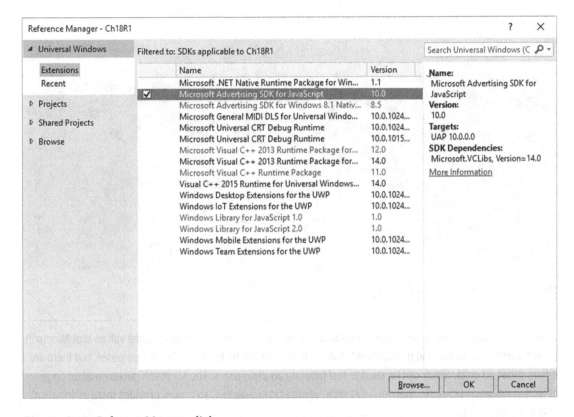

Figure 18-17. *Reference Manager dialog*

4. Open the **default.html** or any other file where you want to place the ads.

5. In the <head> section, after the project's JavaScript references of **default.css** and **default.js**, add the reference to **ad.js**.

    ```
    <!-- Microsoft Advertising required references -->
    <script src="/Microsoft.Advertising.JavaScript/ad.js" ></script>
    ```

6. Modify the <body> section in the default.html file (or other HTML files, as appropriate for your project) to include the following:

    ```
    <div id="myAd" style="position: absolute; top: 50px; left: 0px; width:
    300px; height: 250px; z-index: 1"
         data-win-control="MicrosoftNSJS.Advertising.AdControl"
         data-win-options="{applicationId: 'd25517cb-12d4-4699-8bdc-52040c712cab',
         adUnitId: '10043121'}">
         </div>
    ```

7. Compile and run the app to see it with an ad (see Figure 18-18).

Figure 18-18. *Universal Windows app with ads*

■ **Note**   The application id and ad unit id provided in the earlier code snippet are the test values that Microsoft provides for you to test during development. The application id will be the same for test purposes, but there are different test ad units, which can be used to test different ad dimensions. The Microsoft documentation page at https://msdn.microsoft.com/en-US/library/mt313178(v=msads.30).aspx provides more information about test ad unit ids.

---

8. To generate ApplicationID and AdUnitId in your production apps, follow these steps:

    a. Start the store submission process in the Windows Dev Center.

    b. Make sure that you set the App Category in the App Properties section.

    c. Next, select **Monetization ➤ Monetize with ads** from the options in the section on the left of the page.

    d. On the **Monetize with ads** page, under the **Microsoft Advertising ad units** section, click **Show Options**.

    e. Enter a name for your ad unit. Select the **Ad unit** type and the device family where the ad will be shown. Click the **Create ad unit** button.

    f. Now you have created an ad unit. Copy the application id and ad unit id and paste into the ad control in your app.

    g. Regenerate the package and use the new package in your submission process.

Index

A

Accelerometer tool, 322–323
Adaptive tiles
    AddAdaptiveTiles()event handler
        method, 278
    binding element, 277
    createTileUpdaterForApplication().update()
        method, 279
    default.html, 277
    JavaScript file, 278
    LoadTileandNotifications.js file, 278
    templates, 277
    TileLarge binding, 279
    UWP app, 277
    Windows.UI.Notifications.Tile
        Notification(), 279
    working process, 277
    XmlDocument object, 278
    XML schema syntax, 277
    XML templates, 276
Adaptive UI technique
    fluid layouts
        app.onactivated function, 124
        default.html, 123
        formatDateString function, 122
        ListView control, 121
        output screen, 125–126
        project dialog, 121
        resizeListView, 124
        script file reference, 123
        weatherData.js, 122–123
    reposition
        CSS file, 118
        CSS media queries, 116
        default.css, 118
        default.html, 117
        device targets/screen, 116
        output screen, 119–120
        project dialog, 117
        Windows Mobile, 120
        working process, 117

Additional tools
    accelerometer tool, 322–323
    additional tools feature, 318
    emulator, 319–320
    feature, 319
    location tab, 323, 325
    modes, 323
    multi-touch input, 322
    near field communication, 320–322
    network tab, 325
    real-world interaction, 318
    simulate mouse input, 320
    steps, 322
    Universal Windows Platform tools, 318
    working process, 318
Ad Mediator control, 360–361
Application manifest file
    capabilities, 352
    content URIs, 353
    declarations, 352
    package editing, 350
    packaging, 353
    steps, 349
    tabs, 350
    visual assets, 350–351
    XML file, 349

B

Background task
    BackgroundTaskBuilder class, 214, 217
    BackgroundTaskRegistration.all
        Tasks property, 216
    code snippet, 217–218
    mytask.js file, 215–216
    package.appxmanifest, 218
    solution explorer, 215
    system condition, 218
    SystemTrigger, 213
    task completion, 220
    WebUIBackgroundTaskInstance.current
        property, 216

BackgroundTaskBuilder class, 214, 217
BackgroundTaskProgressEventArgs object, 220
BackgroundTaskRegistration.allTasks property, 216
Badge notification, 286
Bluetooth device
    DeviceCapability element, 289
    GATT device, 289
    Package.appmanifest file, 289
    Windows apps, 289
Built-in Maps app
    Bing Maps control
        AJAX Control 7.0, 245
        default.html file, 247
        default.js, 247
        loadModule, 248
        map.entities.push method, 248
        mobile and web applications, 246
        reference manager, 246
        Windows app, 245, 248–249
        working process, 246
    default.html file, 239
    default.js, 239
    desktop windows, 242
    directions
        bingmaps, 242
        default.html file, 243
        default.js, 243
        desktop windows, 245
        LaunchUriASync method, 244
        Windows device, 242
        Windows mobile, 244
    display maps, 238
    parameters, 240
    Windows Mobile app, 240–241

■ C

Controls
    AppBar control
        appbarevents.js, 77
        default.html page, 76
        functionality, 76
        properties, 77
        syntax, 75
        Windows app, 78–79
    FlipView control
        creation, 59
        data.js file, 59–60
        itemDataSource property, 61
        WinJS app, 61
    ListView control
        cell-spanning layout, 64
        create Universal app, 62
        data.js file, 63
        filtering function, 66
        grid layout, 64–65

        grouping items, 68
        List data source, 62
        list layout, 64
        SemanticZoom, 71–75
    Repeater control
        data.js, 56
        default.html page, 56
        HTML table, 55
        items, 59
        list of, employees, 58
        Windows Mobile emulator, 57
    ToolBar control
        creation, 79
        default.html page, 80
        default.js file, 81
        properties set, 81
        Windows app, 82
Cost-per-million (CPM), 26

■ D, E

Data binding and navigation, 83
Data binding system
    business object
        data properties, 83
        processAll() method, 83
        Project dialog, 84
        Windows Mobile output, 86
        working process, 83–86
    style attributes
        data property, 87
        default.html, 88
        default.js, 87–88
        DOM elements, 86
        project dialog, 87
        Windows Mobile output, 89
    templates
        data item, 89
        default.html, 91
        default.js, 90–92
        DOM element, 89
        project dialog, 90
        Windows Mobile screen, 93
    WinJS controls
        data.js file, 94
        data template, 93
        default.html, 95
        ListView, 93
        project dialog, 94
        style sheet definition, 95
        Windows Mobile screen, 96
Data storage techniques
    create and delete app
        btnSaveClick method, 162
        container, 162
        createContainer method, 161

DataStorageDemo.js file, 161–162
  default.html, 160
  js file, 161
  levels, 159
  local app data store, 159
  Windows 10 app, 159
file handling
  btnDataToFile and btnCreateAFile, 177
  callback function, 176
  createFileAsync method, 175
  create, read and write options, 175
  DatastorageDemo.js file, 177–178
  default.html file, 177
  default screen, 179
  local folder, 175
  local holder file, 179
  MyFile.txt, 176
  readTextAsync method, 180
  roaming folder, 175
  temporary folder, 175
  Universal Windows app, 175
  Windows.Storage.StorageFile class, 175
overview, 159
reading app data
  ApplicationDataContainer.values, 163
  creation, 163
  DataStorageDemo.js file, 164–165
  default.html page, 163
  function, 164
  store and retrieve app, 163
  Windows 10, 165
register and implementation
  ApplicationData.DataChanged event, 173
  applicationData object, 174
  DatastorageDemo.js, 174
  default.html code, 173
  event handler, 173
  working process, 173
retrieve local composite
  ApplicationDataCompositeValue
    class, 166
  composite value class, 166
  Windows 10 app, 166
roaming app data store
  ApplicationDataContainer.values, 169
  btnCreateRoamingContainerClick
    function, 170
  create and read data, 169
  createContainer method, 168, 171
  DataStorageDemo.js, 167, 170–171
  default.html page, 167, 169
  roamingSettings.containers.hasKey
    function, 168
  roamingSettings.createContainer, 167
  Windows Mobile output, 168, 172

Define classes, 21
Design breakpoints, 116
Device capabilities
  app package manifest
    app package.appmanifest file, 288
    DeviceCapability element, 287
    problem, 287
    Visual Studio, 287
    XML editor, 288
  audio stream and output speech
    audio options, 297
    audio_SetUp() method, 296
    controls, 294
    debug mode, 293–294
    default.html page, 293
    drop-down controls, 295
    errorMessage() method, 298
    plain text, 292
    ready() function, 295
    speakFn() function, 297
    SpeechSynthesise.js file, 298
    StatusMessage error message, 296
    text-speech app, 299
    voicesSelect drop-down control, 297
    Windows.Media.SpeechSynthesis.
      SpeechSynthesizer(), 292
  Bluetooth device
    DeviceCapability element, 289
    GATT device, 289
    Package.appmanifest file, 289
    Windows Apps, 289
  Cortana voice commands
    activatedEventArgs, 306
    default.js, 304–305
    foreground, 303
    VCD file, 303
    working process, 304
    XML code, 304
  find availability
    default.html page, 290
    DevicePicker.js, 290
    get enumeration, 291–292
    ready() function, 291
    showDevicePicker() method, 291
    UWP app, 290
    Windows.Devices.Enumeration.
      DevicePicker class, 290
    working process, 290
  speech recognition constraints
    buttonSpeechRecognizer
      ListConstraintClick function, 301
    creation, 300
    custom list, 302–303
    default.html file, 300
    Speechrecognisation.js file, 301–302

Device capabilities (*cont.*)
    speechRecognizer.
      compileConstraintsAsync() method, 302
    UWP apps, 300
    working process, 300
Diagnostic tools
   debug menu, 314
   different options, 315–316
   factors, 314
   GPU Usage tool, 318
   results of, 316–317
   UI responsiveness tool, 317
   Visual Studio profilers, 314
   Windows app, 314
Display text, 50
DOM explorer
   computed tab, 312–313
   debugging purposes, 311
   DOM Explorer tab, 312
   HTML element, 310
   layout tab, 313
   refresh windows app, 314
   Visual Studio 2015, 311
   while debugging, 314
   working process, 311

■ F

Function scope, 26

■ G

Getter method, 21
Getting HTML document, 38
Globalization
   date and time formatting
      DateTimeFormatter, 150
      default.html file, 150
      onactivated method, 150–151
      output, 151–152
   definition, 145
   numbers and currencies formatting
      default.html, 152
      NumberFormatting, 152
      onactivated method, 152
      output, 153–154
   resource string
      add additional language, 148
      app.onactivated function, 148
      default.html file, 148
      default.js file, 148
      default language settings, 146
      English resource file, 147
      folder creation, 147
      French culture, 149

      package.appxmanifest file, 146
      running app, 149
      universal app, 145–146
Global scope, 26
GroupData, 70
GroupKey, 70
GroupSorter, 70

■ H

Hub navigation
   default.html, 106
   default.js file, 107
   element, 105
   hierarchical pattern, 105
   output, 108
   project dialog, 106
Hyperlinks
   HTML, 137
   navigation model, 137
   newpage.html, 138
   working process, 138

■ I

IBackgroundTaskRegistration object, 220
Internet of Things (IoT), 1

■ J, K

JavaScript console window
   commands, 310
   console.log method, 309
   console window, 309–310
   default.js file, 309
   developers, 307
   errors/write debug messages, 307
   local machine option, 308
   log message, 310
   template, 308
   Universal Windows
      Platform app, 307
   Visual Studio menu debug, 307
   warnings and errors, 309
   working process, 307

■ L

Labels, 50
LaunchUriASync method, 244
Lifecycle and navigation model
   hyperlinks
      HTML, 137
      newpage.html, 138
      working process, 138

SessionState
  app activation, 135
  default.html page, 135
  default.js file, 136
  page display, 137
  use of, 135
  Visual Studio, 137
  WinJS.Application.sessionState, 135
  working process, 135
single-page navigation model (*see* Single-page
  navigation model)
states and events
  ActivationKind enumeration, 130
  activation methods, 130–131
  app execution states, 128
  code, 128
  default.js file, 127
  demonstrates, 128
  JavaScript console window, 130
  Universal Windows app, 129
  Windows app, 130
  WinJS.Application.addEventListener
    method, 129
  WinJS.Application.checkpoint event, 129
  working process, 127
termination and resuming
  ApplicationExecutionState
    enumeration, 134
  default.js file, 133
  detail.previousExecutionState property, 133
  ExecutionState, 133
  JavaScript console window, 134
  working process, 133
unhandling exception
  default.js file, 132
  handling app, 131
  Windows desktop, 132
  WinJS.Application.error, 131
  working process, 131
WinJS.Application.sessionState, 135
Localization
  WinJS Controls
    data-win-res, 156
    default.html, 155
    onactivated method, 155
    output, 158
    resource files, 155
    string, 155
    Visual Studio 2015, 155
Location
  current location
    default.html file, 222
    default.js, 223
    getGeopositionAsync method, 221
    getLocation method, 224

    location prompt, 225
    package.appxmanifest file, 221
    Visual Studio, 222
    Windows app, 221
    Windows Mobile app, 225
    working process, 221
  detect user location (HTML5)
    default.html file, 232, 235
    default.js, 232–233, 235
    error message, 234
    getCurrentPosition method, 234
    getLocation method, 234
    Onsuccess method, 237
    package.appxmanifest file, 232, 235
    problem, 231
    updates, 235
    W3C Geolocation API, 235
    watchPosition function, 237
    watchPosition method, 237
    Windows Store app, 234, 238
    WinJS app, 231
    working process, 232, 235
  geolocator location updates
    default.html file, 227
    default.js, 228–229
    desktop window, 231
    getGeopositionAsync method, 226
    getStatus method, 230
    positionchanged event, 230
    problem, 226
    Starttracking method, 230
    Windows Mobile emulator, 230
    working process, 226

■ M

Maps. *See* Built-in Maps app
Master/Detail navigation pattern
  app.onactivated method, 110
  data.js, 112
  default.html, 109
  default.js, 109
  detail.html, 112
  detail.js, 112
  details screen, 113–114
  ListView, 108
  master.html, 110
  master.js, 111
  master screen, 113
  working process, 109
Microsoft Azure Mobile Services
  CRUD operations
    default.js file, 263–264
    del() method, 267
    insert method, 266

Microsoft Azure Mobile Services (*cont.*)
    MobileServiceClient constructor, 266
    remote service, 265
    todo database table, 262
    update method, 266
  database table creation, 258
  data retrieval, 267
  new mobile service creation, 251
  server scripts validation, 270
  sorting data, 269
  WinJS client library, 260
MobileServiceClient constructor, 266
MobileServiceTable, 265
Monetization
  Ad Mediator control, 360–361
  extension and updates dialog, 360–361
  in-app advertisements, 360
  showing ads
    ApplicationID and AdUnitId, 364
    compile and run program, 363
    default.html, 363
    HTML files, 363
    installation, 362
    mediation control, 362
    reference manager dialog, 362–363
  UWP apps, 360
  Windows ad mediation, 361

N, O

Navigational structures
  elements, 98
  hierarchy structures, 97
  hub control
    default.html, 106
    default.js file, 107
    element, 105
    hierarchical pattern, 105
    output, 108
    project dialog, 106
  Master/Detail navigation pattern
    app.onactivated method, 110
    data.js, 112
    default.html, 109
    default.js, 109
    detail.html, 112
    detail.js, 112
    details screen, 113–114
    ListView, 108
    master.html, 110
    master.js, 111
    master screen, 113
    working process, 109
  pages/screens, 97
  Pivot control

    content categories, 98
    default.html, 99
    peer-based, 98
    project dialog, 99
    Windows Mobile output, 100
  SplitView control
    content area, 105
    default.html, 101
    default.js, 102
    helper class, 103
    pane, 100
    project dialog, 101
    working process, 101
Near Field Communication (NFC), 320–322
Notifications. *See* Toast notification

P, Q

Photo gallery app, 59

R

Remote Windows 10 device
  app package, 342
  enabling developer mode, 343
  installation, 342
  package creation, 344
  package file, 342
  remote connection screen, 344–345

S

SessionState
  app activation, 135
  default.html page, 135
  default.js file, 136
  page display, 137
  use of, 135
  Visual Studio, 137
  working process, 135
Setter method, 21
Sharing data
  app declaration
    data types, 197
    guidelines, 195
    package.appxmanifest file, 194
    project title, 196
    Share Charm windows, 197
    share target, 194
    time management reporting app, 195
    working process, 195
  custom data format type
    app UI, 210
    DataSharingDemo.js, 208–209
    default.html, 207–208

JSON and XML format, 208
problem, 207
receiver app, 211
request.data.setData function, 207
set data method, 207
shareDataHandler function, 208
activatedShareHandler function, 209
working process, 207
event handler
    datarequested event listener
        method, 182
    DataSharingDemo.js file, 182
    DataTransferManager object, 182
    DataTransferManager.get
        ForCurrentView() function, 183
    default.html, 183
    source app, 182
handle share activation
    activatedShareHandler, 199
    DataSharingDemo.js file, 199–200
    default.html, 198
    dispReceivedContent() function, 200
    receive plain text, 198
    Share Charm windows, 199
    shareOperation object, 200
    target app, 198, 202
    Windows Universal templete, 198
    working process, 198
image app
    default.html, 190
    demo screen, 192–193
    FileOpenPicker method, 191
    preceding code, 190
    problem, 190
    project title, 193–194
    selectImage function, 191
    selectImage() folder, 192
    selectImageButton control, 191
    selection, 193
    shareDataHandler function, 192
    shareDataHandler() method, 191
    title and description fields, 190
    Universal Windows apps, 190
overview, 181
receive image sharing
    bitmaps method, 203
    DataSharingDemo.js, 204
    event listener function, 204
    getBitmapAsync() method, 203
    package.appxmanifest, 205
    problem, 203
    shareOperation.data.getBitmapAsync()
        method, 203
    target app, 206
    working process, 203

share contract, 181
share plain text data
    charm windows, 187
    DataSharingDemo.js file, 185
    demo screen, 186
    event argument, 186
    OneNote sharing data, 187
    problem, 184
    properties, 184
    request.data.title, 184
    user interface, 185
    working process, 184
web links
    DataSharingDemo.js file, 188
    default.html, 188
    request.data.setWebLink() function, 189
    request.data.setWebLink()
        method, 188–189
    title and description fields, 187
    Windows application, 187
Sideload application
    Add-AppDevPackage file, 327
    confirmation dialog, 328
    developer mode, 328
    installation message, 330
    package and certificate
        Add-AppDevPackage file, 330
        Add-appxpackage command, 336
        browse button, 332–333
        certificate screen, 331
        import process, 334–335
        installation, 330
        pop-up screen, 333
        store location selection, 332
        Windows desktop, 330
        working process, 330
    PowerShell menu, 329
    steps, 327, 329
    traditional desktop apps, 327
    Universal Windows apps, 327
    Windows device, 327
Single-page navigation model
    back button, 143
    default.html page, 141
    files, 141
    home.html page, 143
    href attribute, 142
    navigator.js file, 139
    page1.html, 141
    page1.js file, 142
    pagecontrol home.html file, 139
    PageControlNavigator control, 141
    pages, 138
    simplest solutions, 138
    Universal Windows app, 140

Single-page navigation model (*cont.*)
    Visual Studio 2015, 140
    Windows 8.1 project, 139
    WinJS.Navigate.navigate() method, 142
    WinJS.Navigation class, 143
    working process, 138–139

■ **T**

Tiles
    adaptive tiles
        AddAdaptiveTiles()event handler
            method, 278
        binding element, 277
        createTileUpdaterForApplication().
            update() method, 279
        default.html, 277
        JavaScript file, 278
        LoadTileandNotifications.js file, 278
        templates, 277
        TileLarge binding, 279
        UWP app, 277
        Windows.UI.Notifications.
            TileNotification(), 279
        working process, 277
        XmlDocument object, 278
        XML schema syntax, 277
        XML templates, 276
    default creation
        application package.appmanifest, 275–276
        package.appxmanifest, 275
        problem, 275
        working process, 275
Toast notification
    actions
        AddInteractiveToastNotification()
            method, 281–282
        default.html, 282
        element, 281
        GetControl() method, 282
        interactive app, 283
        problem, 281
        working process, 281
    badge
        AdaptiveTiles() method, 285
        BadgeNotificationto, 285
        default.html, 285
        GetControl()method, 286
        LoadTileandNotifications.js, 285
        tile, 285
        UpdateTileBadge() method, 285
    scheduled tile and toast notification
        AddScheduledTileNotification()
            method, 283
        default.html, 284
        element, 283
        interactive, 283
        LoadTileandNotifications.js, 284
        scheduled adaptive tile, 284
        working process, 283
    Visual content
        AddToastNotification()
            method, 280
        default.html, 280
        GetControl() method, 280
        interactive, 279
        ToastNotificationManager, 279
        UWP app, 281
        working process, 280
ToastNotificationManager, 279
ToggleSwitch control, 40
Tooltip control, 49

■ **U**

UMP apps
    creation, 5
    default.html, 7
    development tools, 3
    device family hierarchy, 1–2
    input handling, 3
    js file, 6
    running
        local machine, 11
        Mobile device, 12
        Windows 10 emulators, 8–10
        Windows 10 simulator, 9
    solution explorer, 6
    universal controls, 3
Universal Windows Platform (UWP), 1.
    See also Navigational structures
    application package/appxupload
        package, 349
    app package, 350–351, 353
        app name selection, 356
        app package wizard, 355
        completion dialog, 358
        context menu, 354
        creation, 354
        manifest file, 349–353
        package details configuration, 357
        remote machine, 358
        Windows Dev Center account, 355
    background task (*see* Background task)
    Windows 10, 349
    working process, 349

■ **V**

Voice Command Definition (VCD) file, 303

■ W

WebUIBackgroundTaskInstance.
     current property, 216
Windows 10 Mobile device. *See* Additional tools
Windows Ad Mediation. *See* Monetization
Windows App Certification Kit (WACK)
     selection, 338
     solution, 336
     start menu, 337
     store app option, 338–339
     test results, 342
     tests applicable, 339–340
     Universal Windows Platform app, 336
     validation, 341
     working process, 336
Windows app developer account
     access account registration
          Visual Studio, 348
          Windows dev center, 347
     developer account online, 347
     upload app, 347
Windows Store
     appxupload package, 358
     process of, 359–360
     Windows Dev Center dashboard, 359
WinJS.Class.define method, 19
WinJS.Class.derive method, 22
WinJS.Class.mix method, 24
WinJS controls
     additional properties, 34
     data-win-control attribute, 31
     DatePicker control
          controldemo.js file, 44–45
          datePattern property, 46
          declaration, 43
          default.html, 44
          monthPattern property, 45
          yearPattern property, 46
     declaration, 31
     display text, 50
     editing text

password input box, 52
     rich text box, 52
     text area, 52
     text box, 52
getting HTML document, 38
JavaScript code
     controldemo.js, 36
     default.html, 36
     IntelliSense support, 38
     maximumRating
          property, 37
     preceding code, 36
     Rating control, 37
TimePicker control
     controldemo.js, 47–48
     declaration, 46
     default.html, 46
     hourPattern property, 48
     minutePattern property, 48
     periodPattern property, 49
ToggleSwitch control, 40
Tooltip control, 49
Windows Mobile emulator, 33
Windows tablet, 32
WinJS features
     create class, 19
     create mix method, 24
     derive method, 22
     encapsulation, 26
     Namespace
          define method, 15
          Developerpublish, 16
          functions, 17
          parameters, 15
          to existing namespace, 18
          WinJSFundamentals.js, 16
     promise function, 29
WinJS.Navigate.navigate() method, 142

■ X, Y, Z

xhr function, 30

Get the eBook for only $5!

Why limit yourself?

Now you can take the weightless companion with you wherever you go and access your content on your PC, phone, tablet, or reader.

Since you've purchased this print book, we're happy to offer you the eBook in all 3 formats for just $5.

Convenient and fully searchable, the PDF version enables you to easily find and copy code—or perform examples by quickly toggling between instructions and applications. The MOBI format is ideal for your Kindle, while the ePUB can be utilized on a variety of mobile devices.

To learn more, go to www.apress.com/companion or contact support@apress.com.